D1710924

Between Home and Homeland

JUDAIC STUDIES SERIES

Leon J. Weinberger
General Editor

Between Home and Homeland

Youth Aliyah from Nazi Germany

Brian Amkraut

THE UNIVERSITY OF ALABAMA PRESS

Tuscaloosa

Typeface: ACaslon

∞

The paper on which this book is printed meets the minimum requirements of
American National Standard for Information Sciences-Permanence of Paper for
Printed Library Materials, ANSI Z39.48-1984.

Library of Congress Cataloging-in-Publication Data

Amkraut, Brian, 1969–
    Between home and homeland : youth aliyah from Nazi Germany / Brian Amkraut.
        p. cm. — (Judaic studies series)
    Includes bibliographical references and index.
    ISBN-13: 978-0-8173-1513-9 (cloth : alk. paper)
    ISBN-10: 0-8173-1513-6
    1. Jews—Germany—Migrations. 2. Germany—Emigration and immigration—
History—20th century. 3. Palestine—Emigration and immigration—History—20th
century. 4. Jewish children in the Holocaust. 5. Zionism—Germany—History—20th
century. 6. Jews—Germany—Politics and government. I. Title. II. Series.
    DS135.G3315A547 2006
    940.53′183508350943—dc22

                                                                    2005030543

In Loving Memory of My Parents
Ruth and Julian Amkraut

The angel who has redeemed me from all harm shall bless the children and shall recall in them my name and the names of my fathers.

—Genesis 48:16

What is more tragic than a child that grows up with tight lips, with secretly clenched fists, with a tormented disturbed soul? . . . From such a fate we must strive with every ounce of our spiritual energy to protect those Jewish children whose parents desire them to have a different home. Those who help now to take German children out of their oppressive surroundings and to plant them into a life that is more free and happy are not only helping the children alone, are not merely diminishing the personal sufferings of individuals, but are helping to diminish hatred itself, which is now, in a thousand different ways, darkening our European earth.

—Stefan Zweig, November 1933

Contents

Acknowledgments

A number of individuals and institutions must receive proper credit for allowing me to finally bring this work to publication. The Interuniversity Fellowship in Jewish Studies sponsored a year of archival research in Israel, and New York University's Institute for Advanced European Studies supported a summer in Germany. My doctoral research was maintained by generous support from the National Foundation for Jewish Culture and the Memorial Foundation for Jewish Culture. An award from Oberlin College's grant-in-aid program allowed me to return to Israel for some additional research.

I owe a tremendous debt of thanks to the many archivists who helped me find relevant documentation, including the staff at the Institut für Zeitgeschichte in Munich, the YIVO archives in New York, the Central Archives for the History of the Jewish People at the National Library in Jerusalem, the Institute for Contemporary Jewry at the Hebrew University in Jerusalem, and the photo archivists from the U.S. Holocaust Memorial in Washington and the Jüdisches Museum Berlin. Special thanks go to Morry Kantor at Yad Tabenkin in Ramat Eph'al, Susan Woodland of the Hadassah Archives at the Center for Jewish History in New York, and Rochelle Rubinstein at the Central Zionist Archives in Jerusalem, who helped me sort through a vast amount of material in a short time.

I have been fortunate to be affiliated with three academic institutions that have encouraged and assisted the completion of this project. The faculty and staff at Siegal College have welcomed me into a pleasant and productive working environment and supported my research. I benefited greatly from a year as visiting professor of Jewish history at Oberlin College, where the history faculty was most supportive and offered helpful advice. And the Judaic studies and history faculty at New York University truly helped set me on the path to scholarship. A number of scholars have helped with their advice and criticism at various stages of this project, including Michael Berkowitz, Robert Chazan, Hasia Diner, and Alan Levenson. Shulamit Magnus, Hagit Lavsky, and Michael A. Meyer reviewed a number of chapters and I thank them for their constructive criticism. A special debt of thanks goes to Stewart Stehlin, who taught me the importance of picking my words with great care. I am most fortunate to have found a mentor of great expertise, scholarship, and understanding in David Engel. He helped guide me through this project from its earliest stages and directed me toward the right questions to ask.

Gloria Horowitz has been tremendously helpful with editorial and substantive advice, far beyond the normal responsibilities of a mother-in-law. Of course, this project would never have gotten off the ground without the tremendous support of my family. Ruthy and Saul probably have not realized how much time their father was away from them in order to complete this book. Davida has endured my nights and weekends spent writing and teaching, and weeks away doing research, not to mention her years working full time and coparenting as I labored in graduate school. The publication of this work is a testament to her perseverance, not mine.

Abbreviations

Arbeitsgemeinschaft	Arbeitsgemeinschaft für Kinder- und Jugend-Alijah (Working Group for Children and Youth Aliyah)
CV	Centralverein deutscher Staatsbürger jüdischen Glaubens (Central Association of German Citizens of the Jewish Faith)
CZA	Central Zionist Archives
ICJOHP	Institute of Contemporary Jewry Oral History Project
IfZ	Institut für Zeitgeschichte (Institute for Contemporary History)
JFB	Jüdischer Frauenbund (Jewish Women's League)
JR	*Jüdische Rundschau*
JWuS	*Jüdische Wohlfahrtspflege und Sozialpolitik*
LBIJ	Archives of the Leo Baeck Institute, Jerusalem
LBIY	Leo Baeck Institute Yearbook
MiHa	Mittleren-Hachscharah (Intermediate Hachscharah)
Reichsvertretung	Reichsvertretung der deutschen Juden (National Representative of German Jews)

RjF	Reichsbund jüdischer Frontsoldaten (National League of Jewish War Veterans)
SA	*Sturmabteilung* (storm troopers; Nazi brownshirts)
SS	*Schutzstaffel* (protective squad; police force of Nazi party)
UPA	United Palestine Appeal
YAA	Youth Aliyah Archives
YVA	Yad Vashem Archives
YVS	*Yad Vashem Studies*
WIZO	Women's International Zionist Organization
Zentralausschuss	Zentralausschuss für Hilfe und Aufbau (Central Committee for Aid and Reconstruction)
ZVfD	Zionistische Vereinigung für Deutschland (Zionist Federation of Germany)

Between Home and Homeland

Introduction

Dealing with the Nazis

While the synagogues were burning throughout the Third Reich on November 10, 1938, not all Jewish institutions were targeted for destruction. In a strange turn of events, Gestapo officials could be found protecting some Youth Aliyah training facilities, where Jewish teenagers prepared for emigration from Germany to the land of Israel. On other occasions, despite complaints by local farmers, young Jews enrolled in emigration programs were permitted by government officials to develop agricultural skills for a future life in Palestine by tilling the soil of the Fatherland, the lifeblood of the Aryan nation according to Nazi ideologues. Even as German Jews' day-to-day movements were restricted and monitored by the Nazi regime, Youth Aliyah's representatives had significant freedom of movement to raise funds in Germany and abroad. These examples and the complete early history of Youth Aliyah in this book do not suggest collaboration with Nazis, but rather demonstrate the many challenges confronting Jewish groups engaged in the task of emigration from Germany and the seeming success that certain Zionist institutions enjoyed relative to other Jewish organizations. Youth Aliyah provides a striking example of the strange nature of Jewish life under Nazi rule and the moral, educational, and economic dilemmas that may confront a humanitarian movement during a chaotic era.

Since the earliest studies of the encounter between the Third Reich and the Jews, the most significant research has focused on the perpetrators of oppression and mass murder. Recently, however, historical scholarship has attempted to provide insight into victims' responses to Nazism as well as emphasizing the roles of so-called bystanders. One of the most comprehensive approaches is *The Years of Persecution, 1933–1939,* volume 1 of Saul Friedländer's *Nazi Germany and the Jews.*[1] Yet much of the literature about German Jews during this period is based on survivor testimony and memoirs rather than academic inquiry. This book considers one specific reaction to the rise of Nazism, Youth Aliyah, which took Jewish teenagers out of Germany and brought them to Palestine. The organization managed to bring in about five thousand young immigrants prior to World War II.[2] The story of Youth Aliyah touches on important human questions regarding the ways that individuals, families, and communities deal with adversity and how they confront the unknown.

Youth Aliyah's assistance to the German Jewish community during these years has received only minimal attention, often in the form of a single line of text or a footnote, in the relevant scholarly literature.[3] The few detailed studies of Youth Aliyah have either focused on the movement's significance for Jewish Palestine and the development of the State of Israel or addressed its pedagogical achievements within the Israeli educational system.[4] These analyses perceive Youth Aliyah as a *yishuv*/Israeli institution. The apparent lack of interest in both its German origins and its role in German Jewish life during the 1930s can be explained as a function of specific Israeli educational/cultural trends.

In a country that has been, in so many ways, obsessed with the Holocaust, the experiences of German Jews have never been perceived as part of mainstream culture in Israel. Even as the catastrophe began to unfold in Europe, some Jewish leaders in Palestine viewed the commitment of Germany's Jews to a foreign culture and identity, and the subsequent Nazi oppression, as vindication of the Zionist idea. Emigrants from Germany to Israel, particularly those who came at a young age, privately proud of their sophisticated cultural heritage, may have felt compelled to repress identification with that past, as the educational and political structure of the Jewish state looked toward its future. Furthermore, despite the fact that many of these teens were rescued via Youth Aliyah and often found ways to contribute to Israeli society, the survival of these few thousands also served as constant reminder of the slaughtered millions, including their family and friends. Not surprisingly, survival in this fashion leaves its mark, both on the individuals and on the broader community. Tom Segev's *The Seventh Million* clearly demonstrates the ambivalence that characterized attitudes toward German Jews who found their way to Palestine and the unique role that the Holocaust continues to play in Israeli society.[5] Perhaps these factors account for the relative lack of material related to the early days of Youth Aliyah and the desire to focus on the movement's achievements in later years without much critical analysis.

The extent to which the Nazis supported Zionist ideas and enterprises and the claim that certain elements within the Zionist parties collaborated with the Nazi regime have been hotly debated, at least in the Israeli media, since the contentious case of Rudolph Kasztner in the mid-1950s. Even while the Third Reich was taking the first steps toward its ultimate confrontation with the Jews, some Zionist leaders recognized that Nazism, as it was understood at the time, and Zionism had certain mutual interests. The most conspicuous point of intersection was in removing Jews from Germany. Of course the Nazis seemed to care little where Jews were going as long as they left German soil, and Zionists were only interested in bringing Jews to Palestine.

This shared goal resulted in the Ha'avara Transfer agreement in 1933. This deal with Hitler's party, which never remained secret as some critics have contended, was bitterly debated in Zionist circles, the main critics coming from Jabotinsky's Revisionist camp, which favored an all-out boycott of Nazi Germany, and the supporters found among Ben-Gurion's circle in the *yishuv* leadership, which viewed Ha'avara as a way of bringing more Jews into Palestine. Ha'avara was particularly helpful as it facilitated capitalist immigration, which would not only bring in essential wealth and population but also not cut into the number of workers allowed to enter under immigration quotas.[6] The Nazis supported the plan for two reasons. Some German officials felt that Ha'avara's specific economic requirements could help offset any negative impact of Jewish boycott efforts. More importantly, the plan helped rid Germany of additional Jews. In the words of Yehuda Bauer, Ha'avara was continued up until the outbreak of the war, "against the wishes of almost all German government economic bureaucrats because Hitler had decided that emigration of Jews was more important than any economic consideration—and that Haavarah was one of the ways to achieve that aim."[7]

Even if one believes that Hitler and his supporters envisioned physically destroying European Jewry at a relatively early stage, as Lucy Dawidowicz has claimed, other historians have more than adequately demonstrated that Nazi policy before the Second World War had the specific goal of promoting Jewish emigration.[8] National Socialist directives regarding Jewish organizations in general, and youth groups in particular, reflected this approach. In January 1934 Nazi security chief Reinhard Heydrich ordered that only Jewish organizations of a purely religious nature or with specifically charitable aims would be allowed to continue functioning. Exceptions to this law were granted on an individual basis.[9]

Organizations focused on immigration to Palestine generally found their activity less hindered by the government than other Jewish institutions. For example, even before the Nuremberg Laws, ad hoc official edicts prohibited Jewish youth groups from publicly wearing uniforms, displaying flags, or distributing literature.[10] Yet a directive from the same police office declared "the activity of Zionistically engaged Jewish youth organizations, concerned with the occupational retraining of Jews [as] agricultural and manual laborers prior to the emigration for Palestine, lies in accord with the National Socialist State leadership." The directive continued, "in any case, the members of Zionist groups, in view of the emigration-to-Palestine directed activity, should not be treated with the same severity as is necessary towards members of the so-called German-Jewish Organizations (Assimilationist)."[11] It is interesting that the Gestapo has, in this document, adopted the term *Assimilanten,* commonly used by German Zionists in reference to their political opponents. Such language demonstrates the degree to which some Nazi bureaucrats internalized Zionist rhetoric, and of course the paragraph in the Nuremberg Laws expressly protecting the Jewish right to fly the Zionist flag can be seen as further demonstration of such support.[12]

Yet Nazi policy could never be clearly understood. In spite of the government's apparent support for Jewish agricultural training in preparation for emigration, in 1934 a Jewish social work agency noted the outright hostility of the rural population and the German bureaucracy to Jewish farming activity. An official resolution against future Jewish work on German land confirmed this animosity.[13] Though this outlook corresponded precisely with Nazi claims regarding the sanctity of German soil, the government's determination to promote Jewish emigration received higher priority.

In February 1934 the minister for agriculture, Herbert Bäcke, wrote to the Gestapo regarding the retraining of Jews for vocational and agricultural occupations, stating that he had "considerable doubts in every respect."[14] The rural population lodged complaints regarding Jewish labor on German farmland. Echoing Nazi anti-Semitic propaganda that could have been lifted from the pages of *Der Stürmer*, the minister cited public concern that Jews were likely to bring diseases from the city to the countryside, notably syphilis, and that despite the local population's aversion to Jewish people, the possibility of racial defilement should not be underestimated. Even if the training were limited to "closed camps," social interaction with the local population would be inevitable. The minister therefore requested, on racial grounds, prohibiting such activity as a matter of policy.

The ministry of the interior responded in June, explaining the situation in blunt terms. "If the Jewish question is going to be settled, from the outset no ways should be blocked that are likely to promote the emigration of Jews who live in Germany."[15] The need for retraining was based on the perception that Jews were disinclined to manual, particularly agricultural, labor, which would hinder emigration. The official reassured Bäcke, instructing him not to worry about Jews remaining in the new Germany as farm workers. The minister for the interior consequently reported that his office had no concerns regarding Jewish retraining activities, even within the Reich, provided they operated in closed camps to further the goal of immigration, especially to Palestine.[16] Youth Aliyah's *hachsharah* (agricultural training) camps were thus assured "favorable" treatment by the Gestapo. In the words of historian Francis Nicosia, "Hechalutz . . . operated over 40 retraining camps (*umschulungslager*) throughout Germany during the 1930s with the knowledge and encouragement of the Nazi police."[17]

The SS, which at this time urged massive Jewish emigration as the best solution to the Jewish problem, specifically promoted Palestine as a destination. Early success achieved by the SS in advancing this position among Nazi leaders may have been due initially to the work of Baron Leopold Itz von Mildenstein, who headed the SS Jewish department until early 1936.[18] Mildenstein even toured Palestine, reporting favorably on Jewish settlement and specifically noting the remarkable independence of Jewish children there.[19] Though the SS officer recommended immigration to Palestine, not only in terms of removing Jews from Germany but also in re-creating the Jews as a nation, the reconstitution of a Jewish state was later recognized as ideologically unfavorable by Nazi authorities and the attitude toward Zionism soured accordingly.[20] At this early juncture, however, the policies of the Third Reich's police forces seemed to find common ground with the immediate goals of Germany's Zionists.

Significantly for Youth Aliyah, this attitude extended to the realm of fund-raising, and in early 1935 the Gestapo decreed that any organizations that engaged in propaganda calling for Jews to remain in Germany would be prohibited from collecting money.[21] Youth Aliyah also benefited from the fact that its work was mostly staffed by women. Females were generally underestimated and considered insignificant by Nazi leaders, and Youth Aliyah activists were allowed to continue their work, including extensive traveling, for the most part undisturbed by government officials.[22] Eric Johnson's study of the Gestapo and the Jews notes that prior to 1939 few Jewish women had Gestapo cases filed against them.[23]

Soon enough, though, even women could not continue their activities on behalf of Youth Aliyah without directly confronting the German police authorities. Late 1937 and early 1938 saw Nazi policy move more decisively against the Jews, and despite its efforts to promote Jewish emigration, Youth Aliyah did not remain immune to this climatic change.

In mid-November 1937 German police detained Friedl Levy, a Youth Aliyah fund-raiser, following a publicity campaign in Konstanz. On November 13 the Berlin police confiscated Youth Aliyah's books and blocked its bank accounts, forcing the organization to rely on support from Jewish institutions of all stripes in Germany to maintain its budget.[24] The criminal police charged Youth Aliyah with violating a 1934 ordinance prohibiting public solicitation of funds by private organizations. The attorney Julius Seligsohn argued on behalf of Youth Aliyah that the government had previously stipulated that Jewish institutions, since they did not benefit from public welfare, were permitted to engage in their own fund-raising activities. He further argued that this money was collected for the sole purpose of promoting Jewish emigration. The specific reasons why may never be known, but the charges were dropped.[25]

In December 1937 the Gestapo summoned Eva Stern, then director of Youth Aliyah work in Germany, to its headquarters at Prinz-Albrechtstrasse, claiming that she had slandered the German government. An officer quoted a speech she allegedly gave in Zurich, which was a tirade against the Nazis.[26] Making such a speech in the first place, not to mention returning to Germany afterward, would have been not only foolhardy but obviously dangerous to both Stern personally and Youth Aliyah as an organization. As a rule, public declarations, even by representatives from other countries, never addressed conditions created by Nazi policy, but rather stressed the need to promote Youth Aliyah from the perspective of supporting Zionism. Prior to the first Youth Aliyah conference in 1935 the following directive was distributed to all participants:

> We should like to point out to you that although the Conference proceedings will be entirely private, no reference of any kind should be made concerning Germany which would in any way affect the German delegation.
>
> Any expression of opinion concerning Germany will endanger not only the representatives from Germany themselves, but also the carrying on of the work in Berlin, and the German delegation would be compelled to leave the conference.
>
> As the German delegation can only be present at the Conference with the official sanction of the German Secret State police, the members will be coming in the expectation that full and careful consideration will be given to their particularly difficult situation."[27]

True conditions in Germany were only discussed in private, though the Youth Aliyah had managed to forward printed material to Zurich without interference from Nazi censors.

When Jewish representatives asked the German authorities whether official charges would be brought against Stern, the reply arrived in the form of a summons for her to see Eichmann. The interrogation consisted of questions regarding the nature of her work for Youth Aliyah and whether she claimed responsibility for the brochures distributed in Zurich. Her affirmative reply led Eichmann to conclude that Stern was indeed engaged in propaganda against Germany and that she must therefore desist from her work for Youth Aliyah. Stern, in consultation with Zionist leaders, decided to organize her immediate departure for Palestine.[28]

In late 1937 Jettka Levy-Stein, a fund-raiser who traveled extensively throughout Germany and Europe, attempted to renew her passport.[29]

According to government regulations, organizations based in Germany needed special approval to collect money abroad. Even though Youth Aliyah claimed that foreign institutions conducted campaigns in other countries and that the money was not necessarily donated to offices in Germany, police forces still interrogated Levy-Stein.[30] Again, however, the government proved unpredictable; as a "Christmas present" the police released the Youth Aliyah's previously confiscated bank account.

The increased tension created by these developments, which demonstrated a specific government interest in Youth Aliyah, necessitated moving the center of European operations away from Berlin, as the organization could no longer effectively orchestrate collections in other lands from inside Germany. Correspondence with the various committees abroad, under the scrutiny of Nazi censors, had become a constant headache.[31] Individual Jews could not predict what language might be deemed offensive, suspicious, or threatening in the eyes of the Gestapo. Not surprisingly, one method of evading the censor was to employ code language.[32] Perhaps par for the course in the Third Reich, an organization established in order to remove young Jews from Germany, seemingly in accordance with the dictates of the government, nonetheless continually feared Nazi intervention.

In early 1938 German authorities increased pressure on the Jewish community to promote rapid emigration. Jewish youths were included in the order of the day that required removing "undesirable elements." That February, Himmler ordered young Jews of Russian origin to evacuate the country within eight days or face internment in a concentration camp.[33] Youth Aliyah could not, in such short time, arrange for certificates and transportation for the threatened youths. In some cases Youth Aliyah staff accompanied these children to the police to request extensions while they waited for Palestine certificates. In cases where the period had expired it was unwise to request an extension lest the teenagers be apprehended on the spot. Youth Aliyah often took responsibility, providing safe homes so the fugitives' whereabouts remained unknown. Such concealment relied on private individuals since the Gestapo watched the training facilities and communal institutions.[34]

Youth Aliyah's preparatory camps also faced stronger regulations from Nazi authorities following the annexation of Austria. Eichmann, arriving in Vienna to "organize" Jewish affairs, apparently shared his predecessor's enthusiasm for Palestine as a haven for Jews. He appointed Josef Löwenherz, previously vice president of the Zionist association, to head the reorganized Jewish community. The SS demanded an emigration figure of twenty thousand between April and May; Zionist and communal institutions promised to fulfill this demand.[35]

Within a few months Eichmann had succeeded in his task to a greater degree than had been accomplished in the *Altreich* (Germany proper) in the past several years. His most notable innovation was the establishment of the Zentralstelle für jüdische Auswanderung (Central Office for Jewish Emigration), which greatly facilitated the emigration process (at the same time fleecing potential emigrants of most of their property).[36] David Cesarani's recent biography of Eichmann notes that the impetus for the streamlined emigration procedure stemmed from Jewish leaders in Vienna, Zionists in particular, who staffed the office. Eichmann nevertheless received credit and achieved such high emigration statistics that following the November pogrom Heydrich hailed this feat as an example to be emulated in Berlin.[37] Youth Aliyah "benefited" from the institution of the Zentralstelle since passports could be issued for potential emigrants in a fraction of the time normally required. Eichmann personally approved the opening of an agricultural preparatory camp for Youth Aliyah near Vienna and justified his decision on the basis of increased emigration prospects.[38]

By mid-1938 it had become impossible to arrange meetings, festivities, excursions, or discussions without Gestapo supervision. The police demanded that all gatherings begin punctually. If they decided that too few people attended or too many appeared late, the entire event would be canceled at their discretion. On one occasion authorities closed all cultural institutions for a week, including the Youth Aliyah School and language courses that were essential preparation for emigration, an example of the often-arbitrary nature of Gestapo tactics.[39] The existence of regulations concerning meetings of Jewish organizations is well documented; yet the strict application of these measures to groups focused on emigration, the cornerstone of Nazi Jewish policy, demonstrates the confusing nature of National Socialist rule, where the regime often created difficulties in the public sphere, for reasons generally unknown to those outside the bureaucracy.

Discerning the attitude of government representatives toward the work of Youth Aliyah remained a constant challenge. Since official government policy promoted Jewish emigration, the Gestapo often supported the organization's activities. Yet unpredictably, as a result of the generally anti-Semitic atmosphere, Nazi authorities would create difficulties. In an attempt to navigate this treacherous terrain and still promote the maximum effectiveness of their work, Youth Aliyah's liaison to the Gestapo adopted a strictly legalistic approach to emigration rather than test the limits of Gestapo good will.[40]

Ra'anan (Rudolph) Melitz, who accompanied the last Youth Aliyah group to leave Germany before World War II, described his absurd interaction with the Nazi security forces regarding his passport:

> I was requested by the local police station in the area in Berlin in which I was living, to appear three times a day, in order to report that I am still there because I was the holder of a passport. I went to the police station and explained to them that it is correct, that I was a holder of a passport, but the passport was actually in the hands of the Gestapo and before I participated in a transit to England, I had to go again with a new letter to the Gestapo in order to receive the passport. Then after I had received the passport, I could get my English visa and after I returned to Germany I had again to hand in the passport to the Gestapo. Thus I explained to the local police station that it's no good for me to report 3 times a day which in any case I could not do because I was working for an organization which took care of emigration and this was considered important enough to let people continue in such an activity.[41]

In comparison to most other Jewish organizations, Youth Aliyah was fortunate to still be functioning by the time World War II began. Undoubtedly the commitment to a perceived set of shared goals with Hitler's regime enabled Youth Aliyah to continue its work, even as the noose tightened around the neck of Germany's Jews. The strange reality of pursing these aims inside the Third Reich demonstrates the complicated nature of Jewish responses to Nazi aggression during these years, and Youth Aliyah's activities provide a window into that turbulent era.

To be comprehensive, Youth Aliyah's work in Germany must be viewed as the confluence of three sets of interactions: those between Youth Aliyah and the German Jewish community, such as local fund-raising and promoting enrollment; those between Youth Aliyah in Germany and its offices in Palestine, including division of labor and distribution of certificates; and those between Youth Aliyah and the German government, specifically obtaining permission for its various domestic and foreign activities. In each of these cases, the evidence demonstrates numerous tensions, reflecting the factioned nature of Jewish responses to Nazism and the difficulty of presenting a truly united front. Constant competition for financial resources complicated Youth Aliyah's attempts to attract broad support among German Jews. Jews of varying ideological and religious orientation competed for inclusion in the youth immigration program. The specific educational or political agenda emanating from Palestine's labor Zionist leadership often conflicted with the expectations of German Jews. And despite their common goal of attempting to remove Jews from Germany, Youth Aliyah officials in Germany could not confidently rely on assistance from Nazi authorities to achieve those goals. Analyzing these many conflicts and attempts to resolve them not only tells the stories of adults and children making difficult choices but also contributes to our understanding of the complex nature of Jewish reactions to Nazi aggression in the years before World War II.

Of course an accurate assessment of Jewish responses to the Third Reich requires at least a basic knowledge of the history of German Jewry prior to the appearance of Hitler. The attitudes of many German Jews and the specific internal dynamics of Jewish organizations and communal bodies during the Nazi era can only be understood as a function of certain political, economic, demographic, and religious factors that developed over many years.[42]

Prior to the nineteenth century Jewish life in Germany generally followed a pattern that had become established during the Middle Ages. Both individual and communal activity depended on the goodwill of the various kings, princes, lords, barons, and other nobility who ruled the hundreds of individual sovereign entities in German-speaking lands. Jews suffered excessive taxation, sporadic violence, property restrictions, and other discriminatory laws common in medieval Europe. During the 1800s, though, political and intellectual developments ushered in radical changes for the status of Jews in Germany, transforming the nature of Jewish community both internally and externally.

The Napoleonic wars brought new freedoms to Jews throughout Europe, including in many cases the promise of full civic equality in accordance with French revolutionary ideals. Yet demands for Jewish emancipation were only realized with the unification of the Reich under

Bismarck and the enactment of the German constitution of 1871. As a result of the ideological and cultural influences of this era, by the late 1800s most German Jews had become more liberal in terms of religious thought and religious practice. Even religious conservatives in Germany tried to assimilate into German life as much as possible within the confines of Jewish law. Almost all German Jews shared the common goal of retaining Judaism as a religious identity, divested of any national characteristics or nationalist aspirations.[43]

Despite the preoccupation of German anti-Semites with "the Jewish Problem" in Germany, Jews never accounted for more than 1.1 percent of the population between 1871 and 1933.[44] After the figures peaked around 1910, the steadily decreasing birthrate among German Jews could not keep pace with the general population. German Jews numbered more than five hundred thousand by 1933, less than 1 percent of all inhabitants, but only as a result of a steady influx of emigrants from eastern Europe, accounting for nearly a hundred thousand German Jews by the end of the Weimar period.[45]

These numbers notwithstanding, Jews nevertheless proved a highly visible element within German society as a result of their geographic and economic concentration. Most conspicuous was the community in Berlin, which by 1933 contained nearly one-third of all German Jews. Jews tended to congregate residentially within certain districts of these large cities, further heightening their visibility and giving rise to the perception that the proportion of Jews in the population exceeded 1 percent. This pattern was most obvious among the *Ostjuden* (eastern European Jews), who were noticeably distinctive with the culture and traditions they brought from eastern Europe.[46]

Jews were further distinguished by an occupational distribution different from that of the general population. Jewish overrepresentation in commerce, business, and free professions, as well as underrepresentation in agriculture and heavy industry, legacies from the medieval past, only intensified during the modern period. The conspicuous Jewish presence in certain lines of work reinforced anti-Semitic propaganda, and this trend continued into the Nazi period.[47]

More significant was the impact that many Jewish figures had on German artistic and intellectual life during the Imperial and Weimar periods. Much of the unique cultural environment that developed in Germany during the 1920s was rooted in trends that were visible even before World War I.[48] Undoubtedly Jews played a remarkable role in this process, with figures such as Freud, Einstein, and Schoenberg having exceptional impact. Between 1905 and 1931 nearly one-third of the German scientists who received Nobel Prizes were Jews. Jews dominated the German stage and were highly influential in the emerging film industry. Equally visible was the Jewish presence in the world of music, no small matter in the land of Bach, Brahms, and Beethoven. Perhaps most influential was the prominent place Jews held in German journalism as publishers, editors, and journalists for such widely read newspapers as the *Berliner Tageblatt, Vossische Zeitung,* and *Frankfurter Zeitung.*[49] As much as individual Jews contributed to German public life, the broader German Jewish population felt itself deeply connected to and identified with a *Deutschtum* (German-ness) that reflected the pinnacle of European high culture and did not exclude those of the Israelite faith.

Yet this success had profound consequences. On the one hand most Jews had consciously divested themselves of the distinguishing characteristics of traditional Jewish life. On the other hand, for anti-Semites, the prominent roles played by many Jews in Germany's public life were not viewed as successful Jewish integration, but rather as alien infiltration and domination that contributed directly to the disastrous military defeat in 1918 and the humiliating Treaty of Versailles in 1919. As opposed to contributing to Germany's success, Jews were charged with ruining the German economy, manipulating political movements, and promoting decadent cultural trends.[50]

The appearance of anti-Semitism in Germany during the 1920s was not a new or even surprising phenomenon. Even though no one could have predicted the tremendous political success that an avowedly anti-Semitic party such as the Nazis could achieve and the radically violent course that its policies would eventually follow, clearly there was precedent for the anti-Jewish elements of the Nazi program. Anti-Semitic parties had been a vocal though hardly successful part of the German political landscape during the 1890s.[51]

Jews responded to this challenge by establishing the Centralverein deutscher Staatsbürger jüdischen Glaubens (CV, Central Association of German Citizens of the Jewish Faith) in 1893, an organization that would shape and reflect the attitudes of most German Jews for the next forty years. The CV's stated mission was to unite all German citizens of Jewish faith in an effort to guard their position in Germany and to foster

German loyalty.[52] This ideology was soon criticized by the Zionist movement in Germany.

Prior to 1933 the Zionistische Vereinigung für Deutschland (ZVfD, Zionist Federation of Germany) reflected the attitude of only a small fraction of German Jewry, perhaps 10 percent of the population. Nevertheless, largely due to the influx of thousands of *Ostjuden,* the interwar era was a period of growth for the ZVfD. In simple terms, the CV viewed anti-Jewish behavior as driven by the Jews' failure to integrate rapidly into German society, whereas the ZVfD perceived Jew hatred as an inevitable by-product of Jewish homelessness and powerlessness. The two groups' responses to anti-Semitism arose directly from these conflicting interpretations of the problem.

During the Weimar period, the political, cultural, and religious life of most German Jews began to change, in part as a reaction to the shifting political climate in Germany. As Michael Brenner has clearly shown, the 1920s witnessed a tremendous awakening of Jewish consciousness in Germany.[53] The more intense renaissance of Jewish cultural activity that resulted from the Nazis' rise to power continued a process that had already been set in motion following World War I. One result of the war experience was a nationwide quest to find a common sense of *Gemeinschaft,* best translated as community, reflective of the camaraderie that many young soldiers found in the army. Prevailing nationalist ideology, however, excluded Jews from this national *Gemeinschaft.* As a result, many Jews began to reevaluate their connection to Judaism and the Jewish community, though these steps should not be viewed as a desire or willingness to cast off their German identities.

The growing influence of Zionism was in fact another example of this Jewish revival. Though still a minority movement, support for a Jewish national home in Palestine made important inroads, particularly among the younger generation. The history of the German-Jewish youth movement had been tied to Zionism even before World War I. The Blau-Weiß (blue-white) youth group, founded in 1916 when young Jews were denied membership in German *völkisch* organizations, emulated the nationalist spirit of German groups. To be sure, these children of the Jewish bourgeoisie were not calling for mass emigration from Germany, (roughly thirty-seven hundred German Jews immigrated to Palestine during the years of the Republic), but the Zionist messages of Jewish pride and strength found a receptive audience in the Blau-Weiß.

The interwar period coincided with the first years of British rule in Palestine. The British permitted Jewish immigration to the Holy Land according to a strict quota system, on the basis of what was considered to be the country's "economic absorptive capacity." By 1933 quotas were set for four main categories of Jewish immigrants. Category A was reserved for "capitalists," which included anyone possessing at least $4,230 in local currency.[54] Category B provided for the entry of a limited number of students and rabbis. Category C, also known as the "labour schedule," set the quota for all manual workers, and category D allowed for immigration of dependents of Palestine residents.[55] The overwhelming majority of labor certificates went to *chaluzim* (pioneers) from eastern Europe for both qualitative and quantitative reasons. Poland alone had a population of 3 million Jews living under an anti-Semitic regime and regularly facing discrimination. Jewish leaders in Palestine viewed Polish Jews as better suited for life in Palestine than western Jews. In general they had greater knowledge of Hebrew and were more likely to support the social ideals of labor Zionism, the dominant political force in the *yishuv*.

Despite the resolution by the ZVfD board in 1912 that every Zionist should "incorporate into their life's program a personal emigration to Palestine,"[56] most German Zionists did not want to leave the land of their birth. Only after the Nazis came to power did ZVfD leaders unenthusiastically immigrate to the land of Israel. Nevertheless in 1913 the CV responded to the Zionists' resolution by declaring that anyone who did not adhere to *deutsche Gesinnung* (German [national] identity) would no longer be welcome in the organization. This antipathy moderated during the closing years of Weimar, and the younger CV leaders were more tolerant of Zionist attitudes and even helped promote some Zionist projects.[57]

Yet the force that would most directly impact the fortunes of German Jewry was the dangerous combination of a dismal economy and ineffective government. The chaotic political and financial fortunes of Weimar Germany, not a great outcry against the Jews, resulted in electoral success for the National Socialist German Worker's Party (Nazis).[58] Those who could not find work, particularly young people just finishing school, acutely felt the impact of the Great Depression. The economic dislocation did lead to a rise in anti-Semitism, demonstrated not only by the increasing popularity of Hitler during elections, but also by overt anti-

Semitic acts and attitudes. Vestiges of Germany's past now appeared to threaten Jews' prosperity and their future on German soil. By 1932, with a government and economy in turmoil, the stage was set for a decisive turn of events, and some Jews in Germany started to feel that the time was ripe for action rather than words.

1
1932—The Decisive Year

The history of Youth Aliyah most accurately begins during Weimar Germany's closing year. Historians of modern German Jewry have recognized 1932 not just as a watershed of German history but also as a time of singular significance for Germany's Jewish population.[1] Yet this chronological classification does not only revolve around the coincident rise of Hitler. Although Youth Aliyah is commonly viewed as a German Jewish response to Nazism, its origins must be understood within the context of Weimar's decline. The unique economic circumstances of this period, coupled with increasingly successful anti-Semitic politics, provided the specific background that inspired the vision behind Youth Aliyah. Under these conditions, large-scale immigration to Palestine was first conceived to ensure the material and spiritual survival of German Jewish youth, not to provide physical security.

The 1929 Depression hit Germany with particular severity, having dramatic repercussions in a country that had only recently recovered from the financial crisis of the 1923 inflation.[2] Unemployment, perhaps the defining characteristic of the Great Depression, grew to unprecedented numbers in Germany. Intensely devastated in this regard was the country's youth, especially those who had only recently completed school.[3] These teenagers faced the prospect of entering a job market that held few opportunities for older, more experienced individuals and offered almost no hope for the young.

As poorly as Weimar's unemployment insurance program functioned in its attempt to cope with the world economic crisis, the existing legislation, and subsequent adjustments to it, discriminated against unemployed youth.[4] Individuals under the age of twenty-one could be required to attend courses and perform compulsory labor in order to receive benefits. Unemployed youths were also excluded from subsistence level "crisis benefits," available to citizens who had already received the allotted twenty-six-week subsidy. In 1930 unemployment compensation for those under seventeen depended on applying a means test to their parents' income. And most decisively, in June 1931, the government of Chancellor Heinrich Brüning disqualified all claims for unmarried unemployed individuals under twenty-one years of age.[5]

Government spokesmen and officials throughout Germany recognized the demoralizing and potentially dangerous consequences of unemployment for the future of the republic, particularly its impact on the younger generation. A ministry of the interior official in 1932 referred to the pressing task of "protecting and helping an endangered generation."[6] These leaders justifiably expressed concern that unoccupied youth would take to the streets and the pubs, venues in which radical political ideologies such as Nazism and Communism proliferated. The government, therefore, sponsored two similar programs to maintain order within the ranks of German youth: compulsory labor (*Pflichtarbeit*) for those receiving welfare benefits, and the Voluntary Labor Service (Freiwillige Arbeitsdienst) providing short-term low-paying work and accommodations. Often the youth camps organized by the voluntary labor service drew on the nationalist traditions of the German youth movements and also incorporated ideas from racist movements. Many churches, hoping to prevent a mass exodus to atheistic Communism, also assisted in implementing voluntary labor schemes with the similar expectation of using this institution to influence an increasingly indifferent young generation.[7]

Despite these programs, widespread unemployment had a psychologically debilitating impact on Germany's youth. Apathy, anxiety, and indifference were major consequences. What type of future did an individual leaving school at the age of fourteen have to look forward to? Those fortunate few in an apprenticeship or vocational training had little prospect of finding gainful employment upon completing the program.[8] In Weimar Germany, unless a family had the means and a child the desire and ability to continue formal schooling, fourteen-year-olds were expected to find gainful employment. Families depended on the extra income, especially during the Depression years. For such children, the outlook was grim and the overall mood could aptly be characterized as one of despair.

The prevailing misery did benefit the politically astute Hitler and his Nazi party, whose electoral successes coincided with continuing economic distress and general dissatisfaction with Weimar administrations, which had unsuccessfully attempted to tackle the problem of unemployment since 1918.[9] Hitler's offer of stability through resolute leadership appealed to voters more than any specific plan for economic reconstruction, allowing the Nazis to capitalize on this deteriorating situation rather than directly causing the demise of German democracy.[10]

The growing success of the National Socialists in Reichstag elections between 1930 and 1932 certainly did not bode well for a Jewish population suffering the financial hardships of the Depression. Hitler's message as well as the anti-Jewish measures in the Nazi party's Twenty-Five Point Program called for complete removal of the Jewish element from Germany's economy.[11] By the final years of Weimar, German Jews in some regions had already tasted the anti-Semitic aspects of Hitler's economic policy. Whenever the opportunity arose, the paramilitary SA (*Sturmabteilung*, storm troopers), even before 1933, organized boycotts against Jewish shops and businesses.[12] Yet before Hitler came to power, Jewish victims could find some comfort from the notion that Nazism was a fringe phenomenon and that Jews did have recourse to the Weimar judicial system.

As the economic outlook that confronted German youth during the last years of the Weimar Republic continued to deteriorate, prospects for Jewish young adults were even more limited. The anti-Semitism of extremist politics filtered down into the streets and the schools as the success of the Nazis and Communists at the polls continued to grow. Jewish youth groups experienced firsthand the terror of Hitler's SA.[13] A number of unions and professional organizations refused admittance to individuals of Jewish background. In addition to rising unemployment levels, young Jews also faced discriminatory hiring practices. Increasing political radicalism among the unemployed masses further aggravated these circumstances.[14]

Jewish employment was concentrated overwhelmingly in the commercial sector, including a large number of independent artisans who operated their own stores. Furthermore, even the large number of Jews who entered professions, such as law and medicine, generally worked independently. Jews were severely underrepresented in agriculture as well as heavy industry. The large presence in the textile and consumer goods sectors, both of which suffered greatly at the onset of the Depression in 1929, resulted in high Jewish unemployment. The percentage of Jews receiving welfare assistance in Berlin reached a level twice as high as the Jewish proportion of the general population and the economic historian Avraham Barkai noted, "Jewish office and factory workers were thus ravaged more severely by the effects of unemployment than non-Jewish workers, and at an earlier point in time."[15]

It is difficult to verify claims that Jews suffered more severely in Weimar Germany, however, because there is no specific statistic for unemployed Jews other than registration at Jewish employment agencies and perhaps as many as half of the unemployed Jews in Germany did not register, either out of pride or hopelessness.[16] Nevertheless in some regions the figures for unemployed Jewish youth, as best as can be estimated from communal records, did elicit a rate higher than that for non-Jews. Frankfurt, for example, showed an unemployment rate of 36 percent for Jews under age twenty-five alongside a rate of 30 percent for young non-Jews.[17] After January 1933 the government took special account of Jews, and the unemployment statistics for mid-1933 show rates of 28 and 46 percent for Jewish white- and blue-collar workers, respectively, as compared to figures of 21 and 32 percent for the entire German population.[18]

Considering the nature of the voluntary work programs, few unemployed young Jews found solace in government attempts to alleviate the situation. Though the original ideals of the German youth movement, specifically that of self-realization, on which the entire Voluntary Labor Service was based, were not prejudiced against Jews, by the early 1930s most German youth groups had adopted a *völkisch* position on the Jewish question. Leaders for the service generally came from German youth groups. The government funded these projects but relied on private agencies, especially those political associations already associated with youth work, to organize accommodations, education, and supervision. In fact Weimar officials instituted the voluntary program with the express intention of involving paramilitary organizations, hoping to tame them.[19] Aside from providing financing, the federal government did not participate in or supervise approved projects. The Nazi government's later policy of continuing and expanding these operations, though on a compulsory rather than voluntary basis, demonstrated support for the pedagogical and social ideals realized at the work camps. Quite understandably, the Social Democratic Party opposed this program, but only in late 1932 did the Jewish *Gemeinde* (official community) of Berlin receive approval from the government to establish an independent Jewish Voluntary Labor Service. This permission was received relatively late as compared to non-Jewish institutions and further reflected the discriminatory trend prevalent in the relief program.[20]

The lack of opportunities for young Jews, who would normally contribute financially during trying times, frustrated and disrupted family life. The story of a boy named Samuel (pseudonyms have been employed in case histories to preserve the privacy of all Youth Aliyah participants and their families) became increasingly common in the wake of the Great Depression. He was born in 1917 in a small upper Silesian town near the Polish border, but the chaos and violence immediately after World War I convinced his father to relocate to Breslau. Soon after setting up a business Samuel's father died, leaving his mother with the care of three children. Unsuccessful at keeping the business running, his mother remarried in 1923. Though a capable student, Samuel did not advance beyond *Volksschule* (comparable to elementary school) because his family could not afford additional education. In school he was often the only Jew and the insecurity led him to try to conceal his Jewishness as much as possible. He was blond and blue-eyed, allowing him to hide his identity—most of the teachers did not even know.

The 1929 Depression hit Samuel's family very hard and their economic situation deteriorated. In 1932, when Samuel was fourteen, his stepfather gave him two alternatives—either earn money and contribute to the household or leave home. Though unable to find work, he did have some social support. Four years earlier Samuel had been introduced to a Zionist youth group. There, for the first time, he did not have to conceal his Jewishness. This group proved to be his salvation when they recommended him for one of the first Youth Aliyah transports.[21]

The atmosphere of 1932 Germany, particularly in urban and industrial regions, corresponds to the situation described by Recha Freier, the woman directly responsible for initiating Youth Aliyah. At that time Freier was a social worker and active Zionist concerned primarily with organizing Jewish youth to support a Jewish Palestine.[22] Though throughout her life she maintained that she had envisioned a mass exodus of

Jewish youth from the diaspora to the land of Israel for some years be-
forehand, this project only received her full attention when she came face
to face with the effects of the Depression.

Born Recha Schweitzer, she grew up in the town of Norden, in east
Prussia, where her father was a teacher. Freier encountered anti-Semitism
in her youth, both in public and in school, where she was mocked for
refusing to write on the Sabbath. She was drawn to the idea of Zionism
through the writings of Ber Borochov, the ideologue of socialist Zionism, which presented Zionism as a force that would radically alter the
conditions of the Jewish people. She came to believe that a Jewish return
to the soil and the establishment of agricultural colonies in Palestine
would enable the Jewish people to live normal lives.[23] Yet her interest in
Jewish nationalism became secondary as she matured, and her husband's
position as a rabbi, in various German cities, as well as in Sofia, Bulgaria,
prevented her from immigrating to Eretz Israel. She studied languages
in university and by the early 1920s her primary professional focus was
the study of Jewish folklore; she initiated a correspondence with the
scholar Martin Buber and often lectured on the subject.[24]

Freier's Zionist interests remained, however, and by the early 1930s
she was active in WIZO (Women's International Zionist Organization)
in Berlin. She served as the representative for Bulgarian Jewry to the
WIZO conference for 1932. In September 1932 she was elected to the
Berlin executive committee for German WIZO.[25] Even when invited to
speak about Jewish folk legends, she often turned to the subject of Jewish
youth and Palestine. People who knew her at that time, and even those
who met her in later years, generally concur in their assessment of Freier
as a woman of vision, a dreamer less concerned with mundane practical
day-to-day matters and focused more on a utopian ideal.[26] While these
qualities often created difficulties for those who had to work for her, they
also allowed Freier to persevere in her quest even as others questioned its
necessity and feasibility. The idea for youth emigration occurred to her
after working-class Jewish boys who had recently found themselves
among the unemployed—for no other reason, they claimed, than that
they were Jews—approached her in early 1932.[27] They came to Freier
because her WIZO activity included leading study sessions on Zionism
for local youths in her apartment near the Alexanderplatz in central Berlin, and her associates knew that Freier was actively seeking practical

solutions for the problems facing young German Jews.[28] The boys hoped Freier could give them advice regarding employment opportunities in the coal mines of western Germany.[29]

Freier wondered how relocation to some other part of Germany, or anywhere in the diaspora for that matter, would compensate for the basic lack of a Jewish homeland where this fundamental right to work and prosper would be guaranteed. Recognizing the growing popularity of Communism's message, one highly attractive to unemployed youth, Freier believed that Zionists had to find a way to offer an even more appealing solution.

This anxiety over the future direction of Germany's Jewish youth and their desperate economic plight had already become a major topic of concern for Jewish social workers during the Depression, as it was similarly a focal point among the Christian population. Though Jewish leaders often perceived the problems of youth as unique to the Jewish community, the difficulties mirrored those facing non-Jews. In addition to German Jewry's occupational distribution, which suggested that Jews were suffering more severely from the Depression, some Jewish social workers concluded that "Jews faced problems that had once been the sole province of the Gentiles," that they had succeeded in acculturating to such an extent that they had adopted the social problems of typical German families.[30]

In a conference held during the closing days of 1931 on the "state of Jewish youth in Germany," Georg Lubinski, a Jewish social worker, Zionist, and socialist, noted that economic and political circumstances were pushing the masses of Jewish youth closer to Communism. This affiliation would result in a practical separation from the Jewish community.[31] Lubinski implored the German Jewish leadership to solve the dilemma facing Jewish youth, to the point of providing subsistence in order to prevent a mass exodus to Communist ranks. Ludwig Tietz, founder of an organization aimed at uniting young German Jews of all ideological orientations, was primarily concerned with degeneracy and demoralization as outgrowths of unemployment. Both Tietz and Lubinski, who worked to improve the lot of Jewish youth during the Weimar period, would later contribute to Youth Aliyah's work in Germany. In 1931 Tietz proposed a three-step program for Jewish communities: establishing unemployment centers to provide a structured substitute for the

social activity that had disappeared along with the workplace and to relieve tension in the home, offering training courses and substitute work,
and promoting efforts to create jobs for those most desperate.[32]

Yet impoverished Jewish communities lacked the means to initiate
these programs effectively. Moreover, Weimar Jewry was highly frag-
mented on many levels. Prior to Nazi rule, Germany's Jews were divided
along geographic, political, and sectarian lines. Though there were attempts before 1933 to unite under one representative body, such endeavors were unsuccessful, and cooperation among the disparate factions was
generally achieved only on an ad hoc basis in response to specific issues.
Social work, of which youth welfare was an essential aspect, was one of
the few realms in which the opposing factions often put aside political
and ideological differences in order to collaborate.[33]

Recha Freier's approach to the unemployment crisis differed significantly from those that other Jewish leaders, both Zionist and non-
Zionist, had taken. She called for the unemployed youths to embark immediately for Palestine, where they would receive training on the land in
collective workers' settlements. This relocation would serve both the material and spiritual needs of these teenagers and assist the Jewish people
in its task of rebuilding its home in Palestine.[34] Previously, individuals
who wished to become *chaluzim* (pioneers) in Palestine would first complete a period of *hachsharah*, usually two years, prior to immigration.
Freier's approach was unique not only in its search for a solution outside
Germany but also in its call for *hachsharah* to be undertaken in the land
of Israel. Specific agricultural instruction would be carried out under the
actual conditions of life in Palestine, and the educational and social components of the training period would more effectively prepare the trainees for pioneer life. This idea represented a major innovation in the
approach to German Jewish social work and in the management of
immigration to Palestine.

The Jewish Agency for Palestine, which distributed immigration permits under the British quota system, preferred to restrict labor certificates to applicants over the age of eighteen who had already completed
hachsharah. This stipulation effectively made it impossible for younger
Jews to take advantage of settlement opportunities in Palestine that
might allow them to escape the economic despair confronting them in
Europe.

Unwilling to accept the prevailing attitude that the crisis confronting

Jewish youth would be solved with an improved economy and the complacent posture that implied, Freier took steps toward realizing her vision of mass youth emigration. She consulted Enzo Sereni, the Berlin *shaliach* (emissary) for both Palestine's kibbutz movement Hakibbutz Hame'uchad (United Kibbutz) and the German *Hechaluz* (pioneer) organization. Sereni, an Italian Jew by birth, was at that time a member of the kibbutz Givat Brenner, many of whose founding members were German pioneers who had come to Palestine in 1928. Sereni and others promoted active *hachsharah* and urban training facilities as well as frequent communication with political movements in Palestine.[35]

Since the founding of the Blau-Weiß in 1916, the history of Jewish youth organizations in Germany was strongly tied to Zionism, and Freier expected to rely on an already established foundation of Zionist-oriented youth activity. Sereni aggressively advocated large-scale immigration of young Jews to Palestine as a feasible solution to the challenges facing them in Germany.[36] He encouraged Freier to contact the *Histadrut* (workers' federation) in Palestine and to investigate which settlements would accept Jewish teenagers from Germany for a two-year training period. With Sereni's name offering her entrée, both the *Histadrut* and some kibbutzim in Palestine took Freier's proposals seriously.[37]

Yet the settlements represented only one element among many that required persuasion. First of all, the children who would actually undertake the journey, as well as their parents, had to be willing to participate. Funds would have to be raised, implying assistance from Zionist organizations in Germany. Initiating the program on a large scale also presupposed cooperation with a responsible body in Palestine, specifically some branch of the Jewish Agency. Finally, the Mandatory government of Palestine had to approve immigration certificates.

Garnering public enthusiasm for a project that, in Freier's mind, appeared logical and, from a Zionist perspective, even compelling, turned out to be complicated. She could not take support even from German Zionists for granted. Despite the rhetoric of a personal commitment to *aliyah* (immigration to Palestine), most self-professed Zionists in Germany were in reality unwilling to commit themselves to mass Jewish emigration. Although enthusiasm grew slightly during periods of economic distress, the probability that Germany's Zionist institutions would champion a program for large-scale emigration of their members' children was undoubtedly slim.[38] For a predominantly middle-class community, the prospect of uprooting children and educating them many miles away in socialistic settlements was frightening indeed. Zionism, as it had developed in Germany, did not demand emigration, despite the rhetoric. If true for Zionists, this attitude was even more intense among the majority non-Zionists, who viewed Jewish history on German soil as an example of increasing acceptance and integration within the larger society. They perceived emigration in general, and affirmation of Jewish as opposed to German nationality, as a step backward and a complete reorientation of ideals.[39]

In extreme instances some German Jews during the early Weimar period even viewed Zionism as asocial behavior. One mother, for example, requested that her son be admitted to a correctional educational institution in order to cure him of his abnormal desire to become a farmer and settle in Palestine. As Claudia Prestel noted, the fact that the institution's board of trustees generally supported this mother's reaction illustrates that her position was less radical than one might initially suspect.[40] A young adult harboring Zionist ideals or sympathies could find himself in complete disagreement with his or her parents regarding the correct personal course for German Jews. In a society where youth culture in general rejected the ideals of the preceding generation, this scenario was not uncommon. Religious considerations frequently led parents to oppose Zionism in toto, and even more so the perceived atheistic socialist Zionism of kibbutzim.[41]

The conventional institutional solutions proposed by Jewish social workers seemed to be more popular among adult German Jews than Freier's ideas to assist the growing number of unemployed Jewish youth. The Berlin *Gemeinde*'s youth and welfare office established its own counseling center for young Jews. Only a small minority affirmed the idea that young Jews would be better off leaving Germany in order to protect their prospects for earning a living.

Freier was nevertheless surprised to find only minimal backing from leading Zionist personalities in Germany. In later years she described their attitude as one of apathy toward the plight of Jewish youth in Germany, "the first sacrifice of a flood of anti-Semitism." She even wrote that, unlike her, these leaders did not recognize the signs of impending doom. Freier correctly recalled that her scheme was initially received unenthusiastically. According to Izzi Eisner, a rabbinical student in Berlin at the time, prior to 1933 Freier's plan only found support among the *shlichim* from Palestine.[42] However, her memoirs portray a German-Jewish establishment that hindered the success of Youth Aliyah throughout the pre-war Nazi era. Her sharp criticism of Germany's Jewish leadership stemmed from post-Holocaust hindsight as well as personal embitterment for not receiving proper credit for her contributions, and there is no documentation to support her extremely critical suggestion that she conceived of Youth Aliyah as a means of rescuing young German Jews from an imminent death that *only* she foresaw.[43] Obviously, Freier enjoyed the luxury of hindsight when writing after World War II that she perceived the impending doom as early as 1932. While certainly possible, it is highly unlikely that Freier foresaw even large-scale physical oppression, much less the "forthcoming catastrophe" (*ha-shoah ha-omedet lavo*). Freier could easily have interpreted the general antagonism toward her personally during the ensuing years of youth emigration activity as reflecting a refusal to accept her accurate assessment of prospects for young Jews as early as 1932. When assessing Freier's memories, it is impossible to avoid the ongoing feud between her and Henrietta Szold (and as Freier perceived it, the Zionist establishment after Szold's death) over who deserved credit for creating Youth Aliyah.[44]

Eva Michaelis-Stern, who directed Youth Aliyah's European operations for most of the period in question, offered a more sober assessment of German Jewry's initial reaction to Freier's ideas. German Jews, even after Hitler's appointment as chancellor, could not have foreseen their calamitous future. Stern contradicted Freier and noted the strong support from Zionist leaders in Germany as soon as it became apparent that responsible people in Jerusalem would direct the needs and education of the children in Palestine.[45] In fact some Jews in Germany did notice that the coincidence of economic depression in the diaspora with an economic boom in Palestine presented an ideal opportunity to settle large numbers of young Jewish workers from Germany in Palestine.[46] Most adults, however, recognized a difference between sending nineteen- to twenty-year-old workers to help build the Jewish homeland and authorizing a program for unaccompanied, less mature youngsters to immigrate without a reputable agency in Palestine taking responsibility.

But prior to soliciting guarantees from Palestine, Freier's more pressing task was to gauge enthusiasm for her plan among young Jews. She approached Selma Schiratzky, who headed the Jewish Rykestrasse School in Berlin, and received permission to address pupils who were in their final year of study. Considering the school's reputation, it represented a prime recruiting spot. The school's stated mission was "to educate towards a national Judaism with a strong emotional and rational connection to Palestine and the Jewish work of construction [*Aufbauwerk*] there."[47] Many of the students' parents were known Zionists, and the faculty was outspokenly Zionist. Freier noted that the students responded eagerly to her proposal, with parents and children showing up at her apartment in the days following her presentation inquiring where one should go to sign up.[48]

The organized Zionist *Jugendbünde* (youth groups), particularly those affiliated with the Palestine labor movement, enthusiastically backed the notion of youth immigration to agricultural settlements. Both during the economic crisis and before, one goal of the Jewish youth movements in Germany, of all ideological backgrounds, had been *Berufsumschichtung*, occupational retraining, in order to restructure a Jewish community that was overwhelmingly engaged in the commercial sector. Among organized Jewish youth, manual labor was seen not merely as an alternative to limited white-collar employment opportunities but rather as a value in its own right.[49] However, the catchword *Berufsumschichtung* was more commonly used in connection with preserving the Jewish presence on German soil than with preparation for life abroad.[50] The youth groups seemed to be more impressed than their elders by the rising anti-Semitism in Germany and its possible ramifications during the late Weimar period. Because of the political instability in Germany, the Zionist youth group Kadimah, for example, chose to hold its 1932 summer camp in Czechoslovakia.[51]

Youth groups tended to be more radical, compared to the older generation, in their commitment to personal realization of Zionist ideals. These organizations maintained that Palestine offered a viable solution to the crisis confronting youth. However, as a public appeal from a dozen groups in the pages of the *Jüdische Rundschau* showed, they needed the support, mainly financial, of the older generation in order to promote programs that would enable the *yishuv* to absorb young immigrants.[52] Indeed, a number of Zionist youth groups in Germany were affiliated with specific political parties and ideological movements in Palestine and perceived a program to complete agricultural preparation on the kibbutz as an ideal scenario.

Freier's earliest contacts with Jewish institutions in Palestine, though seemingly positive, did not provide the assurances that Jewish leaders in Germany desired. Freier learned in the spring of 1932 that the agricultural settlements Ein-Harod, Geva, Degania, and Nahalal were interested in absorbing Jewish youth from Germany, and the monthly cost of maintaining the children would be approximately seventeen dollars per person. Kibbutz Ein-Harod, in June 1932, negotiated with Freier to arrange for the transfer of a group of twenty-five youths.[53] Subsequently Bachad (*Brith Chalutzim Dati'im*), the religious pioneering organization, contacted Freier regarding placing German Jewish youth in a farming colony that observed Orthodox religious practice. Even before receiving positive replies from prospective host communities in Palestine, Freier was confident enough to begin raising money. She solicited support from charitable funds and wealthy Jews in Germany and neighboring countries.[54] Yet the apparent willingness of a few collective settlements in Palestine to accept teenagers from Germany failed to convince the Zionist leadership in Germany that their children would be properly supervised and educated.

Georg Landauer, secretary of the ZVfD, recommended that Freier contact Henrietta Szold, who was in charge of the Jewish Agency's social service department.[55] If the agency would put its name and resources behind the project, German Zionists would endorse it as well. However, when first contacted by Freier in the summer of 1932, Szold refused to support the plan. As Szold put it, she could not in good conscience, at that time, promote the immigration of unaccompanied children, citing "the tremendous need of children in Palestine itself and the helpless inadequacy of educational facilities."[56]

Szold's initial negative reply, which Freier later referred to repeatedly, had ramifications other than simply deterring the German Zionist leadership. According to the quota system, the Jewish Agency was responsible for requesting immigration certificates from the Mandatory government. Without agency support there seemed little chance of arranging to send pioneer youth below the age of eighteen. The agency was empowered to distribute certificates to its representative offices in the diaspora. For demographic and qualitative reasons, the Jewish Agency generally preferred to dispense certificates to applicants from eastern Europe. For the second half of 1932, of 2,100 workers' certificates issued, 980 were allocated to pioneers from Poland as opposed to only 48 for German *chaluzim*.[57] The certificates were distributed in a ratio of about 20:1, whereas the corresponding ratio of Jewish populations was approximately 6:1. Thus pioneers from Poland were considered worthier either because Jewish oppression there was more severe or the individual emigrants comprised better raw material. In any case, the agency's hesitancy to endorse the youth immigration project seemed to present a major roadblock.

Nevertheless, Freier did not despair. During July 1932 her quest was aided by the arrival in Berlin of Siegfried Lehmann, who directed the Ben-Shemen Youth Village in Palestine. As a "closed" institution, according to the requirements of the Mandatory immigration policy, Ben-Shemen could request student immigration certificates under category B directly from the Palestine government, bypassing the Jewish Agency altogether. Lehmann's pedagogical work was well known in German Jewish circles. In 1916 he had founded the Jüdisches Volksheim for homeless Jewish youth in Berlin. By 1932 a number of young German Jews had completed training at his Palestine institution, and the village received considerable financial support from the *Waisenhilfe* (orphans-aid) society in Berlin. As early as January 1932, some Zionists in Germany had recognized the importance of Lehmann's establishment in terms of creating a "living, concrete connection between Jewish youth and Palestine."[58] The youth village now offered the possibility of preparing young Jews from Germany for a successful future in Palestine in line with the general tenets of Freier's plan.

Lehmann met with Freier and some of the youths who had hoped to proceed to Kibbutz Ein-Harod and offered twelve certificates for Ben-Shemen. Though not the ideal scenario, Freier recognized that these twelve initiates would constitute a beginning, and in November 1932, accompanied by a joyous celebration of singing and dancing at the train station, the first group of teenagers departed.[59]

Freier then renewed her efforts to gain support for her project from responsible Jewish officials in Palestine. She maintained that the successful transfer of one group of young German Jews to a kibbutz would establish the basis for a mass movement. Freier stressed that all her early candidates were members of Zionist youth groups and thus uniquely qualified to contribute to the upbuilding of Jewish Palestine.[60] But political developments proved to be more critical than her continued efforts. Zionist leaders in both Palestine and Germany would change their attitudes only in response to the decisive shift in Germany's fortunes in early 1933.

2
Spreading the Word

As the Weimar Republic collapsed during the early 1930s and while Recha Freier envisioned a mass exodus of young Jews to Palestine, Chanoch Reinhold (later Rinnot) seemed destined to follow the path of the stereotypical bourgeois German Jew. Though an ardent Zionist and former member of the youth group Kadimah, at the beginning of 1933 Reinhold lived in Vienna, studying at university, presumably destined for a middle-class professional career back in Germany.[1] Reinhold's path demonstrates the turbulent nature of Jewish life in Germany during the first year of Nazi rule. By February 1934 this law student found himself teacher and guide for sixty German Jewish teenagers, leading the first official Youth Aliyah group to Kibbutz Ein-Harod.

In early 1933 the new political leadership in Germany ushered in unprecedented changes, bringing great anxiety and uncertainty to German Jewry. During the first year of National Socialist rule, as Jews in Germany assessed their prospects, Youth Aliyah was transformed from Freier's idealistic vision into an organization dedicated to transplanting groups of children from Germany to agricultural settlements in Palestine. In order to realize this program, Youth Aliyah set out to accomplish three main tasks: promoting interest in the program among thousands of young German Jews; working to gain the support of Zionist and communal institutions and leaders in Germany; and initiating fund-raising efforts in Germany and abroad to support the project.

Youth Aliyah's activity reflected both the Jewish community's desire to ensure the future of its younger generation and the response to challenges from sources inside and outside Germany in attaining this goal.

The growing number of young Jews hoping to immigrate to Palestine, as well as the numerous older individuals who labored to realize this objective, reflect the rising interest in both Zionism and immigration to Palestine in response to Hitler's assumption of power.[2]

The emotional scene that accompanied the Ben-Shemen group's departure from the Anhalter train station in Berlin inspired the Zionist youth groups to promote large-scale youth immigration programs to ideologically compatible agricultural settlements.[3] Specifically, the groups Kadimah and Brith Haolim, which would merge in February 1933, the religious Zionist youth group Zeire Misrachi (Mizrachi youth), the Werkleute, and the smaller Hashomer Hazair (Young Watchmen) agreed to cooperate and facilitate the project.[4] On January 30, 1933, the same day Adolf Hitler was appointed chancellor of Germany, the Jüdische Jugendhilfe (Jewish Youth-Aid), representing the interests of the Jewish youth groups, registered as a legal corporation in Germany. Freier was elected president and Adam Simonson of Brith Haolim was elected secretary. With the future of Jewish institutions in Germany undetermined, the founders deliberately chose to avoid assigning any ideological labels to the new corporation, lest they be shut down before they could even begin their work.[5]

The Jüdische Jugendhilfe was incorporated with the following mission: "The vocational training of unemployed Jewish youths in Germany and their settlement in Palestine." This cautious approach, as opposed to immediate panic and flight, reflected most German Jews' attitude to the change in the country's leadership. Jewish organizations in Germany shared an anxiety regarding how they would be treated in the new order, and each group initially maintained that its particular ideological outlook was best suited to confront the new political reality.[6]

The Zionist establishment had no clear perception of how National Socialism would treat its institutions. Contacts with Nazi officials led some Zionists to anticipate the imminent dissolution of their organizations.[7] They feared that Hitler's regime would give preference to Jews affiliated with the right-wing Verband nationaldeutscher Juden (League of German Nationalist Jews) led by Max Naumann, who, in contrast to the Zionists, contended that German Jews had not immersed themselves deeply enough in Germany and its culture.[8] On the other hand, both before Hitler assumed power and during the initial months of 1933, other Zionist leaders believed a Nazi government would recognize the

ZVfD as the most suitable partner for resolving the Jewish question in Germany. According to this theory Nazis and Zionists shared the view that Jews were really a separate nation living as foreigners in Germany. The new government's ambiguous attitude toward Zionism was characterized by authorities working with Zionists and simultaneous Nazi violence directed at Zionist establishments.[9] For supporters of the nascent Youth Aliyah movement, however, Germany's changing political fortunes merely supported the argument that young Jews in Germany could only secure their future through physical and spiritual rebirth in the land of Israel.

In the aftermath of Weimar's political collapse, Zionist youth in Germany who now shared Recha Freier's vision committed themselves to promoting youth immigration to kibbutzim, even though Jewish communal leaders did not yet fully support the project. The youth groups remained confident, especially in light of the changed political circumstances, that immigration certificates for Palestine would soon be forthcoming. To facilitate preparing an initial group of sixty youths for Ein-Harod, each of the participating youth groups dispatched delegates to a special conference organized to determine the constituency of this first group.[10] The Jugendhilfe provided a forum through which competing Zionist groups of various ideologies could cooperate.

In accordance with the practice of Hechaluz, which prepared older candidates for immigration to Palestine, the youth groups used the principle of selection. In theory, an applicant's acceptability for youth immigration would be determined not by his or her social or economic status, but rather by that individual's dedication, diligence, and adaptability to communal living. Even before pioneers arrived in Palestine, this program hoped to promote a collective activist attitude in contrast to the perceived traditional passive approach of diaspora Jewry.

Though certainly wary of the new regime's attitude, the Jugendhilfe did not anticipate direct opposition from the government. Yet the initial plans immediately confronted obstacles from Nazi authorities. The Jugendhilfe, hoping to train the groups in security beyond the reach of Nazi anti-Semitism, arranged for the first group of sixty to undergo preparatory training at a facility in Denmark.[11] However, Baldur von Schirach, the Nazi official charged with supervising all matters pertaining to youth within the Third Reich, prohibited all youth groups from traveling abroad without express permission, which he refused to grant the Jüdische Jugendhilfe. This typifies the confusing nature of Nazism, which called for Jewish emigration, yet continually found ways to impede that process.[12]

Within weeks of Hitler's appointment, Zionism grew more and more attractive to young Jews, and membership in Jewish youth groups of all ideological persuasions flowered. In contrast to non-Jewish Germany, where youth groups were either dissolved or "coordinated" (*gleichgeschaltet*) into the Nazi order, by August 1933, ninety-seven new Jewish youth organizations had registered membership.[13] The Nazi emphasis on a community of blood, which by definition excluded Jews from membership in the *Volk,* spurred the growth of Zionist groups that recognized the Jews as a distinct national entity. In mid-February the leadership of the groups Brith Haolim and Kadimah decided to unite into a larger group under the name Habonim, Noar Chaluzi (the Builders, Pioneer Youth). This merger represented the first time since the dissolution of the Blau-Weiß in 1927 that a Jewish pioneering group could claim three thousand members.[14] Yet only after Hitler's assumption of power did the popular Zionist youth groups actively and realistically prepare for a life outside the Reich. Prior to the 1930s most young German Jews, even if aware of their Jewish roots and consciously identifying with them, were optimistic regarding ultimate integration into the general population. The atmosphere promoted by Nazi rule convinced many young Jews that Zionism's message was eminently practical.

The teenage Ludwig, for instance, described this transformation from his early childhood in Lower Silesia: "[my] father was a doctor for all the local villages. . . . I felt very much at home with my friends. My parents were assimilated Jews and we were not taught anything about Judaism. I felt no need of such knowledge because we were the only Jewish family in that part of the country. . . . There were very few occasions in my childhood when I had reason to feel that I was different from the other boys. . . . One day, however, while I was quarreling with a friend, he suddenly shot out at me with 'Judenjunge'! [Jew boy]. . . . Father told me then that we were Jews." Ludwig's family had been in Germany for many generations—his father had fought during World War I and was highly assimilated but ended the conversation with the warning: "Watch out! Always remember that you are a Jew!"

Ludwig's sports club embraced Nazism and when he heard anti-Jewish songs he left. His friends explained: "It isn't you we want to get rid of. You have always lived here. It's the dirty Jews who came to Germany after the war." These comments caused Ludwig to resent immigrant Jews.

> That summer [1932] I spent my vacation with my married sister in Berlin, and met Jewish boys for the first time. I did not like their way of talking nor their manners. I much preferred my friends at home. . . . When Hitler came to power, I began to take an interest in politics. I had many talks with a Catholic friend who was an active Storm Trooper. We tried to find a practical solution for the problem. . . . On June 30 I went home to visit my parents. That night ten S.S. men came to our house and arrested my father. He was sent to a concentration camp. When my brother-in-law visited us, I told him that though I loved Germany dearly, I had begun to feel like an alien. Then he told me that he had returned from Eretz Israel only a few weeks previously, and described what the Jews were doing there. . . . I too wanted equality, freedom, and a share in building up a Jewish country. . . . He told me about the Youth Aliyah to Palestine. A few days later I went back to Berlin with him.[15]

Ludwig's tale of disillusionment and his desire to find a home was shared by many of his peers. Nine months later Ludwig received notice to report to *hachsharah*—six months later he was in Palestine.

The increase in Zionist activity was paralleled in the adult Jewish population as well. By late 1935 the ZVfD counted 22,500 members compared to only 10,000 three years earlier. The growth is even greater when the emigration of about 7,000 long-standing Zionists is factored in.[16] The Zionist *Jüdische Rundschau* repeatedly stressed that economic conditions in Palestine had never been more favorable. Zionism, it was claimed, offered the Jews the only real escape from the economic hopelessness that prevailed in Germany. Financial prospects could draw Jews out of the very dire spiritual and material straits of diaspora life and help construct a strong Jewish community in Palestine.

Yet the outlook of German Zionists was certainly not monolithic. Many were not yet willing to concede that the Jewish people could no longer contribute to German society. As the government took steps to eliminate Jews from Germany's economy, even some Zionists continued to hope that normalization would help preserve a Jewish presence.[17] If Zionists in Germany could not form a unified position at this early stage, one could scarcely expect to find agreement within the larger German Jewish community regarding the most effective solution to the threat posed by Nazism, both as it affected young Jews specifically and German Jewry as a whole.

The government's desire to weaken the stability of German Jewry and the increasingly limited possibilities of earning a living elevated public interest in emigration as a solution for the crisis facing the younger generation. Eliyahu, a member of the first Ein-Harod Youth Aliyah group, recalled that his family's economic circumstances drove him to explore emigration possibilities. In 1932 he was the only Jewish student in his class at the Karl Marx School in Berlin. As a young socialist whose allegiance lay with the proletariat rather than any religious or national entity, Eliyahu originally had no ties to Zionism, and in fact disparaged the idea because of its avowed nationalist character. The depressed financial situation in his house and school first brought him in contact with Jewish life and culture as he found free meals with the Union of Russian Jews in Germany. The changing political climate, particularly the suppression of leftist politics, compelled Eliyahu to consider emigration. After the Nazis came to power, of the forty students from his class (the school having been renamed the Kaiser Friedrich Realgymnasium) only nine remained. Hoping to join a group he heard was training in Denmark, Eliyahu registered with the Jugendhilfe during the summer of 1933, without realizing that the program's ultimate goal was the land of Israel. The two-year commitment to Palestine did not deter him, for he was grateful to find any means of leaving Germany.[18]

This case notwithstanding, most of the earliest recruits for Youth Aliyah had at least a rudimentary affiliation with Zionism, if not wholehearted enthusiasm for it. Avraham, for example, claimed that the drive to immigrate to Eretz Israel stirred within him from the age of nine, when he joined Kadimah in Leipzig. His parents' home had been a focal point for local Zionist activity and he drew upon their inspiration. At fourteen he left school and, in a chance meeting with a friend, heard about a program to bring young Jews to Palestine. He was excited by the idea and wrote to Freier, begging to join the group. Some months later he received an invitation to attend the preparatory camp at Gut Winkel near Berlin.[19]

Anti-Semitism also prompted some young Jews to embrace Freier's vision. Pnina was in secondary school when she first experienced anti-Semitism. She recalled one of her classmates saying to the Jewish girls: "Shut up. We want to talk!" Nor did the headmaster of the school make any secret of his anti-Semitic feelings. On one occasion he too barked at her, "Shut your mouth." For many young Jews, experiencing anti-Semitism firsthand brought home the messages that Zionist groups had been imparting for many years. Pnina belonged to the youth group Makkabi Hazair (Maccabee Youth) and the leaders sent her to Freier's apartment for an interview.[20] Both public sentiment and the laws enacted against Germany's Jews began to make youth emigration appealing to a small but growing number of young Jews and their families.

Max, for example, was born to Orthodox *ostjüdische* parents, who sent him to a religious secondary school in Hannover. Max had joined the local Brith Ha-No'ar, a religious Zionist youth group. In the spring of 1933 Max's parents felt compelled to remove him from school—the business in their small shop had become so meager that Max needed to contribute some income. The boy's Zionist connections found him a job in a bakery just over the border in Holland. Before taking the job, Max had applied to Youth Aliyah, for which he was eventually selected, joining the first Orthodox group to immigrate.[21] By early May 1933 the Jugend-hilfe had already received 250 applicants for an anticipated initial allocation of 60 certificates.[22]

The government's early Jewish policy became clear enough, particularly in the aftermath of the April 1 boycott and the introduction of the Aryan paragraph into Nazi legislation with the Law for the Restoration of the German Civil Service on April 7. This initial decree was soon followed by others that increasingly restricted Jews engaged in the free professions, notably lawyers, doctors, teachers, and professors. These developments, combined with traditional anti-Semitic propaganda against Jewish commercial activity, reinforced the youth groups' perceptions that young Jews needed to reorient their occupational interests.

During these first months of Hitler's rule, many German Jews hoped to adjust to and accommodate the new regime, and the April 1 boycott was a complete shock, in Shulamit Volkov's words, "a genuine earthquake."[23] For many, this event represented the first time they truly felt like unwelcome strangers. Despite current scholarship, which generally highlights the failure of the boycott from the Nazi government's perspective and the lack of public support for this action (or less support than the Nazis anticipated), its impact on Germany's Jewish population was still strong.[24] The appearance of SA men in front of Jewish shops and offices and the public identification of these businesses as Jewish succeeded in convincing many Jews to flee Germany, regardless of the degree of public support for the boycott. And even if not particularly effective in the short term, the boycott signaled the beginning of a trend that would result in the liquidation or "Aryanization" of 60 percent of Jewish business even before the November 1938 pogrom.[25] While some Jews found comfort in the fact that not all Germans supported the boycott, the fact that many Germans turned away from their Jewish neighbors could only be viewed as disheartening. A Jewish World War I veteran who owned a department store in Wesel described the boycott as "an action felt by countless number of Jews as a personal humiliation to such a degree that they considered their lives robbed of all meaning."[26] Particularly outside of Berlin, violence accompanied the boycott and heightened individual Jews' sense of isolation. The boycott reinforced efforts by German Jews to create the institutional framework for organized emigration as well as general economic assistance.[27]

Some Jewish leaders in Germany, among them non-Zionists, consequently began to support Freier's youth emigration idea, and a joint appeal committee was established in late May directed by Hans Lubinski.[28] A pediatrician by training, Lubinski was no stranger to helping young Jews in need of assistance. In 1929 he reopened and directed the Jewish reformatory school at Wolzig, which had been closed by the government for pedagogical and hygienic reasons. Lubinski encouraged treating youths who found themselves in trouble by addressing the root causes, rather than focusing on symptoms.[29] His willingness to promote youth immigration to Palestine corresponded to this pedagogical philosophy.

The joint action committee, titled Arbeitsgemeinschaft für Kinder- und Jugend-Alijah (Working Group for Children and Youth Aliyah), from which the name Youth Aliyah was derived, would assume overall responsibility for activity in Germany and ensure the practical needs of organizing youth immigration. Three separate elements comprised the larger body: the Jüdische Jugendhilfe, under the leadership of Freier, represented the various youth groups in Germany and determined which candidates would be sent to which settlements in Palestine; the Waisenhilfe, represented by Wilfrid Israel, of the department store family Israel, supported the youth village Ben-Shemen, and claimed responsibility for transferring German youth to that institution; and the third constituent was the Berlin children's home Ahawah, soon to be relocated in Haifa.[30] Aside from transplanting Jewish youth from Germany to Palestine, the Arbeitsgemeinschaft's by-laws stated its purpose as making foreign and domestic propaganda and minimizing competition among those interested in supporting Youth Aliyah.[31] Despite the formal three-way partnership, the guiding voice in the new organization and its leadership came from the organized youth movements.

Centralization of Jewish organization and cooperation among the many factions had been a longtime goal of many German Jews, and by September 1933 an umbrella organization was established, with Zionist supporters and sympathizers holding leading positions. Reichsvertretung der deutschen Juden (National Representation of German Jews), composed of representatives from various Gemeinden, religious bodies, and ideological/political organizations, hoped to speak on behalf of German Jewry through a single voice.[32] Although the Reichsvertretung opposed a mass exodus from Germany and aspired to ensure a Jewish individual and communal presence in Germany, which indeed reflected most German Jews' desires, Youth Aliyah's proponents could take heart in the Reichsvertretung's stated aims. These goals included restructuring the abnormal (overly commercial) Berufsschichtung (occupational distribution) with particular emphasis on agriculture and manual trades, and helping German Jews develop Palestine for the benefit of German Jewry.[33] Of course such declarations do not demonstrate total espousal of the Zionist idea, but they do illustrate sympathy for Zionist projects. In general, most German Jews supported emigration as a solution for the young and for others incapable of earning a living in Germany.[34]

The Arbeitsgemeinschaft provided Youth Aliyah with respectability among German Jews by coordinating its work with the Palestine office of the ZVfD and with the community's nationwide organization for social welfare, the Zentralausschuss für Hilfe und Aufbau (Central Committee for Aid and Reconstruction), and by late 1933 with the Reichsvertretung as well. The Zentralausschuss, directed initially by Ludwig Tietz and the Zionist Werner Senator, subsequently by Wilfrid Israel and Georg Lubinski, all of whom fully supported Youth Aliyah, further reinforced the connection between professional social service activity and the youth movements.

Georg Lubinski, who from 1933 to 1938 headed the Zentralausschuss's department for social work and occupational retraining, recognized the importance of Palestine for German Jewry's younger generation. In his words, only those young Jews "who found the way to the land of Israel, or were educated in and promoted the spirit of Zionism or at least the spirit of upbuilding Palestine, had found meaning in their lives."[35] At this stage Lubinski perceived Zionism as representing a viable alternative to Communism. After 1933 he saw immigration as essential to the movement's positive influence on Jewish youth. Lubinski himself went to Palestine after the November 1938 pogroms.[36]

When the Arbeitsgemeinschaft was organized, the crisis confronting Jewish youth had become further aggravated by the Law against the Overcrowding of German Schools and Universities published on April 25. Five to six thousand young Jews were completing their compulsory schooling at the same time many other Jewish students were expelled from state schools in accordance with Nazi legislation. Jewish social workers felt obligated to provide for these teenagers.[37] Although the law did not bar all Jewish children from attending state-run elementary schools, Jewish pupils no longer enjoyed the same rights as the so-called Aryan children. No Jewish child in a school could win a scholarship as long as there was an Aryan child in the school without a scholarship.[38] A general atmosphere of anti-Semitism, which in many cases had lain just beneath the surface, now began to pervade most German educational institutions, reinforcing the Jews' feeling of isolation from the surrounding society. In the historian Werner Angress's words, many young Jews regarded each school day as a "heavy psychological burden."[39] Although initial legislation did provide exemptions for many Jews from the quotas, the message of sanctioned anti-Semitism compelled large numbers to leave voluntarily. In Württemberg, for example, where only 10 percent of young Jews were directly affected by the April legislation, 58 percent decided to leave state-run schools as a result of the anti-Jewish atmosphere.[40] Jewish children also faced social ostracism to a great degree outside the school environment, as they soon found themselves restricted from sporting and cultural activities.[41] Ironically, these quotas positively impacted Jewish education in Germany. The number of Jewish schools grew consistently between 1933 and 1937, as did the proportion of Jewish children attending these schools.[42] Many parents welcomed the possibility of finding a Jewish school environment, even if their children were legally permitted to attend government schools.

Debórah Dwork, in her study of Jewish youth in Nazi Europe, tells of a girl from Nuremberg who was exempt from the quota because her father was a war veteran. Soon enough, though, her non-Jewish class-mates would say, "No, I can't walk home from school with you any-more. I can't be seen with you anymore." Eventually she could no longer take the abuse: 1935 "seems to have been the year when the consciousness of my Jewishness and the differences, and the fact that I was disadvan-taged came home to me." She transferred to a Jewish school and joined Habonim.[43]

Though hesitant in some ways, many parents showed great interest in plans to relocate their children outside of Nazi Germany, at least tempo-rarily. In response to parents' concern for their children, the Zionist press argued that only the *yishuv* was prepared to accept large numbers of young Jews, though the papers generally omitted the fact that British policy was unlikely to permit mass immigration in the face of Arab op-position. And despite the growing hostility Jews confronted in Germany, fear of Arab violence did surely deter many from looking toward Pales-tine for refuge.

Before committing its resources to back Youth Aliyah, representatives of the ZVfD demanded that the Jewish Agency accept responsibility for the children in Palestine. Logic might dictate that the *yishuv*'s leaders would change their attitude because of Hitler's assumption of power. Yet the process was more forcefully set in motion by two related events: Chaim Arlosoroff's visit to Berlin in May 1933 and his assassination in Tel-Aviv one month later. Arlosoroff was the head of the Jewish Agency's political department and a rising star in the *yishuv*'s labor Zi-onist leadership. Additionally, having grown through the ranks of the Zionist establishment in Germany, at one time directing Hechaluz, Ar-losoroff had tremendous influence among German Zionists. Arloso-roff's support for organized immigration of German youth to Palestine became even more important after his death.

Immediately following Hitler's ascension to the chancellorship, Ar-losoroff argued that the rise of Nazism represented a catastrophe for all European Jewry but a unique opportunity for Zionism that should not be squandered.[44] In immediate response to the April boycott, Arlosoroff spoke with the high commissioner for Palestine, Sir Arthur Wauchope, stating the immediate need for supplementary immigration certificates to relieve German Jewry. Even though British policy based Jewish immigration to Palestine on the country's economic absorptive capacity, Arlosoroff sought to convince Wauchope to consider political developments in Europe as well. During the last few months of his life, Arlosoroff dedicated himself to promoting Palestine as a haven for German Jews.[45]

Arlosoroff departed for Germany on April 26 and remained until the end of May. In an interview published in the May 23 *Jüdische Rundschau*, under the title "What Can Palestine Offer the German Jews?" Arlosoroff offered his vision for solving the crisis, prefacing his remarks with the caution that while he indeed was submitting an organized plan, he would not engage in debate whether or not Palestine represented *"the [sole] solution"* to the challenges facing German Jewry (emphasis in original). Nevertheless, he declared, Palestine would be neither a temporary answer nor an emergency shelter (*Nachtasyl*), but rather, as the Jewish national home, could offer a permanent solution for those able to take advantage of it.[46]

The first question he addressed was "What can Palestine, according to this plan, accomplish for the education of Jewish children from Germany?" Arlosoroff suggested three possibilities: boarding schools (*Internate*), schools on agricultural settlements (*Siedlungsschulen*), and settlements that were schools (*Schul-Siedlungen*) in and of themselves. The first solution he recognized as possible for only a small number of students, due to the high cost. The latter two, on the other hand, could potentially absorb large numbers. At minimal cost, declared Arlosoroff, agricultural colonies such as Ein-Harod, Beth Alpha, or Nahalal could provide education along with practical preparation. The only drawback he foresaw was lack of suitable accommodations, which would have to be constructed. The third option was an institutional one along the lines of Ben-Shemen youth village, where his own daughter had been a student in 1931.[47] In fact, Arlosoroff suggested not merely expanding Ben-Shemen but also establishing ten new *Schul-Siedlungen* along this model. These new institutions could thereby offer places for two to three thousand young immigrants.[48] Considering the financial resources required to construct other youth villages, immediate implementation was unlikely. Since a few agricultural settlements had previously expressed interest, and were already constructing the necessary housing units, the second option appeared most feasible.

From what source did Arlosoroff find inspiration for this plan? Of course the notion of rapid mass immigration was not new and could be seen in the proposal raised by Zionist leader Max Nordau in 1920 to bring five hundred thousand Jews to Palestine in the wake of World War I. In 1929 Hashomer Hazair's Mordechai Shenhavi had called upon Polish Jewry to view Palestine as an "educational center" for Jewish youth, with little impact.[49] Arlosoroff does not seem to have been influenced by these plans. One possibility, that he met Recha Freier during his tour of Berlin, must be ruled out, as Freier was actually in Palestine at that time. In fact Arlosoroff never credited Freier or any other individual for originating the idea of large-scale youth immigration.[50] However, as he did meet with Zionist leaders in Germany, who were at least aware of Freier's scheme, and since the idea had been raised in the *Histadrut* prior to his Berlin trip, one may speculate that Arlosoroff had been exposed to the basic framework of this plan. Even before the article's appearance and the wider publicity given the scheme following Arlosoroff's death, other figures seriously considered organized immigration to Palestine as a solution to the crisis facing Germany's Jewish youth.[51] In the May 4 issue of the Palestine Hebrew daily *Davar*, the journalist Yosef Aharonovitz wrote, "I advise establishing an organization, which will focus all its efforts to rescue the Jewish children of Germany and transfer them to the Land of Israel. By Jewish children in Germany I refer to children from the ages 6–7 to 15–16."[52]

Arlosoroff's support provided the necessary spark to create the organizational framework allowing Youth Aliyah to function. Arlosoroff could justifiably be considered the movement's architect, rather than its creator.[53] The Jewish public's association of youth immigration with Arlosoroff served to increase awareness of both the specific problems confronting young Jews and a possible solution via organized transfer.

Upon his return to Palestine Arlosoroff immediately pressed Wauchope on the issue, visiting Ben-Shemen with him in order to demonstrate the possibilities for youth immigration. This initial discussion elicited a positive response from the high commissioner. Though no papers were signed, Arlosoroff and Wauchope informally agreed to obtain certificates for youth emigration from Germany.[54] As this tour coincided with the last day of Arlosoroff's life, some leaders in the *yishuv*, including Henrietta Szold, perceived Youth Aliyah as Arlosoroff's legacy and a testament to his vision.

Zionist leaders in Germany now had the proof they had earlier demanded that the Jewish Agency would support Freier's program. The Jüdische Jugendhilfe consequently concluded an agreement in midsummer to be organized as the Jugend- und Kinderalijah department of the Berlin Palestine office. Since the Palestine office was traditionally responsible for distributing immigration certificates allotted to Germany, this arrangement increased Youth Aliyah's visibility and lent the plan an air of greater legitimacy. Primarily through the pages of the *Jüdische Rundschau*, Youth Aliyah was now presented to the German Jewish public as a well-conceived, educationally and organizationally sound program rather than as a utopian scheme.

The Jewish press gave Youth Aliyah a forum for explaining its function and purpose to promote interest and to increase its basis for financial support. The picture of Youth Aliyah painted in the *Jüdische Rundschau* differs somewhat from Freier's simple construction of providing training on collective agricultural settlements. Youth Aliyah's propagandists now offered a vision more in tune with the educated middle-class German lifestyle, a perception most likely cultivated to appeal to the more socially conservative German Jewry. Accordingly, even though the newspaper noted that Youth Aliyah was "concluding" negotiations with Ein-Harod and Rodges, the article did not mention that these colonies were kibbutzim, thereby avoiding raising the specter of socialism. Similarly, when the two-year training program was described, the first year of instruction was summarized as follows: "special emphasis will be placed on knowledge of Hebrew, history, literature, study of Palestine [*Palästinakunde*] and general education [*Bildung*].[55] A large portion of the educational program is devoted to natural sciences, such as biology, chemistry, physics, botany, and physiology. . . . A great value is placed on the cultivation of music and physical fitness."[56] During the second year the children would receive training in "various occupations." The language was designed to appeal to teens and parents who envisioned obtaining professional skills and training in fields such as veterinary medicine, agronomy, botany, or zoology, rather than in the agricultural sector.

This curriculum, emphasizing traditional studies and addressing the occupational crisis facing German Jewish youth, did not seem to represent the ideological aspirations of a fifteen- to sixteen-year-old member of a Zionist youth group. Rather, Youth Aliyah was promoted as offering an attractive educational opportunity in the best German pedagogical tradition. The Zionist goal of pioneer life as an agricultural worker in Palestine and the rigors and difficulties associated with it received little attention. Similarly, alongside its agricultural operations, Ein-Harod was described as possessing various vocational workshops. (The kibbutz did have such workshops, but the Youth Aliyah immigrants were to receive their *hachsharah* in the fields as farmers). Training in a particular trade, perceived as a more marketable and valuable skill than farming, was prized by Jewish parents in Germany, whereas agricultural preparation was understood to have only limited value and reflected a lower social status.

These descriptions of the various opportunities available through Youth Aliyah appear deliberately misleading. Youth Aliyah, now organized within the Palestine office, was presented as legitimate, respectable, and appealing to a wider constituency. As complaints later registered by parents demonstrate, the high expectations were sometimes unfulfilled.

Whether due to Arlosoroff's interest or to the basic urgency of the situation, by mid-1933 the idea of an organized youth emigration from Germany had achieved enough attention to be raised at the Eighteenth Zionist Congress in Prague. Recha Freier recalled that during her stay in Palestine, at a time when Arlosoroff was in Berlin, one of the few leading personalities in the *yishuv* to support her idea had been sociologist Arthur Ruppin.[57] According to the recollections of Georg Landauer, Ruppin, though inclined to bring in large numbers of young Jews, initially did not consider the responsibility for educating these youths as falling within the purview of the Jewish Agency.[58] Perhaps Arlosoroff's legacy prevailed when Ruppin spoke at the congress and stressed the important role Palestine could play in relieving German Jews' distress, particularly that of the younger generation, despite the small percentage of world Jewry this represented.[59] Ruppin not only reported on the plight of Jews in Germany but also offered specific suggestions on immigration. The congress subsequently passed the following resolution: "As it is very important that the young immigrants from Germany, who have passed the obligatory school age, shall receive a technical education, especially preparation for agricultural work, the Congress welcomes the fact that all sections of the *yishuv* are endeavouring to facilitate the admission of immigrants to the rural farmsteads." The congress then requested the Jewish Agency Executive "to see to the centralising of this activity under conditions that render possible a proper education and its supervision, as well as to use its best endeavours to facilitate the immigration of youth into the country."[60]

Specific work in Palestine on behalf of youth from Germany fell under the auspices of a larger office also created during this congress, the Central Bureau for the Settlement of German Jews in Palestine, nominally under the direction of Chaim Weizmann in London and run by Ruppin in Jerusalem. Responsible to the Jewish Agency Executive, this new section was known simply as the German Department. Szold, who until this point had opposed mass youth immigration, was prevailed upon by the Central Bureau to undertake direction of the program in Jerusalem. The seriousness with which the Jewish Agency regarded this aspect of emigration from Germany is evident by the fact that the first item on the budgetary proposal presented to the Central British Fund for German Jewry was a $106,000 allocation for youth immigration, including capital investments for new construction. This appropriation represented the largest single budgetary item aside from land purchase through the Keren Kayemet Leyisrael (Jewish National Fund).[61]

During the summer of 1933 the Arbeitsgemeinschaft planned for the first wave of teenagers to be transferred to Palestine via Youth Aliyah. Anticipating a speedy allocation of certificates, the Jüdische Jugendhilfe had already selected the first candidates, and in September this group trained at a preparatory camp, owned by publishing magnate Salman Schocken, at Gut-Winkel near Berlin.[62] Subsequently the group of Orthodox youths destined for Rodges underwent a six-week training course at the Sonderhof farm near Hamburg.[63] The Arbeitsgemeinschaft's initial proposal to the Jewish Agency called for an immigration of five hundred between September 1933 and March 1934. The cost was estimated at a little over one hundred thousand dollars, of which from one-fourth to one-third would be raised in Germany to be used for travel and preparation.[64]

While the group destined for Ein-Harod had completed its preparatory course and anxiously awaited permission to depart, Yitzchak Ben-Zvi, president of the Va'ad Le'umi (the *yishuv's* national council), and Szold negotiated for certificates with representatives of the Palestine government but were unable to achieve tangible results.[65] For the Ein-Harod group, this delay was psychologically debilitating. One teenager's diary entry from October 1933 noted the boredom and monotony that characterized this waiting period. Disappointedly he recorded that hours previously dedicated to learning Hebrew at the Winkel training facility were now passed reading and smoking.[66] Whether on his own or sharing a cheap apartment with a comrade, his spirit withered. According to his description, this waiting period could be characterized in the following manner: "A [departure] date would be set, approach and pass. A new date would be set, and then it too would pass. Organized activity was impossible. Grumbling arose. We began to doubt the entire enterprise. Week after week passed, more than three months."[67] Solace could be found, though, in the prospect of at least recapturing the atmosphere of community he had grown to love during his three weeks at the preparatory camp. During this interim, between completion of the training camp and departure for Palestine, a number of the teens rented an apartment in Berlin and lived communally. In this way they found some measure of social and spiritual fulfillment in an otherwise bleak environment. Yet every postponement darkened their mood.[68]

Though unaware of the ultimate ramifications of leaving Germany, those who had registered for Youth Aliyah did understand that a new life in Palestine offered opportunities and optimism simply unavailable to Jews in Nazi Germany. Young Eliyahu internalized every delay, perceiving that not just his trip to Palestine but his very future rested on the success of this project. The stress made him recognize the very real implications that relocating to Palestine could have for a young man. His commitment waned. If he were so inclined would he be able to return to Europe to study at a university after completing his kibbutz training? When his mother told him of a group of young Jews preparing to leave for a three-year training program in Holland, he seriously considered the proposal. Indecision weighed upon him until late December when the Mandatory government approved the application for youth certificates.[69]

In October 1933 the *Jüdische Rundschau* devoted a full page to the subject of Jewish youth in Palestine, highlighting the youth village Ben-Shemen. The next issue of the newspaper printed an article focusing on the third partner in the Arbeitsgemeinschaft, the children's home Ahawah, noting the Berlin institution's decision to construct a home in Palestine where it could provide children with better opportunities.[70]

Using the Jewish press in the diaspora, particularly through visual imagery and language, was recognized as an effective tool for promoting immigration to Palestine.[71]

In an article printed on November 3, conspicuously adjacent to another piece addressing the problems of occupational retraining in Germany, Eva Stern, then in charge of the Arbeitsgemeinschaft's publicity, provided a comprehensive description of Youth Aliyah as a solution to the questions worrying Jewish parents in Germany.[72] The public could be adequately reassured of the venture's serious nature through Youth Aliyah's ties to the Berlin Palestine office as well as the Zentralausschuss, and through the Jewish Agency's assumption of responsibility under the direction of no less a figure than Chaim Weizmann, the leading statesman of the Zionist movement.[73]

Utilizing the language of professional social work, Stern highlighted the tremendous contrast between the future confronting a young Jew remaining in Germany and one who would realize the dream of immigrating to Palestine. By acclimating the individual at an earlier age, Youth Aliyah would ensure a more successful absorption than the conventional scheme of joining Hechaluz and training in the diaspora. Further psychological advantages would be gained by removing the young Jew from the harmful environment of a hostile society. The project was thus presented not as a short-term solution of two training years, but rather as a long-range project to incorporate Jewish youth into a community (*Gemeinschaft*) that needed the strength and cooperation of young pioneers.

As Stern later recalled, any early opposition Freier may have encountered from the German Jewish community stemmed from general concern with taking young people out of their homes and separating them from their families rather than an inability or unwillingness to see the approaching storm.[74] The common Jewish (and German) conception of family as the center of life created a psychological barrier to enthusiastically embracing Youth Aliyah, and Stern's articles and brochures attempted to overcome this resistance.

Eva Stern (later Michaelis-Stern after her marriage to Adolf Paul Michaelis in 1938), who composed these articles and edited most of the public relations material produced by Youth Aliyah, was perhaps second only to Recha Freier in consistently and continuously trying to achieve youth emigration from Germany. In terms of administrative responsibilities and daily activities, her practical contributions surpassed Freier's. A woman whose efforts are generally missing from histories of Youth Aliyah, Stern's unique path to this calling deserves specific attention.[75]

In 1904 Eva Stern was born into an assimilated German-Jewish family in Breslau. Her grandfather Sigismund Stern had been active in the Reform movement in Germany and her father, Wilhelm Stern, was a renowned professor of psychology in Breslau, Hamburg, and finally Durham, North Carolina, where he died in 1938. Her family also included a brother, Günther, who married the philosopher Hannah Arendt. (They divorced in 1937.) From 1935 to 1939, while she still supported the Zionist movement, Arendt was the secretary general for Youth Aliyah's Paris office, most likely brought to this position by her connection to Eva Stern.

Stern's upbringing included few ties to any Jewish communal organizations, as her father did not support even the CV or the Reichsbund jüdischer Frontsoldaten (National League of Jewish Veterans). On the other hand, Wilhelm Stern had left Breslau during World War I because he had refused to accept baptism as a means of academic advancement, claiming that he would never change his religion just to further his career. The family moved to Hamburg where Stern enrolled in the Jewish Girls Lyceum, headed by the liberal poet Ya'akov Löwenberg. Her parents chose this school because of its reputation as a progressive educational institution and because of its proximity to their flat in Hamburg, not because of its religious identification. In fact her father had petitioned the school to exempt Eva from learning Hebrew. Nevertheless, this introduction to Jewish life and culture attracted her and at the age of fourteen she joined the Jüng-jüdischer Wanderbund, which later became the Zionist group Brith Haolim.

After finishing secondary school Stern received certification as a gymnastics (physical education) instructor. She worked in this capacity from 1924 to 1928 in Hamburg and volunteered to teach gymnastics in the Jewish Volksheim in Altona. This activity brought her into contact not only with young eastern European Jews but also with Siegfried Lehmann from Ben Shemen, who invited Stern to live and work at his youth village in 1928. Though thrilled with the prospect of relocating to Palestine, even as "the only German Jewess at Ben Shemen," her *aliyah* was unsuccessful. She did not adjust well to the summer climate at Ben Shemen and returned to Germany later that year, finally settling in Berlin. Stern's experience was not necessarily atypical; many German *olim* found conditions in Palestine too trying and returned, a phenomenon less characteristic of emigrants from eastern Europe.[76]

Stern's work with Lehmann and the youth village, the fact that she had firsthand knowledge of Palestine, and her enthusiasm for the Zionist cause made her a valuable asset to the team of activists beginning to organize youth immigration, and she agreed to join the staff in late 1932.

In accordance with the Arbeitsgemeinschaft's mission in 1933, Stern appealed to the wider Jewish public to support Youth Aliyah. Not only was it necessary to cover the basic costs of the emigration and education, notably transportation and two years of room, board, and instruction, but the settlements and institutions in Palestine also required capital investments. The costs for two years of training were broken down as follows (in dollars):

Support costs, first year	104
Support costs, second year (taking into account work done by student)	86
Building investment per child	72
Travel costs, preparation in Germany, administrative costs	98
Total	360[77]

Half the candidates would be selected from families capable of paying the full cost. In order to provide for those in more severe financial straits the Arbeitsgemeinschaft required charitable contributions. This plea was aimed not merely at concerned parents and Zionists but at German Jewry in its entirety. By appealing to a broad constituency, even during those early months, Youth Aliyah's leadership presented the movement as a means of uniting, through understanding and practical aid, a divided community confronted by a common fate.[78]

Ludwig Tietz, the youth leader and social worker, played a significant role in demonstrating Youth Aliyah's broad base of support. Though strongly identified with the CV, Tietz nevertheless sympathized with the work being carried out in Palestine. Tietz, who had always been convinced, despite economic challenges, that young Jews could find their destiny in Germany, also recognized the unprecedented threat of Nazism. As a young doctor in 1921 he helped found the Deutsche-Jüdische Jugend-Gemeinschaft, an organization that stated its goal as educating young Jewish men "in common work for Germany and Judaism."[79] Indeed Tietz's ideological journey from an outspokenly *deutsch-jüdisch* position to one of sympathy though not outright support for Zionism, epitomized the transformation experienced by many German Jews of his generation during the early 1930s. Tietz's willingness to work for Youth Aliyah during the summer of 1933, while it was still unknown to most Jews in Germany, had enormous influence in bringing the movement to the attention of leading German Jewish figures outside the Zionist establishment.[80]

During these same months, the periodical *Jüdische Wohlfahrtspflege und Sozialpolitik,* issued by the major Jewish social work organization, supported the notion of Palestine as a rallying point to unite German Jewry, specifically as a means of providing a future home for Jewish youth. Georg Landauer claimed that all conflicts within the Jewish community were silenced when people were confronted with the Palestine question and the hope it offered Jewish youth, emphasizing the need to support Youth Aliyah, which presented immediate settlement opportunities.[81] In addition, according to the social worker Shalom Adler-Rudel, *Berufsumschichtung,* the more conventional approach to the economic crisis, succeeded most effectively among those individuals preparing to immigrate to Palestine. The ideological and spiritual commitment to life in the land of Israel motivated young Jews more strongly than simple economic considerations.[82]

Youth Aliyah was indeed attracting wider circles of German Jewry to the Zionist idea. Expanding the base from which it could draw potential trainees also assisted Youth Aliyah from a practical perspective. The organization expected that increased interest in the program would attract a sufficient number of parents capable of providing full financial support for their children during the two-year training period in Palestine.[83] Three months into its work, the Arbeitsgemeinschaft noted that applications for youth emigration far surpassed the expected number of certificates. Yet only one-fifth of the applicants could guarantee payment for all maintenance costs. Most potential emigrants had already reached a point of economic desperation, while those Jews who still had the means to live comfortably were less likely to flee the country. Candidates from families without means sometimes sought to raise the required money independent of the Jugendhilfe and thus be included as "paying" participants.[84]

Despite oversubscription, the Arbeitsgemeinschaft continued to seek out new applicants. Such expansion served three distinct purposes. Hopefully additional affluent parents would be convinced to enroll their children, thus alleviating a financial burden. Furthermore, a larger pool of applicants would improve the quality of candidates selected for relocation in Palestine. Finally, increased enrollment would demonstrate to the Palestine authorities the need for more youth certificates. Favorable publicity for the youth immigration project was reinforced when Henrietta Szold came to Berlin in 1933.

Though Youth Aliyah provided Szold a tangible legacy among a new generation in Jewish Palestine, this contribution was merely the capstone to a lifelong commitment to the Jewish people, the Zionist movement, and the *yishuv*. Though Szold's life and work has been extensively documented elsewhere, a few biographical details will highlight why she was well suited to head Youth Aliyah and how she was able to serve so effectively in this capacity.[85]

Perhaps most importantly, Szold's position as head of the Jewish Agency's child welfare and social services department gave her invaluable insight into the pedagogical and practical challenges Youth Aliyah would face in Palestine. As a relatively neutral figure in *yishuv* and Zionist politics, Szold's appeal reached across party lines, a significant factor as Youth Aliyah sought moral, political, and financial support throughout the Jewish world. So too was she one of the few figures able to straddle that middle ground between Orthodox and secular Jews in Palestine, a relationship already strained by the 1930s. One must also consider Szold's role as founder of Hadassah, the Women's Zionist Organization of America, and the philanthropic implications of that relationship. Whether this connection was factored into the equation when she was initially asked to direct Youth Aliyah, Hadassah's contributions would prove essential.

When she agreed to direct the Jerusalem office of Youth Aliyah at the age of seventy-three, Henrietta Szold decided to travel to Germany in order to evaluate firsthand both the crisis confronting German Jewry and the young Jews' desire to come to Palestine. She claimed that direct discussion with the Arbeitsgemeinschaft was essential in order to determine the division of labor within the organization as a whole. Her visit provided unique opportunities from a fund-raising perspective and furnished effective public relations material. Szold's work in improving public health in Palestine was legendary, going back to Hadassah's earliest contributions, and she was respected by the competing ideological movements within German Jewry. Her appearance gave a tremendous spiritual lift to the members of the Arbeitsgemeinschaft, the Jugendhilfe, and those young Jews hoping to be included in Youth Aliyah.[86]

Szold met with representatives from the Arbeitsgemeinschaft, the Palestine office, the Jüdische Jugendhilfe, WIZO, and various youth groups. She criticized the many partners within the Arbeitsgemeinschaft for acting independently without any sort of organized plan. Regarding the Jüdische Jugendhilfe's claim to represent organized Jewish youth, she did note that the association included representatives of the religious youth, but membership was essentially limited to Zionists, thus failing to represent organized German-Jewish youth in its entirety.[87]

During the course of Szold's negotiations with the Arbeitsgemeinschaft, a number of resolutions were passed. All parties agreed that Youth Aliyah could only succeed through closer contact between Germany and Palestine and the establishment of corresponding centers of operations with clearly delimited responsibilities. Szold resolved to organize such an office in Jerusalem within the framework of Ruppin's German Department. The center in Palestine would obtain all certificates for immigrating youth, particularly for those not going to Ben-Shemen or Ahawah, and find appropriate means of accommodating the young people in Palestine; it would continually supervise these accommodations; it would take sufficient measures, if the living conditions were deemed inappropriate, to find other means to integrate the youths; and finally it would administer funds remitted to Palestine by the Arbeitsgemeinschaft according to mutually established guidelines.[88]

Szold agreed to find appropriate host kibbutzim and moshavim. With the approval of the Jugendhilfe, the Palestine bureau would sign contracts with these settlements. At the Jugendhilfe's request, the general desires of the German youths to be brought to specific collective workers' settlements would also be considered. The Arbeitsgemeinschaft would retain control of sending children to Ben-Shemen and Ahawah. Szold's office would accept the "moral responsibility" for hygienic, pedagogic, and professionally engineered accommodations in Palestine. Observations of immigrant youth would be conducted in conjunction with the Palestine school inspectors. At the discretion of the Palestine bureau, and at the expense of the Central Fund, one or more social workers would be employed to secure adequate supervision.[89]

The Berlin offices granted certain functions they had previously ful-
filled to Szold's bureau within the Jewish Agency. Specifically, communications with settlements in Palestine, which had been carried out from
Berlin as early as Recha Freier's negotiations with Ein-Harod, would be
conducted from Jerusalem. Other than a willingness to take the ideological backgrounds of the German youths into consideration, there was
no contractual obligation to send members of particular youth groups to
corresponding settlements in Palestine. However, the Jugendhilfe, representing the various *Bünde,* retained responsibility for selecting suitable
candidates.

The determination to restrict Palestine immigration only to individuals deemed appropriate "material" (this was the word used by Zionist
leaders) for building up the land of Israel was a distinct feature of the
yishuv's Labor-dominated political leadership at that time.[90] The kibbutzim demanded that Youth Aliyah candidates be screened on the basis of
qualifications determined in Palestine, not in Germany. While the selection issue indeed received consideration before 1933, the installation of a
Nazi regime and the concomitant dramatic rise in applications to the
Palestine office forced Zionist leaders for the first time to face the real
possibility of mass emigration from Germany.[91] Nazi policies, however,
compelled some individuals, even in the *yishuv,* to perceive selectivity in
a new light, not merely as a function of physical training and Zionist
indoctrination. Specifically, even a politically neutral Zionist such as
Ruppin stressed that age, education, marital status, and property qualifications should also be considered.[92] With the number of applicants to
Youth Aliyah far exceeding the anticipated allotment of certificates,
leaders of the Arbeitsgemeinschaft anticipated sending only individuals
of the "highest quality" to Palestine.[93]

Over time, the moral dilemma raised by selectively determining immigration candidates intensified and sparked debates among Zionist
leaders in Germany and Palestine. The historian Avraham Margaliot
noted that Hechaluz in Germany, in contrast to the wishes of the Histadrut, did not support immediate mass immigration, and referred to
immigration to Palestine without the prerequisite training as "a Zionist
crime."[94] Errors in preparation and selection could lead to emigration
from Palestine, which was absolutely unacceptable from a Zionist perspective. Suitability for life in Palestine generally received heavy consideration in determining which two-thirds of those who requested

immigration permits from the Palästina-Amt (Palestine office) were rejected. The guiding principle behind the selection process, according to the physicians who supervised candidates' medical screening, was that "Youth Aliyah is a national enterprise (*miph'al le'umi*) and not a philanthropic enterprise."[95] Even though youth leaders in Berlin supported the selection ideal, at least theoretically, the goal was hardly achieved to the satisfaction of Youth Aliyah's office in Jerusalem.

While Szold visited Berlin, the Jugendhilfe negotiated with the Reich Economics Ministry for the transfer of funds to Palestine. The British government would not allow minors to immigrate unaccompanied without a guarantee of financial support provided in Palestine pounds. Owing to Germany's fiscal laws, notably the *Reichsfluchtsteuer* (flight tax) and blocked bank accounts, special arrangements would be necessary to convert the sums raised by Youth Aliyah in Germany to Palestinian currency.[96] Duly aware of Nazi economic policy, the Jugendhilfe nevertheless made a special request, noting that its organization worked for the removal of young Jews from German soil.[97]

In a letter addressed directly to the proper government ministry, Simonson requested permission to transfer the sum of 1,000 pounds ($4,240) monthly to Palestine. The funds would be forwarded directly to the German department of the Jewish Agency. Following the successful transfer, the Jugendhilfe promised to furnish a list of the young Jews scheduled for immediate relocation in Palestine.[98]

The language of this inquiry, particularly the request for 1,000 pounds, equivalent to the required sum for individual capitalist immigrants, and the request to wire funds directly to the Jewish Agency, demonstrates Youth Aliyah's hope of using the Ha'avara transfer agreement.[99] The purpose of Ha'avara, concluded on August 7, 1933, was to enable *olim* from Germany to remove a larger portion of their capital holdings than was generally permitted in accordance with the flight tax. Funds transferred to Palestine via the Jewish Agency would be used as credit to purchase German manufactured goods. Germany's government supported this scheme since it not only promoted Jewish emigration but also had the practical benefit of increasing exports. Two weeks later, the Reich Ministry of Finance stipulated the transfer be carried out by the appropriate fiscal institutions, showing that the Ha'avara permitted Youth Aliyah to use some of the funds raised in Germany for directly subsidizing maintenance costs in Palestine.[100] The Palästina-Amt, having received assurances from the Ministry of Finance that Youth Aliyah could use the transfer, believed the German government viewed the youth immigration program in a positive light.[101]

In November 1933 the Palestine government announced the distribution of 350 immigration certificates for German Jews between the ages of fifteen and seventeen, but demanded a financial guarantee of $611 for each child to cover the entire two-year training period.[102] The Palestine government, choosing the side of caution, estimated the monthly outlay per child at $25.50, whereas Szold claimed the Jewish Agency could care for a child at half that cost.[103] Regardless, Youth Aliyah had to provide these financial guarantees in addition to the expense of preparing the host settlements to receive young German Jews.

Thus the project's success depended considerably on Youth Aliyah's ability to locate sufficient funding. While trying to find immigration candidates from families able to cover these costs, the Arbeitsgemeinschaft also initiated fund-raising activities in Germany and abroad. As early as the summer of 1932, Freier toured Jewish communities in France, the Netherlands, and elsewhere, with some success, in order to find financial support for her project.[104] By early 1933 these neighboring countries began to receive the initial wave of Jewish refugees fleeing Germany and, considering the economic circumstances prevailing throughout all of Europe, had little desire to see continued immigration.[105] This factor, in addition to the deepening unemployment crisis confronting German Jewry, led the Arbeitsgemeinschaft to expect that its campaigns abroad would provide more income than those in Germany. Yet Germany's restrictive economic policy and Youth Aliyah's desire not to aid the Nazi economy by importing valuable foreign currency forced the Arbeitsgemeinschaft to conclude that activities and operations conducted on German soil would be financed only by contributions raised domestically. International campaigns would fund operations in Palestine.[106]

Initially all the traditional philanthropic bodies that helped facilitate *aliyah*, specifically the Keren Kayemet Leyisrael (Jewish National Fund) and the Keren Hayesod (Foundation Fund), refused to finance Youth Aliyah. Even German Jewry's own Zentralausschuss, which provided money for immigration to Palestine, did not originally allocate funds for youth immigration.[107] As Martin Rosenbluth recalled, though they operated within the same Central Bureau for the Settlement of German Jews in Palestine, from 1933 it was apparent that Youth Aliyah had to rely on special grants and donations, outside normal Zionist channels. Rosenbluth, who was dispatched to London by the ZVfD in April 1933 to work with the Jewish Agency on matters concerning Jewish emigration from Germany, recalled how surprised he was that Youth Aliyah had to compete aggressively with other Jewish philanthropies for contributions.[108] Eventually Youth Aliyah became so successful in raising money that the other Palestine-directed funds considered it a source of competition.

Logistics and practicality became Youth Aliyah's priorities. The two elements receiving the most consideration, both at this early stage and throughout the prewar years, were selecting candidates and collecting funds. Since youth certificates were received directly from the Mandatory government and assigned to individual immigrants by name, rather than distributed by the Palästina-Amt, the Jugendhilfe had to forward the names of their acceptees to Jerusalem prior to departure. This process created technical difficulties since Berlin generally submitted the names to Szold's office prior to the final selection process. Thus Simonson informed Jerusalem in mid-January 1934 of discrepancies between the lists originally sent from Berlin and the final numbers. Of a group of twenty-four destined for Kibbutz Rodges, four candidates were dismissed during the screening period at the preparatory camp. Another group scheduled to depart for a training farm run by Rachel Yanait (Ben-Zvi) was reduced from thirty-seven to twenty-four.[109] These figures underline the serious commitment to selectivity. However, the removal of candidates from organized groups meant that initially some slots for potential immigrants remained unfilled.

Additional technical problems resulted from the Palestine government's demand for a prepaid guaranty of $611 per immigrant, as opposed to the Jewish Agency's initial estimate of $153 per year for each child. Despite the agreement concluded in November, the German and Palestine offices of Youth Aliyah already found themselves in conflict. Szold's office expected maintenance costs to be provided by Berlin, either from the parents directly or through subsidies raised in Germany. But the Arbeitsgemeinschaft claimed that the economic hardships confronting Germany's Jews prevented the Berlin office from covering the full cost. It was hoped that the Jewish Agency could prevail on some other philanthropic body, such as the American Jewish Joint Distribution Committee to provide the balance.[110] According to Rosenbluth, the first groups' departures were only secured through a last-minute $75,000 contribution from the philanthropist Meyer Weisgal.[111] This debate between Szold's office and the Arbeitsgemeinschaft over financial responsibility parallels the claims of other Zionist organizations in Germany that the *yishuv* did not fully appreciate the challenges confronting German Jews.[112]

By February 1934 the Jugendhilfe had overcome the initial logistical and financial obstacles to enable the first organized group of teenagers, destined for two years training on Ein-Harod, to leave Berlin. The delay, however, reduced the group's size from sixty-one to forty-three, as a number of candidates reached their seventeenth birthday, making them ineligible for youth certificates.[113] The need to act expeditiously in the future was clear.

During the twelve months following Hitler's assumption of power, Youth Aliyah realized some tangible results. The Jugendhilfe succeeded in convincing some Jewish teenagers, parents, and communal leaders in Germany that Youth Aliyah offered a practical solution to concerns regarding young Jews' futures. Responsible figures founded the Arbeitsgemeinschaft to provide the essential material support for the immigration program. These fundamental elements of the movement's mission continued to form the backbone of Youth Aliyah's activity in Germany during the next few years, even as German Jewry's changing needs compelled the organization to address additional issues, some unforeseen, directly related to youth welfare and emigration.

3
Emigration or Welfare Movement?

Though Nazi policies became more oppressive, not all Jews were yet convinced that the time had come to evacuate. Even for those seriously considering emigration, Palestine was not generally viewed as the optimal destination. Among younger Jews, however, the notion of a new life in the land of Israel grew increasingly attractive. This generation gap had significant consequences. In many cases boys and girls became deeply committed to a new life in Palestine while their parents had tremendous difficulty overcoming their negative preconceptions regarding Zionism. As Eva Stern described it: "A Youth Aliyah group from Germany includes young people who receive no further support of an educational, cultural and economic kind from their own family. This generation has nothing to lose and nothing to renounce."[1]

Rosemarie, for example, was born close to the end of World War I. Her family was wealthy and completely assimilated, they believed, into German society and culture. Her parents had concealed their Jewish origins and took great pride in the "fact" that they were pure Germans. As a young teenager Rosemarie rebelled against her parents' world and ideals, joining Habonim at age thirteen and studying the Hebrew language and Zionist ideology with great intensity. Her parents had only contempt for Zionism, a movement anathema to the ethos by which they had modeled their lives. The constant conflict between parents and daughter led Rosemarie to run away from home—she was persuaded to return by her youth group leader.

As early as June 1933, when she turned fifteen, Rosemarie applied for

Youth Aliyah. Naturally her parents refused to sanction such a "disgraceful project." Though she could not be accepted for immigration without her parents' consent, the Jugendhilfe kept her application on file in the hope that her parents would change their minds. Throughout the next year her parents only seemed to become more obstinate in their refusal to permit Rosemarie to go to Palestine. By early 1935 the family's economic position had so deteriorated that her parents relented, though emphasizing that the Zionist cause ran counter to their outlook. In July 1935 Rosemarie left Germany with Youth Aliyah for two years of training at Tel Hai in the Upper Galilee.[2]

Rosemarie's tale highlights both the difficulties Youth Aliyah continued to face in convincing German Jews to support the program and the fact that economic and pragmatic considerations often outweighed the ideological arguments either for or against Zionism.

On the evening of February 12, 1934, the Jüdische Jugendhilfe's first group left Berlin for Palestine under Youth Aliyah's auspices. This first successful transfer, along with the prospect of additional certificates, invigorated Youth Aliyah's promotional work. Between early 1934 and the promulgation of the Nuremberg Laws in September 1935, a period sometimes viewed as relatively calm with respect to the Third Reich's Jewish policy, Youth Aliyah dramatically increased its activities.[3] Adam Simonson's article in the *Jüdische Rundschau* the day after the first group's departure reflected the new focus of Youth Aliyah's public relations agenda. Even more so than the previous year's campaign, the Jugendhilfe appealed to German Jewry in its entirety. While stressing the individual teenager's specific qualifications for the journey to Palestine, Simonson also attempted to demonstrate that the first group's demographics reflected the diverse composition of Germany's Jewish youth.[4] According to Simonson, the group had few *Ostjuden* (eastern European Jews) because there were few "genuine *Ostjuden*" of the appropriate age in Germany. From an individual intimately acquainted with the composition of German Jewry, this claim seems surprising for three reasons. That the *Ostjuden* comprised 20 percent of Germany's Jewish population, a significant minority, was known at that time, and this percentage was even higher in Berlin. Second, *Ostjuden* had always been overrepresented among German Zionists. Third, Jewish sociologists in Germany were well aware of the community's disproportionate age structure, weighted heavily toward the older population.[5] Jews from eastern Europe, who did not share the bourgeois predilection for small families, would have been overrepresented within German Jewry's younger generation.

In fact Youth Aliyah continued to receive many applications from young Jews of eastern origin, as those families more recently arrived in Germany generally experienced greater hardship as a result of the Depression and Nazi policy. A girl named Beate, for instance, was the oldest daughter of *ostjüdische* parents in Dresden. Since her family had applied to the Jewish community for financial assistance, Beate had been placed with foster parents in a middle-class home. After January 1933, as their own economic fortunes waned, the foster parents could no longer support her and pay for her school. With no apparent prospects, and considering the financial burden she represented to both families, she decided to immigrate to Palestine. Beate joined Habonim and the group recommended her for Youth Aliyah in 1934.[6]

Another story is that of Esther, born into a lower middle–class family of seven who had come from Poland. Her father struggled with a small shop and some of the children worked to help support the family. Soon after 1933 the parents decided to send the children to Palestine and hopefully join them at a later date, so Esther too joined Habonim. Though she had very little education, Jewish or otherwise, in April 1934 she immigrated with Youth Aliyah to the Girl's Farm in Talpiot outside Jerusalem.[7] In both these cases the applicants did not seem to wrestle with the decision to go to Palestine. They did not see the move as a permanent separation from family, but as relief from financial burdens confronting their parents. Young Jews of eastern European origin had less vested in German culture or nationalism, so the idea of emigration was more palatable.

If the *Ostjuden* represented a sizable portion of Youth Aliyah immigrants throughout the prewar era, why did Simonson downplay their role? Perhaps Simonson qualified his claim by using the word "genuine" to differentiate between those teenagers of eastern European origin who were visibly identifiable as such, and others who had integrated more fully into mainstream German Jewish society. Apparently, his goal was to present Youth Aliyah as an attractive option even for Germany's assimilated Jews. This effort aimed to change the perception of the typical pioneer as a Polish Jew. Statistically speaking, even during the Nazi era, most immigrants to Palestine, especially those arriving as workers, continued to come from eastern Europe.[8] However, the Jugendhilfe, along with other Zionist organizations, hoped to demonstrate that German Jews, despite their strong identification with western European culture, could also contribute to building up the Jewish homeland.

Accordingly, Simonson noted that the first group's members came to Youth Aliyah with little knowledge of Hebrew, as was generally the case among "*assimilierten Westjuden*," and that although most came from religious families, the children generally rejected this outlook.[9] This portrait of the average candidate probably coincided with many readers' assessments of their own children. The main impact of the first group's departure, however, was to demonstrate the feasibility of the program as a whole, with an eye toward future expansion.

The Arbeitsgemeinschaft distributed a pamphlet titled *Jugend-Alijah* in 1934, with the stated purpose of creating "a living (*lebendig*) personal connection between [Youth Aliyah's] sponsors and the lives of the young people in Palestine."[10] Periodic reports and excerpts from letters written by these young pioneers would help achieve this goal. Not surprisingly, the pamphlet reiterated that Youth Aliyah could only continue if the Palestine government received insurance that the entire training period would be financially guaranteed.[11]

Quite naturally feedback regarding the group's first experiences in Palestine appeared in the Zionist press. The arrival on the shores of Palestine, the process of clearing customs, and the first moment on the soil of Eretz Israel were described as proceeding without difficulty. Even the rainy weather that accompanied the youngsters' arrival was portrayed in a positive light, providing the much-needed water for Palestinian agriculture. One writer even commented on the "exemplary ease" with which the young Jews settled into the new surroundings, "a further sign of the discipline and order prevalent in the Jewish youth groups in Germany."[12] Absorption was not always a smooth process, but publicizing that fact would not have supported the public relations campaign.

Szold sent a letter to both the Palästina-Amt and the Jugendhilfe describing her visit to Ein-Harod before the first group's arrival.[13] She assured the offices in Germany that the barracks constructed specifically for Youth Aliyah were the highest quality, and she hoped that the parents would be so informed. By publishing this letter in the press, Youth Aliyah attempted to show the Jewish public that its children were not destined for a barren wilderness but that the host settlements were civilized in all respects. While this public relations campaign is quite logical, it contradicts the more conventional rhetoric of labor Zionism that stressed sacrifice, toil, and creating a new society. Especially when addressing segments of the population only recently attracted to Zionism, much effort was put forth to portray Palestine as an acceptable destination for the cultured youth of Germany.

Attempts to heed German Jews' demands that accommodations reflect a high standard of living created difficulties. Even the wooden barracks at Ein-Harod as described by Szold were deemed unsatisfactory in Berlin, many parents demanding the erection of sturdier permanent structures. In early 1934 they did not yet consider themselves beggars, but rather believed they had the luxury of being choosers. Concurrently, the Jugendhilfe pressed Jerusalem to approve additional sites in Palestine interested in accepting Youth Aliyah groups. Szold maintained that these demands were contradictory and that only by using the same provisional methods as applied in Ein-Harod could immediate settlement be assured.[14]

By mid-March 1934 Youth Aliyah had filled only 96 of the 350 certificates granted in November 1933. Szold reproached the Berlin offices for not supplying the necessary names for the remaining certificates, which would expire in May.[15] Yet Szold continually pressed the Arbeitsgemeinschaft and its constituents to employ extreme selectivity. This situation highlights the dilemma over mass *aliyah* from Germany: should greater emphasis be placed on qualitative or quantitative considerations for immigration? In general the correspondence from Palestine, especially before November 1938, favored a selective policy, reflecting historical assessments of Zionist and *yishuv* policy at the time. In early 1933 labor leaders in Palestine disparaged the inferior human material that comprised most potential emigrants from Germany. Despite the well-known intensification of Nazi anti-Jewish policy, this attitude prevailed until the outbreak of World War II.[16] Youth Aliyah did not have the luxury of substituting higher-quality candidates from eastern Europe to fill the youth certificate quota.

Conflicts between Berlin and Jerusalem were further compounded by financial considerations. Fund-raising in Germany, including the sums provided by parents, proved insufficient to provide the full maintenance guaranties demanded by the Jewish Agency. Not only did Szold's office need a list of potential candidates in order to apply for certificates, but it also expected Berlin to forward the necessary payments. By the beginning of April the lists of participants were arranged, but Simonson wrote that the Arbeitsgemeinschaft was unable to transfer the money for the final 100 certificates.[17] Despite the Ha'avara agreement, the Third Reich's currency regulations continued to impede the transfer of Youth Aliyah funds from Germany to Palestine. In June 1934, according to Marduk Schattner, then in Prague beyond the scope of Nazi censors, Jewish institutions in Germany had tremendous difficulty exporting even petty sums as small as four Reichsmarks ($1.58). He suggested that communications refrain from suggesting that Youth Aliyah in Germany had any foreign currency at its disposal, lest Nazi censors demand such funds be turned over to the state.[18] Even if the Arbeitsgemeinschaft succeeded in raising sufficient money in Germany, it could not remit the currency to Palestine.

The quantity of youth certificates allocated appears most significant when compared with the overall figures for emigration from Germany, excluding the essentially unlimited possibilities under the capitalist category. For the first half of 1934, when Youth Aliyah received 350 certificates, a total of 884 workers' certificates were available to the Palästina-Amt, mainly for young males age eighteen to thirty-five. Youth Aliyah obtained almost half as many certificates as were available for noncapitalist German Jews of all ages.[19] The disparity between the number of certificates available for pioneers from Germany compared to the 15,000 individuals who registered with Hechaluz by the end of 1933 reinforced the strong demand for selectivity.[20] This fact no doubt further drove young Jews to consider Youth Aliyah, which, based on these figures, offered better odds for reaching Palestine than waiting to join Hechaluz.

In May 1934 Simonson announced his upcoming resignation as director of the Jüdische Jugendhilfe in order to pursue his own *aliyah*.[21] A number of prominent Zionist personalities, such as Kurt Blumenfeld and Georg Landauer, had left Germany soon after Hitler came to power. While these individuals continued to work on behalf of German Jewry from their new homes, leadership of the movement was turned over to less experienced successors. This pattern was repeated at regional and local levels as well as within the various youth movements. Ironically at a time when the message of Zionism began to appeal to a wider audience within German Jewish society, the individuals most capable of presenting this outlook were leaving.

Georg Josephthal, who replaced Simonson in June 1934, soon complained about this constant loss of organizational stability.[22] He claimed that as the best of their comrades departed for Palestine, the full burden fell on the shoulders of a weakened leadership.[23] According to one former Habonim *madrichah*, the leaders generally knew little more than the younger group members. This situation continued to degenerate over time, and by October 1938 youth leaders in Germany complained that all the individuals capable of properly inculcating the membership with the requisite ideals and knowledge had already made *aliyah*.[24] Youth Aliyah was fortunate to find competent and motivated individuals to step into its positions of responsibility. In early 1934 Eva Stern and Marduk Schattner, a *shaliach* from Kibbutz Ein-Harod, officially overtook direction of the Arbeitsgemeinschaft. Josephthal, the new head of the Jugendhilfe, brought extensive experience working for Hechaluz in Germany.

One of Josephthal's first acts in early July was to rewrite the contract signed by Youth Aliyah parents. The original forms stated that if parents defaulted on payment or if trainees were deemed unfit in Palestine, the Jugendhilfe reserved the right to terminate participation three months prior to the deadline that had already been paid for. The remaining funds could be used by Youth Aliyah to return the child to Europe.[25] At the earliest stage, those directing the movement did not conceive of the dangers awaiting children who were returned from Palestine. In mid-1934, though, Josephthal replaced the clause with one stipulating that only in cases where the son or daughter endangered the well-being of the settlement, particularly the welfare of the other youths of the kibbutz, would the training be terminated and the individuals returned to Europe "or to a place determined by the parents/guardians."[26]

The new director of the Jugendhilfe noticed that emigration took its toll on the quality of youth the organization attracted alongside the aforementioned drain on leadership. By April 1935, despite the increasing number of young Jews registering with Youth Aliyah, the level of talent, particularly among the *madrichim*, was diminishing. Josephthal blamed this deficiency on the fact that the earliest groups were largely composed of individuals with longstanding commitments to Zionism who had grown up within the ideological environment of the *Jugendbünde*. Freier described the attitude of the new recruits to the Zionist youth groups as being led, "not by the spirit of the movement, but by the events of the time."[27] The Jugendhilfe established the Youth Aliyah School in 1934 with the aim of reversing this trend.

The school was one of two institutions Youth Aliyah sponsored for the purpose of intensifying the preemigration training that young Jews could receive in Germany. In addition to its school, Youth Aliyah instituted a program known as *Mittleren-Hachscharah* (intermediate preparation, also known as MiHa) in early 1935 in cooperation with Hechaluz.[28] Operating along the lines of traditional *hachsharah* programs, MiHa provided an outlet for young Jews enrolled in Youth Aliyah who failed to pass the initial screening process. Most teenagers who participated in MiHa had only recently been exposed to Zionism and were unfamiliar with the youth movement lifestyle. Many were enrolled by their parents specifically for the purpose of learning a trade without concern for the institution's ideological underpinnings. By directing young Jews down a path that combined academic instruction and vocational training, this program served in one historian's words "to partly solve one of the most severe problems facing Jewish youth in Germany."[29] The training was much more intense than the preparation received by Youth Aliyah groups, which operated from the assumption that real *hachsharah* would be received in Palestine.[30]

Both MiHa and the Youth Aliyah School exemplified an increasingly popular trend among Jewish educational institutions in Germany. Elementary schools traditionally provided instruction until the legally required age of fourteen. As a result of Nazi policies, many Jewish schools, some newly established and others recently expanded to handle the flow of students forced out of public schools, decided to institute a ninth school year. According to the Reichsvertretung's school department, many students opting for the ninth year hoped to participate in Youth Aliyah. For many students this extra school year led to an additional tenth year, which emphasized training for Palestine.[31]

Yet the Jugendhilfe's programs and the ninth year offered by some schools did not function solely as preparation for emigration, but attempted to solve a communal problem already apparent to the nascent Reichsvertretung in late 1933. Recognizing the flow of Jewish students out of the schools, Ismar Elbogen, a leading scholar of German Jewry, hoped that many young Jews could find direction in youth groups. In cases where Jewish youth did not follow this path, caring for the continuing education of these idle Jews would remain the responsibility of individual communities.[32] The *Gemeinden* evidently failed to satisfy this need by mid-1934, and schools such as the Youth Aliyah School began to fill this gap.

Students in Germany generally completed compulsory schooling at fourteen or fifteen. Yet according to immigration regulations, Youth Aliyah students would only be allowed to enter Palestine after they had passed their fifteenth birthday. The school grew out of a series of courses developed by the Jugendhilfe to address the needs of those candidates still too young to immigrate. Classes intensified the preparation process and occupied the trainees as they approached the required age. Since these courses were offered in Berlin, the Jugendhilfe also established a boarding house, known as the Mittleren-Beth-Chaluz to accommodate young Jews from outside the area.[33] As the number of applicants increased to four thousand by July 1934, most would clearly not be able to immigrate with the next groups, so the Jugendhilfe expanded its individual course offerings into a full school program.[34] By bringing together students from diverse backgrounds, the school demonstrated Youth Aliyah's potential to help unify a factioned Jewish community, providing a place where young Jews from small villages sat next to city-dwellers, where the very Orthodox learned together with radical socialists, and where children with no previous identification with Jews or Judaism, some of whom had even been baptized, worked alongside those whose families had identified with Zionism and Palestine for many years.[35]

This unique school has perhaps most accurately been described as an educational "transit-station," as it could not be categorized in traditional pedagogical terms.[36] While there was a faculty and set curriculum, the student body was constantly in flux. The school's director, Franz Ollendorf, pointed out two specific cases to illustrate this phenomenon: "Moses' father was shot in a concentration camp, the mother took her own life. When will be the first opportunity to send this dismayed youth to his new life? Marcel was a member of a communist youth group when he was a student at the Karl Marx School. Yesterday one of his comrades was arrested." As a result of dire circumstances and intense preparation, such students received permission to emigrate after a few months.[37] These examples also demonstrate the contrast between the pressure to emigrate and priority for those in immediate need, glaringly evident to those in Germany, and the demand to reduce the number of problem cases from Youth Aliyah in Palestine. One can easily imagine that such experiences as those described above took a psychological toll on the children, which could inhibit normal social development after immigration. At times urgency outweighed long-term considerations. The focus on preparation was clearly evident from the emphasis on language instruction. Alongside basic language skills, the school also accommodated advanced students, encouraging Hebrew instruction in the traditional academic disciplines, such as mathematics and science. Youth Aliyah did not hesitate to emphasize the similarities between its curriculum and a classical German education.

The Reichsvertretung strongly emphasized this connection between education and emigration. Recognizing the need to consider *Berufsumschichtung* and the likely relocation of young Jews when creating new Jewish schools, it allocated significant resources to instruction in manual trades and foreign languages. When the Reichsvertretung distributed its educational guidelines for Jewish schools in mid-January 1934, the renaissance of Jewish life in Palestine was given particular attention in the curriculum, as was training in Hebrew language.[38] Originally most Jewish schools functioned merely to replace the course of instruction typical of German schools, albeit in a Jewish social setting. This new orientation in the Jewish schools, even those not outspokenly Zionist, fostered an atmosphere in which an increasing number of young Jews became more receptive to Zionist ideas.

The complete promotional effort presented Youth Aliyah within the tradition of Jewish social welfare rather than as a movement centered only on realizing Zionist goals in Palestine. Articles promoting Youth Aliyah's endeavors focused more on the specific services the program offered German Jewry than any contribution the young pioneers would make to building up the Jewish national home. The concluding passage from an article in a Hamburg communal newspaper stated, "Youth Aliyah is a way towards repairing the career and life distress of our young."[39] Recognizing the difficult conditions of life in Palestine, the article suggested that only physically strong and spiritually sound individuals would adapt. Therefore the Jews of Germany must provide the opportunities either through schools or youth organizations for young Jews to attain the necessary state of preparedness. According to at least one historian, Zionism in Germany had served this function throughout the interwar period.[40]

The Jugendhilfe organized propaganda evenings in Jewish schools and continued to push for increased coverage in the Jewish press. As a result, 20 percent of the candidates the Jugendhilfe prepared for immigration came from the ranks of unaffiliated youth.[41] Advocates stressed that among Jewish youth of varied backgrounds, the idea that agricultural or vocational training in Palestine represented the only way, or at least the most likely way, to fulfill the physical and psychological needs of young Jews was gaining increased support.[42]

In May 1934 Szold wrote, "all the Jewish youth organizations of every shade of political and religious opinion united [together] in a federation."[43] While this portrayal, which was applied to Youth Aliyah even many years after the Holocaust and the establishment of an independent Jewish state, may have promoted fund-raising, particularly outside the borders of Germany, the evidence demonstrates that some Jewish groups in Germany even during these early months found themselves in conflict with Youth Aliyah.

Religious orientation, for example, proved a persistent stumbling block to achieving unity of purpose.[44] Even though Orthodox groups, with their own committees and educational goals, were represented almost from the outset, this union was only maintained with difficulty. Religious pioneering movements targeting younger Jews were a relatively new phenomenon in Germany. Prior to 1933 Bachad had generally limited its activity to those eighteen or older. Parents were not easily convinced to permit their children to emigrate. "We attempted to convince even many of our own people, the mizrachi, and also people in the communities or in the Reichsvertretung who did not want to know from [Youth Aliyah]."[45] Most Orthodox Jews in Germany did not affiliate with the Zionist movement, and the largest independent Orthodox organization, the Agudat Israel (the Agudah), originally committed to defeating Zionist aims, could be described as having moved to a moderate position of non-Zionism by the 1930s.[46]

Yet even before the rise of Hitler, a faction within the religious youth group Esra, an organization originally formed in 1918 for the purpose of bringing new blood into the ranks of Agudat Israel leadership, had already turned to Zionism.[47] The new political circumstances after 1933 raised the general issue of emigration within this youth movement and caused many to believe that Palestine offered the best solution.[48] As early as March 1933 *Der Israelit*, the Frankfurt-based organ of the Agudah, criticized British policy that allowed the Jewish Agency to monopolize distribution of certificates and requested that Palestine be opened to young Orthodox Jews as well.[49] In July 1934, in the hopes of realizing a youth immigration within the framework of its particular religious/political ideology, the Agudah created its own Arbeitsgemeinschaft für religiöse Jugend-Alijah.

The news that a non-Zionist body was establishing its own youth immigration program caused anxiety within the German Youth Aliyah offices for two reasons. First, if this new institution could convince the Jewish Agency or the Palestine government to provide youth certificates, the result would likely be a reduction in the number available to Youth Aliyah, which had already committed a quarter of its certificates to Orthodox youth. Second, the Arbeitsgemeinschaft was tremendously concerned about competition in terms of fund-raising. It expected Agudat Israel to solicit donations for their youth immigration scheme by attacking Youth Aliyah.[50] Eventually, the two sides reached a compromise.

The Arbeitsgemeinschaft viewed its work not only as serving the needs of future pioneers but also as beneficial to the whole community, particularly those in dire financial straits. Of the young people enrolled, 40 percent came from impoverished middle-class families and an additional 25 percent from working-class families. The organization emphasized its aid to families in which the parents had been unemployed for a number of years and to children from public homes and institutions, including illegitimate children and orphans. As Claudia Prestel noted in her study of Jewish reform schooling in Weimar Germany, this emphasis on at-risk children reflected longstanding trends within the social welfare establishment.[51] Youth Aliyah would alleviate the financial strain felt not only by those families in particular need but also by the community at large.

Jewish social workers promoted Youth Aliyah as a way to alleviate the economic burden shouldered by struggling families in Germany. Compared to the expense of similar technical or agricultural training in Germany or continued instruction in a private educational institution, the monthly cost of supporting Youth Aliyah students was relatively small. The Zentralausschuss newsletter expressed the hope that individuals receiving the proper technical and professional training through Youth Aliyah would soon be in a position to assist the immigration of their relatives.[52]

This approach can be seen in the case of Ernst Loewy from Krefeld whose parents turned to Youth Aliyah in the middle of 1935. In response to the anti-Semitism of his classmates and teachers at the Krefeld Real-gymnasium, Loewy registered with the Jugendhilfe, his parents hoping their son's new life in Palestine would facilitate their own immigration. They were soon informed, however, that in all likelihood their son would need two additional years of work following the two-year training period before he could expect to bring his parents over.[53] Given the political realities in Germany during 1935, most parents could reasonably expect to persevere long enough for their emigrant children to establish themselves in new lands and then join them. In this respect Youth Aliyah represented hope for entire families, not just the young.

Prior to 1938, however, the atmosphere of Nazi Germany more often exacerbated the generation gap between parents and the growing number of Zionist children. Parents feared that sons and daughters would abandon their families and immigrate to Palestine on their own. In some families children had daily contact with and exposure to the increasing hostility, whereas parents, particularly if unemployed, could retreat into the cocoon of home life. Jewish teenagers, well-aware of the rapidly changing environment in Germany, criticized parents' failure to perceive the growing danger. In more acculturated families, such as those where fathers had performed military service in World War I, the children's espousal of Zionism, a rejection of German nationalism, could create bitter tension.[54]

In addition to these ideological debates, Youth Aliyah also found itself in the midst of economic conflicts aggravating German Jewry. The leaders of traditional Zionist philanthropies viewed the new circumstances in Germany as an unprecedented opportunity to attract contributors. An independent fund for youth would mean competition for these resources. Yet Youth Aliyah was not subsidized by any Zionist organizations in Germany and therefore relied, almost exclusively, on its own fund-raising abilities. Expanding to include education and training programs in Germany combined with continually growing registration and demands from Palestine for more money forced the Arbeitsgemeinschaft constantly to search for new avenues of revenue.

Looking beyond the borders of Germany, the Youth Aliyah staff clearly recognized the importance of America as a philanthropic resource, despite the persistence of the Depression, and consistently expected great contributions from American Jewry, particularly from individuals who were not regular contributors to Zionist projects. In fact, Youth Aliyah was seen as a way of bringing non-Zionist circles to contribute to Jewish Palestine.[55] During 1934 representatives of Hadassah, the Women's Zionist Organization of America, first expressed interest in taking a significant role in Youth Aliyah.[56] Szold counseled Hadassah to focus its efforts elsewhere, as its membership was already committed to supporting various other important projects in Palestine. She suggested that Hadassah, as a large donor, would demand a voice in disbursing the funds it raised; she only acquiesced to Hadassah's involvement provided they merely contributed money and did not participate in the decision-making process.[57]

Szold repeatedly warned Rose Jacobs, Hadassah's president, that Youth Aliyah would differ from every other Hadassah venture in that Berlin and Jerusalem "could brook no interference from America."[58] According to an agreement finalized during the summer of 1935, Hadassah would be recognized as the sole representative for Youth Aliyah in the United States provided it cover the cost (thirty-six thousand dollars) of transferring and maintaining one hundred German Youth Aliyah students. If Hadassah did not succeed in coming up with the required sum, Youth Aliyah would remain free to carry out its own campaign in America.[59] Hadassah proved monumentally successful in marshaling its broad membership to raise contributions, far surpassing those collected in Europe. By 1938, working in association with film and radio star Eddie Cantor, Hadassah could raise more than twenty thousand dollars at a single event.[60]

Louis Lipsky, on behalf of the American United Palestine Appeal (UPA), feared that if only Hadassah raised funds for Youth Aliyah, it would appear that the UPA had no involvement in the program and its philanthropic drives would suffer as a consequence.[61] In December 1935 Hadassah entered into a contract with the UPA stipulating the following: "Hadassah will in its literature, stationery and publicity make prominent reference to the fact that it is engaging in the Youth Aliyah activity as part of the United Palestine Appeal and for the program of the Keren Hayesod."[62] Hadassah, for its part, continually asserted that separating its Youth Aliyah drives from the UPA and Zionist Organization of America's campaigns assured contributors that funds would not be skimmed off for general operating expenses.[63]

Despite its successful fund-raising apparatus abroad, Youth Aliyah became increasingly dependent on the Jewish institutions in Germany, specifically the Reichsvertretung, to finance its expanding domestic programs. Jewish community institutions in Germany clearly recognized that training for work in Palestine held a special position in the occupational restructuring of German Jewry. A report by the Zentralausschuss declared that the normalization of Jewish career distribution was "only possible in Palestine"; particularly for those young Jews interested in vocational or agricultural occupations Palestine had unique significance.[64]

Though cooperation with the Reichsvertretung was essential, Youth Aliyah's success also depended on an international network of public relations and philanthropic organizations. The fund-raising aspect propelled Youth Aliyah from a local movement onto the world stage. It gained support, perhaps to a degree unmatched by other philanthropies, by presenting the specific needs of Jews living under Hitler's rule to the Jewish communities of the world. Indeed the legacy of Youth Aliyah in America was such that a historian of Zionism in the United States wrote, "The most famous relief project initiated by Zionists was Youth Aliyah."[65] Regardless of the accuracy of this statement, by 1935 the program's growth led to a call for an international conference in support of Youth Aliyah to be held in early September 1935, immediately following the World Zionist Conference in Lucerne.

During the Nineteenth Zionist Congress, Arthur Ruppin said in his introductory remarks, "I should like particularly to emphasise the remarkable results of the immigration of the younger people from Germany, of whom already 700 between the ages of 15 and 17 years have come to Palestine and have thus been saved from a soul-destroying existence and afforded the possibility of free development with the prospect of a happy future."[66] In fact, a significant portion of the German Department's report to the Congress addressed Youth Aliyah's accomplishments. This document concluded that Youth Aliyah had already achieved a resounding success and viewed the task as "serious and sacred."[67] For 724 Youth Aliyah immigrants, the Central Bureau for Resettlement of German Jews allocated more than $85,000 for construction costs in agricultural colonies, which translates to more than $120 per trainee. At the same time, the German Department spent $133,255 in similar housing costs to settle 2,576 adults, corresponding to $51.70 per person. The agency invested twice as much money per capita in Youth Aliyah as it did for the average adult emigrant from Germany.[68]

Notwithstanding the claim, reiterated during the congress by Zalman Rubishov, that Youth Aliyah presented a unique opportunity for uniting opposing factions within the Zionist camp, support was not unanimous. Meir Grossman, spokesman for the right-wing State Zionist party, complained that efforts to aid German refugees focused exclusively on absorbing German Jews into labor Zionism. Grossman specifically criticized Youth Aliyah, which brought middle-class German youths to socialist settlements.[69] Indeed some critics claimed that kibbutzim rushed to volunteer to host Youth Aliyah groups, not as a means of assisting diaspora Jews in distress, but rather to receive the coveted financial subsidies and capital investments that accompanied the teenagers from Germany.[70] Statistically at least, Grossman's complaint was accurate, as Youth Aliyah did not seem to offer emigration opportunities for young Jews unwilling to adopt socialist Zionism.

However, as a tool for reaching out to previously untapped sources, Youth Aliyah proved highly effective, and was recognized as such.[71] It seems logical that new converts to the Zionist idea, attracted by Youth Aliyah, would be drawn to labor Zionism as opposed to other ideological positions. Youth Aliyah could be viewed as a tool used by labor Zionists to alleviate the distress of German Jewry while promoting their own interests both in Palestine and abroad.

By augmenting its emphasis on propaganda, the movement attracted more young Jews to apply for youth emigration and increased its visibility and fund-raising activity within the larger Jewish community. Indeed the interest in Youth Aliyah surpassed the organization's ability to realize emigration, forcing its leadership to create institutions in Germany to administer to the general educational and social needs of Jewish youth, thus providing a valuable service to German Jewry within the Reich during a time of increasing despair.

During the first half of 1935, in terms of new edicts and actions, Hitler's government showed little overt concern with the Jewish question. Nevertheless, Germany's Jews experienced a renewal of sporadic spontaneous anti-Jewish violence. This new wave of brutality, reminiscent of early 1933 and generally perpetrated by dissatisfied party members, found support from radical elements within the National Socialist leadership. According to leading figures such as Julius Streicher, editor of the rabidly anti-Semitic *Der Stürmer,* this new outburst of violence demonstrated the German people's demand for the government to take more decisive action toward solving the Jewish problem.[72] Not only had Jewish emigration decreased following the large wave of 1933, but early 1935 also witnessed a large number of Jews returning to Germany. Over the course of that summer rumors surfaced suggesting that Nazi legislators were drafting important new edicts concerning the legal status of German Jewry.

At the annual Nazi party rally in September 1935, Hitler presented this new legislation at a special session of the Reichstag. The first citizenship law, which recognized de jure that Jews in Germany were not citizens, along with the Law for the Protection of German Blood and Honor, which prohibited marriage or sexual relations between German gentiles and Jews, are known collectively as the Nuremberg Laws.

For the history of Youth Aliyah, the Nuremberg legislation's impact lay in its direct influence on German Jews' sense of safety and security. Saul Friedländer noted that Heydrich hoped the new legislative measures would direct more Jews to Zionism and strengthen the drive to emigrate. Jewish reaction to these laws, often based on the psychological impact they produced, demonstrates the new legislation's significance for German Jewry.[73] As on earlier occasions, different segments of the community reacted in accordance with their own particular perspectives; yet these new laws also increased the basis for common action. Many German Jews believed that the Nuremberg Laws, their severity notwithstanding, would provide a concrete basis for Jewish existence in Germany. This attitude echoed the official explanation for the enactments provided by Nazi leaders.[74] Yet the editors of the *CV-Zeitung* also stressed that this latest setback signaled the end of shared communal life for Jews and Germans, reporting that Jews received the news with a profound sense of shock. Indeed, this new stage in Nazi policy caused the CV to adopt a more positive stance on Jewish immigration, particularly that directed to Palestine.[75]

The Reichsvertretung's responses to the Nuremberg Laws clearly demonstrated a strong sympathy toward the Zionist position. While the primary reaction was a renewed focus on emigration, Palestine as a preferred destination for young immigrants received special attention.[76] The Reichsvertretung's educational committee, for example, stressed the need to include knowledge of Zionism and the *yishuv* in Jewish schools' curricula. In fact, the Reichsvertretung's new program emphasized activity in five separate sectors: education, emigration, welfare, economic continuity, and building Palestine.[77] Youth Aliyah was actively engaged in every one of these activities, with the exception of the struggle to ensure financial stability in Germany.

When the Nuremberg Laws appeared, Henrietta Szold was in Berlin, en route to Palestine following the First World Youth Aliyah Conference in Amsterdam. Szold's presence in Berlin, at a seemingly critical juncture for German Jewry, brought Youth Aliyah to the attention of wider circles within a Jewish community becoming increasingly concerned with emigration.[78] The Nuremberg legislation compounded the degenerating financial circumstances in which most German Jews now found themselves, no doubt compelling many who had previously felt secure to consider emigration.

Willy's case demonstrates the impact of the Nuremberg Laws in this respect. He came from a middle-class Jewish family in Berlin; his father had made a comfortable living selling refrigerators. Though they identified themselves as Jews, the family only attended synagogue on the high holidays. The Nazis' success in 1933 caused the parents to reevaluate their commitment to Jewish life even though they were not yet directly affected. Though Willy's father remained ambivalent, his mother joined the Zionist organization and sent her two sons to the Theodor Herzl School. When Willy completed school, he planned to train at a bakery. Though the boys joined Makkabi Hazair, immigration to Palestine was not an immediate objective. After the father lost his German citizenship as a result of the Nuremberg Laws, it was he, not the mother, who went to the offices of the Jüdische Jugendhilfe and signed his children up for Youth Aliyah. Willy immigrated to Kiryat Anavim in March 1936.[79]

In terms of immediate impact, the Nuremberg Laws can be deemed successful, as the last quarter of 1935 saw a tremendous rise in the number of Jews fleeing Germany, reacting as Willy's father had. Yet the pace of emigration slowed, relatively, during 1936 as Germany attempted to downplay its Jewish policy while hosting the Olympic games, and this trend continued during 1937 and most of 1938. Thus, aside from the months immediately following the promulgation of the Nuremberg Laws, emigration statistics in general for the period between September 1935 and November 1938 remained on par with those of the preceding years, and annual figures still remained below the thirty-seven thousand Jews who had departed in 1933.[80] On the other hand, the number of young Jews requesting immigration certificates for Palestine increased dramatically. While total annual Jewish emigration from Germany to Palestine remained around eight thousand during these years, Youth Aliyah experienced continued growth.[81] In January 1936 Josephthal referred to Youth Aliyah as the only truly successful Zionist emigration program from Germany, since few workers' certificates went to German pioneers, and the weakening financial position of Ha'avara slowed the flow of wealthier emigrants.[82]

Events in the land of Israel, however, augmented the burden shouldered by Youth Aliyah in Germany. In November 1935 the Jewish Agency requested 350 additional youth certificates from the Palestine government, and by March 1936 had received the full complement. In May the Jewish Agency expected the Mandatory government's immigration department to approve its request for 450 certificates, noting the demand in Germany and the growing number of suitable host settlements in Palestine. This petition was rejected due to the outbreak of the Arab rebellion in Palestine in the spring of 1936, which resulted in a temporary cessation of Jewish immigration, including Youth Aliyah, and the appointment of a royal commission to investigate possible solutions to the Palestine crisis.[83] During the summer of 1936 a number of Youth Aliyah groups arrived in Palestine, but only by virtue of the certificates that had been allotted during 1935.

This suspension of youth immigration affected hundreds in Germany who had already completed their preparatory training and anticipated placement with a Youth Aliyah group through certificates expected in 1936. Parents who had felt some relief that their children would soon leave Germany again grew anxious. The situation also created an additional financial burden as these groups had to be maintained in Germany.[84] Youth immigration resumed during the winter of 1936–37, and the Palestine government continued to allocate youth certificates throughout 1937 and 1938, thereby relieving one source of pressure facing Youth Aliyah.

The Jugendhilfe reported that demand for youth emigration had increased 65 percent following the Nuremberg Laws. The expanding interest in Youth Aliyah was further exemplified by the remarkable rise, approximately 90 percent, in applications from medium-size and small communities.[85] While organizers reflected approvingly on the increased interest shown by smaller communities, they also recognized that these areas were generally more impoverished and the applicants needed greater financial support than the Jews in larger cities. As the Jugendhilfe relied on the *Gemeinden* to help defray the many costs associated with sending their children to Palestine, incorporating many young Jews from more remote areas presented new economic challenges. In response, the Jugendhilfe sought to find temporary refuge for young Jews hailing from these locations by providing boarding houses and even employment opportunities.[86]

A Jewish child's need to escape Nazi domination was felt most acutely in rural areas. Jews living outside the protective environment of large urban communities experienced a greater sense of alienation and oppression; communal leaders recognized the specific needs of isolated Jewish youths from these areas.[87] In order to accommodate the increasing number of applicants from towns and villages who wished to begin their training while still in Germany and thereby increase their chances of passing the selection process, Youth Aliyah established a number of *batei-hechaluz* (pioneer houses). Considering the terror that young Jews confronted living in isolated locations compared to the comfort offered by strong communal support in the cities, these homes often represented physical sanctuary as well as a springboard to emigration.[88]

The case of a boy named Heinrich demonstrates this trend. He was born and raised in a small provincial town in southern Germany. He had few friends, as there were few Jewish families and no organized Jewish life. His father had died when Heinrich was quite young, and by early 1934 his mother was no longer earning money. The Jugendhilfe, considering Heinrich's background, decided not to place him directly in a preparatory camp, where he would have been out of place among children from large cities who had some prior exposure to Jewish education. He was sent to the Bet-Halutz in Mannheim, where he attended a Jewish school and met other Jewish children his age. After six months, at the age of sixteen, he was sent to a *hachsharah* camp and then on to Palestine.[89]

The *batei-hechaluz* proved quite successful in providing security for young Jews from towns and villages.[90] Based on the model of communal homes established by Hechaluz in urban centers, which provided a gathering point prior to agricultural training, Youth Aliyah organized three *batei-hechaluz* in Berlin, each accommodating twenty to thirty youths, plus one additional youth house for religious children run by Bachad. Similar houses were also located in a number of German cities, such as Frankfurt, Hamburg, Leipzig, and Mannheim. These institutions also housed individuals from outside the cities who had already been selected for Youth Aliyah but had not yet received certificates. Freier compared the atmosphere in the *batei-hechaluz* to a waiting room, with people constantly coming and going and everyone asking, "When is it my turn?"[91] The waiting period could last as long as a year.

In contrast to the homes for adult members of Hechaluz, which often served merely as hostels, the Jugendhilfe established its *batei-hechaluz* for youth with specific pedagogical goals in mind. These houses provided unique educational opportunities, including close interaction with *madrichim* who would participate in the selection process. To a greater degree than attending the Youth Aliyah school, living in the *batei-hechaluz* provided applicants the means to demonstrate their worthiness for emigration.

Considering the stakes, the selection meetings could be contentious and heartrending. Typical reasons for rejection included: "this applicant is not Zionist enough"; "this one is not mature enough"; "this one is from Hashomer Hazair and there were problems with the last mixed group." For example, if the rest of the group came from the Werkleute youth group, that could be reason enough to delay an acceptable candidate's immigration. Freier retrospectively noted that such results could be tragic if an individual was forced to go to Mittleren-Hachscharah and never found the opportunity to leave Germany. Reflecting on the selection process as a whole, she conceded that mistakes often occurred but were unavoidable. "It was clear that a period of three or four weeks [in a preparatory camp] was insufficient really to get to know a person. . . . The situation was much better regarding the children we knew from the [Youth Aliyah] school and the *batei-hechaluz*."[92] These homes along with the Youth Aliyah School provided a meeting ground for a diverse Jewish population, many only recently identified as Jews, growing increasingly attracted to Zionism.

The following example further demonstrates the change in attitudes that occurred by later 1935. Before the Nuremberg legislation, Ilse Wechsler, a fund-raiser for the Arbeitsgemeinschaft, reported on two separate occasions that instituting effective appeals in the city of Düsseldorf would not be possible, as the community actively sponsored other causes.[93] A year after the Nuremberg Laws were announced, the *Gemeindezeitung* of Düsseldorf's Jewish community printed the text of a speech by Henrietta Szold and other propaganda material sent by Youth Aliyah.[94]

While the Nuremberg Laws may have provided renewed impetus for emigration and augmented the number of applicants, Youth Aliyah depended on the Palestine government for certificates, and the selection process remained highly competitive, as reflected in the constant rejection of applicants for medical reasons. At a meeting of the Jüdische Jugendhilfe in late September, leaders seriously considered the suggestion of returning Youth Aliyah's problem cases to Germany.[95] A report from Jerusalem stressed that selection in Germany needed to be controlled more carefully, particularly with respect to mental health, emphasizing that "*Rachmanut* [compassion] should not be used."[96]

But abandoning those who did not immediately qualify did not seem to be the answer. Since applications increased whereas the number of available certificates did not, the Jugendhilfe renewed its emphasis on educating young Jews in Germany.[97] This focus on continued instruction would increase the quality of young pioneers transferred to Palestine and also provide hands-on and academic training for those not immediately chosen. In early 1936 Youth Aliyah worked closely with the Reichsvertretung and local school committees to expand the number of Jewish schools offering a ninth school year.[98] The Reichsvertretung offered financial subsidies to teachers who left their jobs to lead Jewish youth in Mittleren-Hachscharah camps. The individual communities as well as the Reichsvertretung recognized identification with Palestine as an intrinsic element of Jewish education, providing hope and optimism in response to the new circumstances.[99]

By December 1935 the Jugendhilfe estimated requests for enrollment at 250 to 300 per month.[100] Even compared to an overly optimistic expectation of fourteen hundred certificates per year, most applicants would be either rejected or deferred. Nevertheless, through educational programs such as MiHa, the Jugendhilfe hoped to train those individuals for eventual immigration to Palestine. The financial burden of operating Youth Aliyah's programs, particularly the expenses incurred in Germany, outweighed the actual cost reflected in the number of young immigrants. Additionally, since most fund-raising efforts abroad, particularly Zionist ones, did not wish to send contributions directly to

Germany and thereby assist the German economy, Youth Aliyah operations within Germany were financed almost entirely by German Jews.

Perhaps due to Szold's organizational talents, Youth Aliyah seemed to operate with greater economic efficiency than the more conventional training programs, both in Germany and abroad. For the *Gemeinden* and the Zentralausschuss, the monthly cost for each Youth Aliyah participant would be $10.00 for the first year and under $8.40 for the second year. Agricultural training in more traditional settings would cost those institutions between $16.00 and $20.00.[101] From this most basic perspective, regardless of ideological orientation, and disregarding considerations of social or spiritual contentment, Youth Aliyah was appealing.

According to professional social workers in Germany, the importance of Youth Aliyah did not lie merely in the seven hundred immigration certificates provided annually. This number would be irrelevant if the training program in Palestine were not deemed successful from social, cultural, educational, and economic perspectives.[102] Rather than rely on theoretical arguments, such as the benefits of Youth Aliyah versus traditional *hachsharah* or Palestine's untapped potential for absorbing immigrant youth, supporters used the experience of the previous year and a half to provide concrete examples of Youth Aliyah's achievements. With hundreds of young German Jews already undergoing training in more than a dozen locations in Palestine, Youth Aliyah's activists in Germany not only spoke about the opportunities that lay in the future but also referred to current successes. Similarly, Youth Aliyah seemed confident that these initial results would help relieve concerns that German Jews might have regarding supervision in Palestine.[103]

To demonstrate the positive impact Youth Aliyah had on the lives of the young trainees in Palestine, the words of the children themselves as well as the reports of leaders and observers in the settlements were reprinted for the benefit of German Jewry. In early 1936 an additional propaganda tool documenting the absorption of these young pioneers into Jewish Palestine appeared—a Youth Aliyah film. This movie provided a visual connection between Jewish audiences in Germany and the young immigrants in Palestine, with celluloid images of life on the kibbutz. The documentary showed young Jews, reared in the cities of Germany, hard at work in the fields and classrooms of Ein-Harod, expressing their spiritual and cultural freedom through play and dance.[104] The Arbeitsgemeinschaft used the screening of this film, titled *Aufbruch der*

Jugend, as the main attraction of an informational and fund-raising evening in Berlin on May 25, 1936.[105] On this occasion, the keynote speaker was Rabbi Leo Baeck, arguably the leading figure in the Jewish community.[106] The support of such a prominent individual, whose appeal transcended the boundaries of factionalism, demonstrated the growing support for Youth Aliyah among mainstream German Jewry.

The Arbeitsgemeinschaft hoped to capitalize on the success stories from Palestine by compiling a brochure titled *Jugend-Alijah in Briefen,* consisting of letters received by the Jugendhilfe from potential candidates and excerpts from letters by the young pioneers to their parents, their friends, and youth groups and organizations in Germany. Forty-four ten- and eleven-year-old students from a Jewish primary school in Kassel sent a request to the Jugendhilfe for permission to go to Eretz Israel. Kurt, in East Prussia, described how he was the only Jewish boy in his town who had finished school and did not have a job. He read about Youth Aliyah in a newspaper and applied without his parents' knowledge, hoping to surprise them with good news. Aron in Munich was frustrated attending school in his hometown. As he was fit and capable of working the land, he hoped for a new start in the land of Israel. Numerous letters described the joyous receptions that greeted Youth Aliyah immigrants upon their arrival in various settlements in the land of Israel.[107]

In response to the outbreak of violence in Palestine, Youth Aliyah sought to reassure its supporters that its young *chaluzim* remained committed and dedicated to realizing the ideals of their training, which for some now included standing alongside kibbutz veterans in defense of their settlements.[108] As the number of Youth Aliyah graduates in Palestine increased, the movement proudly revealed that more than two-thirds elected to remain in the agricultural sector; thus the movement could claim success.[109] For committed Zionists, Youth Aliyah appeared as perhaps the best way to ensure productive emigration for young Jews. At the same time, Youth Aliyah was presented as an attractive option, certainly from a social and economic standpoint, for those who perceived most emigration schemes as well as retraining programs for continued life in Germany as moderately successful at best.

Jewish social workers did not ignore other suggestions for solving the crisis confronting Jewish youth in Germany, and indeed the Zentral-wohlfahrtsstelle focused on this larger issue.[110] But Palestine consistently appeared as the most logical solution when considering economic as well as spiritual and psychological factors. Josephthal, no longer directing the Jugendhilfe, further emphasized the unique role played by youth immigration to Palestine: "The Youth Aliyah offers not only the best, but also the most comprehensive attempt to solve the problem of those leaving school."[111]

As a direct result of Nazi legislation, children from mixed marriages were lumped together with that of the Jewish population. Though many considered themselves part of non-Jewish Germany, wanting, for example, to join the Hitler Youth, the Third Reich had cast them out. Theoretically the Jewish *Gemeinden* had no obligation to support these "new Jews." Youth Aliyah, however, effectively reached out to a number of these children, many of whom faced strained relations at home, and enabled them to receive immigration permits.[112]

Indeed many young Jews with two Jewish parents felt equally committed to their German identities. Adelyn Bonin, for example, was born into a highly assimilated German-Jewish family; her parents had embraced German identity to such a degree that they had Bonin baptized. Though maintaining no relationship with Judaism, Bonin was asked to leave her school in early 1934, at age thirteen. Considering her parents' outlook, her enrollment in a Jewish school that stressed the German aspect of a dual heritage is not surprising. Accordingly, the philosophy of the school strongly opposed Zionism. This atmosphere did not offer any positive connection to the Jewish element of Bonin's newly discovered identity, and by December 1934 she had become disenchanted.[113]

In Bonin's words, "into this mood of dissatisfaction, bordering at times, with typical teen-age volatility, on despair, like a fresh breeze came the idea of Zionism. . . . Here, finally, was an idea that promised a future, was optimistic, and was ready to put theory into practice. Best of all, following its premises, we could leave our dreary present in a country which despised us and start a new life in a new land, building on our own ideals with the work of our own hands. Instead of waiting for better times while trying to avoid being noticed, we could be proud again and carry our heads high."[114] Bonin obviously contrasted the optimistic message of Zionist activism, popular among younger Jews, with the more complacent wait-and-see attitude of her parents' generation.

Without consulting her parents, the girl explored available options for immigration to Palestine and decided to join Youth Aliyah. The for-

midable task of convincing her father to sign permission papers was
aided by both the promulgation of the Nuremberg Laws and the family's
deteriorating financial status. To begin her preparation, Bonin enrolled
in a Zionist school in the fall of 1935; half a year later she completed
Youth Aliyah's four-week preparatory course at Rüdnitz by Bernau just
outside Berlin. She recounted that students understood the importance
of passing the camp's screening process in order to ensure immigration
to Palestine; she referred to the selection announcements as "judgment
day." The *shlichah* Yocheved Bat-Rachel, recalling her observations from
Youth Aliyah's camp at Schniebinchen near Sommerfeld, similarly noted
the trepidation accompanying final selection.[115]

Since applicants realized the significance of the screening process,
some acted in whatever fashion they believed would most likely lead to
an early emigration. This zeal to emigrate could include disguising one's
religious or political outlook or both. The truth would often be revealed
only after the journey, when Youth Aliyah immigrants requested transfer
from one settlement to another more attuned to their own ideological
inclinations.

For example, a girl originally placed on the secular moshav Nahalal
was transferred, at her own request, to a girls' home run by the religious
Mizrachi organization.[116] Szold noted that young immigrants who hid
their true religious convictions during the enrollment and selection process in Germany complained to Zionist authorities, even while en route
to Palestine, regarding the difficulty of conforming to their traditional
religious observances on antireligious settlements.[117] By 1937 this practice
had become so pervasive that Szold described an overall trend, rather
than isolated cases, of religious children having been included in groups
settled on radical *kevutzot* (collective settlements, smaller than kibbutzim).[118] Religious deception also occurred in the other direction. For
example, the Ivdi home, an Orthodox institution, complained that a
number of students refused to adhere to religious strictures and recommended they be relocated.[119]

How does this pattern of deception shed light on the attitudes of
Jewish families in Germany? Since applicants' parents participated in the
enrollment process, these hidden identities suggest a few identifiable
causes. Parents, in their haste to see their children accepted, adopted the
position most likely to accelerate the emigration process. By 1939 Szold
noted that this behavior persisted as parents and their children affirmed

whatever outlook would result in the coveted certificate. Accordingly she wrote, "The circumstance that the supply of religious places in Palestine falls below the demand in Germany has influenced parents and their children to conceal the desire for the traditional Jewish life. They fear that they may lose the chance of redemption. Religious young people thus find themselves in radical surroundings, the subsequent removal from which presents almost insurmountable obstacles."[120] Since the names of the various settlements in Palestine accepting Youth Aliyah groups were publicized in Germany, families that paid attention would know which political/religious organizations were receiving the most certificates. Conversely, as even some non-Orthodox parents questioned the moral values or nonreligious character of many host settlements, they may have demanded that children who did not hold deep religious commitments request assignment to religious institutions. Moreover, the notion of Orthodoxy as opposed to liberalism, the common religious division among German Jews, differed from the dichotomy in Palestine of religious versus secular. The problem generally remained hidden because the common threat of Nazism and the desire to leave the Third Reich overshadowed these conflicts, which only resurfaced after the participants had succeeded in fleeing Germany.[121]

Of course, there is little doubt that Youth Aliyah was inexorably bound with the workers' movement in Palestine, and among different left-wing Zionist youth groups, Youth Aliyah bridged political conflicts and also brought formerly unorganized youth into the ranks of labor Zionism. One young immigrant reported that her training cadre at the Schniebinchen *hachsharah* farm was composed of two groups, one from Makkabi Hazair and another consisting of Habonim and unaffiliated youth. The camaraderie forged within the training unit created stronger bonds than former ties to specific youth groups, reflecting the social ideal that Palestine Zionists promoted.[122]

In 1936 Yocheved Bat-Rachel was called upon to fill a dual function as *shlichah*. Aside from the traditional duties of the emissary, mainly educational and organizational, particular focus was placed on the need for female representation in Germany, as all of her predecessors were men. Bat-Rachel's diary, if she can be considered representative, demonstrates that these *shlichim* for Hechaluz were not solely concerned with propagating the message of Zionism and knowledge of life in Palestine. They came to Germany with the additional goal of spreading a socialist ethos.

The importance of Zionism was, for them, tied inexorably to the social outlook of the kibbutz movement, and they hoped to bring this collectivist ideology to a Jewish community strongly wedded to middle-class ideals. Bat-Rachel, for instance, noted with dismay that a group of potential young *olim* she met in September 1937 envisioned the kibbutz as merely a transitional stage along the path toward the final goal of a comfortable bourgeois family life in the city or village.[123]

Bat-Rachel recognized Youth Aliyah as a possible means of attracting German Jews to the kibbutz ideal. Even before *hachsharah*, children could be set along this path through instituting common meals within urban groups, thus forging communal responsibility.[124] Mittleren-Hachscharah proved particularly successful in this regard. Even though many *madrichim* had limited pedagogical backgrounds—most either recruits from older Hechaluz groups or individuals with experience in classroom instruction—the specific social circumstances of communal living would imbue the trainees with kibbutz ideals such as commitment to self-government by the entire group with regard to social and work issues, as well as the communal fund (*ha-kupah ha-meshutefet*). Bat-Rachel therefore hoped that MiHa could provide a core of German emigrants dedicated to the kibbutz movement's philosophy. Especially when compared to Jewish emigration from Poland, German representation on agricultural settlements was very weak.[125]

The degree to which at least some potential *olim* adopted this attitude can be seen from the following letter a young girl from Nuremberg wrote to her friend:

> If we want to live in a community, we must all be strong enough to settle our personal affairs with ourselves. I believe, I mean, if we are somewhat depressed, we shouldn't use the *hevrah* [community] as a scapegoat. We must draw a clear line between our personal concerns and those of the community. For I believe, if everyone dumps his personal junk on the community's back, then the community is bound to break down. We must be careful not to let this happen. . . . We do not want to merely go there so as to "build up Palestine and make it fruitful," as the nice phrase runs, but also to look for a certain way in which to do that. It is not the same whether we build the country within the framework of a *hevrah,* or as individuals. *Nor is it the same whether one lives in a city or a village.* . . . I believe

Youth Aliyah to be for us a great step forward on the road to our great target. Now we can prove whether we are capable of translating all that we have learnt to formulate so well in theory, into action.[126] (emphasis added)

Despite this indoctrination, many young Jews arrived in Palestine expecting Youth Aliyah to provide vocational training for an urban trade. In May 1936 Szold criticized fund-raising literature that stressed *Berufsausbildung,* and noted that a large number of Youth Aliyah trainees complained when they did not receive such instruction.[127] Indeed the contract signed between parents and the Jugendhilfe claimed that Youth Aliyah would provide *Berufsausbildung,* a phrase perceived by most German Jews as a reference to manual trades.[128] According to Szold, the leadership in Berlin fostered this impression, perhaps to attract wider circles of German Jewry, even as she reiterated Youth Aliyah's commitment to the agricultural sector. Bat-Rachel recognized that most parents believed their children's future would be more secure with qualifications as skilled tradesmen. For this reason many parents of MiHa trainees preferred to send their children to urban *batei-hechaluz* rather than to agricultural *hachsharah.*[129] Josephthal, in a report to the Histadrut, remarked that the pioneering movements could not overcome most German Jews' preference for skilled trades. As he noted: "The mentality of the Jews in Germany has worked against us. 'The man who has a trade can go anywhere.'"[130] Many parents did not view Palestine as a final goal per se but rather recognized that Youth Aliyah could provide the immediate means for their children to escape from Germany.

As the months passed, even emigration programs suffered under the growing restrictions imposed by the Nazi authorities. For example, the 1935–37 period saw increased difficulties in transferring Youth Aliyah funds from Germany to Palestine. The German authorities favored facilitating financial transfer when they recognized a direct correlation between the release of funds and the number of Jews emigrating. Moreover, the exchange rate, though better for immigrants to Palestine through Ha'avara than for immigrants to other lands, continually declined.[131]

In addition to transferring funds to Palestine, the Arbeitsgemeinschaft also remained focused on continued appeals to support operations in Germany. In early 1936 Zionist economists devised a method to allow German Jews residing beyond Nazi rule to help support Youth

Aliyah without sending foreign currency: the *Sperrmark-Aktion.* German financial policy prohibited the removal of Reichsmarks from Germany without a heavy penalty, thereby severely reducing the value of these funds. The government placed liquid assets of German Jews who had emigrated in special blocked accounts, known as *Sperrkonten.*[132] The contents of these accounts, Sperrmarks, possessed little value outside Germany. During 1936 the rate of exchange for the Sperrmark, for those who migrated to lands other than Palestine, averaged 26.8 percent.[133]

Youth Aliyah recognized that these funds retained their value within the Third Reich and hoped emigrants would donate their blocked cash and help sponsor immigration to Palestine. In this way foreign currency would not be imported into Germany nor would Jewish assets be redeemed below fair value. The Arbeitsgemeinschaft instituted a systematic campaign, hoping to contact all owners of blocked accounts throughout the world in order to elicit their support for Youth Aliyah.[134] Potential immigrants to Palestine were also approached to sell their blocked assets to Youth Aliyah for repayment in Palestine pounds via Ha'avara, thus providing German currency to fund its domestic operations. Since Palestinian Jewry could benefit directly from this drive, particular emphasis was placed on collecting Sperrmark donations from German *olim.*[135]

The success in raising money both in Germany and abroad was paralleled by institutional support. By early 1936 the Zionist establishment strongly endorsed Youth Aliyah. The ZVfD conference held in February 1936 resolved to inform all Zionists of the growing importance of Youth Aliyah and to demand that they support the Arbeitsgemeinschaft as strongly as possible.[136] As the *C.V.-Zeitung* of February 20 reported, by this time Youth Aliyah could also count among its friends Otto Hirsch, leader along with Baeck, of the Reichsvertretung.[137] In November 1936 Josephthal wrote that Youth Aliyah was the most popular issue of all Zionist activities in Germany and more successful than Keren Hayesod and Keren Kayemet. Youth Aliyah had even created a group of supporters that were not ideologically committed to Zionism.[138]

By the second international Youth Aliyah conference in the summer of 1937, the Arbeitsgemeinschaft apparently attained its goal of "getting more and more Jewish circles to take an active interest in Youth Aliyah." Stern gave the following presentation on the activities of the Arbeitsgemeinschaft: "I think it was about two years ago when we had to admit that the Youth Aliyah was not yet receiving the general backing of the Jewish population in Germany. Things have changed since then. It has now been realized that the Youth Aliyah is the only large-scale organization engaged in the work of juvenile emigration. . . . In the year 1935/36 appeals for funds were organized in 95 towns in Germany, and in 120 towns in the year 1936/37."[139] At a time when the number of Jews living in small towns was diminishing and organized Jewish communities were dwindling, Youth Aliyah expanded its geographical base of operations in Germany. Bat-Rachel, for example, recalled her surprise upon encountering a small Jewish community well versed in the questions confronting the Youth Aliyah offices in Berlin and Jerusalem.[140]

Despite the increasing popularity, in late 1937 Stern noted a financial crisis facing the Arbeitsgemeinschaft. She explained that Jewish leaders responsible for Ha'avara demanded that Youth Aliyah provide funds for transfer to Palestine, while the Arbeitsgemeinschaft needed all its assets for programs in Germany.[141] Youth Aliyah's leaders confronted the perennial dilemma regarding the essential purpose of Zionism. Should the movement focus solely on the needs of Jewish Palestine or did it have an obligation to address the immediate concerns of Jews everywhere, even in the diaspora? Stern's attitude reflected the latter position.

Even those in the *yishuv* who supported Zionist work in the diaspora, however, did not limit their attention to the beleaguered Jews of Germany. Members of the Jewish Agency viewed Poland, with its large Jewish population suffering harsh economic conditions, as an ideal addition to the Youth Aliyah program. Youth Aliyah representatives had traveled to Poland in early 1936 to explore the possibility of instituting the program in that country. They reported that linguistically and culturally Polish youths were much more connected with Palestine than those in Germany.[142] Leaders of the *yishuv* may also have recognized that young Jews in Poland were more likely to share the socialistic ideals of the Jewish labor movement in Palestine. Stern supported extending Youth Aliyah to Poland provided Polish Jewry could provide funding.[143] Yet the British government, which granted youth certificates, would not recognize that the Jews of Poland faced discrimination on a par with German Jewry. In reality, political developments during the course of 1938 would force Youth Aliyah to pursue its expansion in other directions, as Hitler's first steps toward European conquest brought additional hardships for the Jews living under Nazi rule.

When German soldiers marched peacefully into Austria in March 1938, both Youth Aliyah's role and its basis of support within the Jewish community had expanded, and its mission had significantly increased as well. From its initial aim of immediately transporting hundreds of young Jews to Palestine, Youth Aliyah was now recognized as an essential element of the Jewish educational and welfare apparatus within Germany, compensating for the Jewish communities' inability to adequately address the social and pedagogical needs of Jewish teenagers.

Youth Aliyah was not immune to current events, neither to the legal changes confronting Jews in Germany nor to the growing instability in Europe and the Mediterranean. Youth Aliyah leaders tried to instill in these young pioneers the sense of historic importance and responsibility that they placed on the youth immigration program. The following words appeared in a letter from a pair of *madrichim* on the eve of the group's departure from Germany in late 1935:

> Jewish destiny and Jewish obligations are today the same for everyone, whether you are only 15 or 17, or already 23 or 27 as we are. Previously people of your age group could walk through life much less burdened than today. They were provided for, and did not have to care for anything. But today, you too are in the forefront, and Youth Aliyah puts demands on you, just as if you were grownups, although you aren't yet, really. Therefore we can also speak to you as we would speak to adults. We cannot spare you today the unpleasantness of considering things which preoccupy us at this hour. . . . We expect from you the same as we do from us: restless devotion of the individual to the common ideal. To the group, the settlement, to Eretz Israel and the Zionist movement.[144]

4
After the Pogrom

From a confidential interview given by a Youth Aliyah representative in Austria: "Hitler entered Austria on a Friday and many were taken to Dachau. From one family all four sons disappeared—they are still in Dachau. The youngest is a girl who is now left alone with her parents. When the Youth Aliyah office offered to give her a certificate, the mother dully repeated: 'she is all I have left. Take her and I will have no reason for living.' The daughter remained. . . . The father, who was destitute, received 10 marks from the community for each of his sons to get them food at Dachau. He knows that the greater part of this pittance does not reach them, but stands in line for hours to get it in the hope that some small part will reach them."[1]

After March 1938 the need to provide refuge for young Jews increased dramatically. Youth Aliyah not only faced the challenge of incorporating groups from Austria but also confronted accelerated persecution in Germany. During these same months, German Jewry witnessed the world's inability or unwillingness to provide asylum for masses of Jewish refugees. With its unique capability to shelter young Jews and the potential to bring out even greater numbers than in previous years, Youth Aliyah took on an increasingly important role.

Though historians generally agree that November 1938 represented a turning point in the encounter between the Third Reich and the Jews, a number of scholars recognize the pogrom as the apex of a campaign the Nazis began earlier that year, one that signaled radicalization of the regime's approach to the Jewish question.[2] Following the annexation of Austria, or Anschluss, German Jewry experienced a renewal of anti-

Semitic terror, including a boycott in Frankfurt during April and pogroms in Berlin and other cities in June. Yet the violence did not approach the brutality perpetrated against Jews in Austria.

In retrospect, considering what is known about the differing histories
of anti-Semitism in Austria and Germany, one should not be surprised
that the public excesses against Austrian Jewry in the days immediately
following the Anschluss were more extensive and more vicious than
those that had befallen German Jews.[3] Perhaps the most significant factor separating the experience of Jews in Austria from that of German
Jewry is the pace at which each community confronted Nazi aggression. Relatively speaking, the Jews in Germany had become accustomed
gradually to life under the Hitler regime, whereas the immediate oppression of Austria's Jews has been aptly described as *Blitzverfolgung*, light-
ning persecution.[4] Not blind to the Nazi menace, the Jews of Austria
were already trying to flee on the night of Chancellor Kurt Schuschnigg's
resignation speech, March 11, yet the degree of persecution to which
they were immediately subjected must have shocked even them. When
Himmler arrived in Vienna the following day in order to arrange for
mass arrests, the Jews found themselves at the top of this list.[5]

Perhaps the Jews of Vienna were caught off guard. One might have
expected, as had been the case in Germany during 1933, that the first
victims of Nazi oppression would be the political opposition, the Communists and socialists. The fury of the pogroms that accompanied the
Anschluss would not be seen in the Altreich until the Kristallnacht riots
in November. The savage nature of these actions in Austria is generally
attributed to a widespread popular (as opposed to political or official)
anti-Semitism more prevalent in Austria than in Germany.[6] That a
large-scale outburst of this type, never before seen in a "civilized" country, could occur in cultured Vienna accounts for the fright and despair
exhibited by Austria's Jewish population, demonstrated by the tremendous rise in suicide rate. The "Aryanization" of business holdings along
with the confiscation of housing and other properties accompanied the
extreme violence and public humiliations.

After five years of National Socialist rule, Jewish children in Germany
had not yet been completely excluded from attending state-run Aryan
schools. In Austria, separation of Jewish students into their own schools
was successfully accomplished within two months. Whereas the German
experience demonstrates a gradual forced retreat into an exclusively Jew-

ish milieu, for the Jewish youth of Austria the transformation was often instantaneous. Quite rapidly, children had to accommodate themselves to a new social order, based on Nazi racial criteria.

Gertrude Schneider recalled that the day following Schuschnigg's resignation, her best friend of four years approached her and said, "I cannot be your friend anymore. . . . My father . . . told me never to speak or play with Jewish children."[7] Often the social dislocation, more than any specific government initiatives, brought home the new reality. A Jewish boy who came on Youth Aliyah from Vienna reported, "it was the Hitler Youth—boys even of [my] own age—who were in the forefront of the destruction, incited to bestial acts by their leaders. . . . There were women who took part, and the women were even worse than the boys."[8] Practically overnight Jewish children were forbidden the use of public spaces and prohibited from sitting on roadside benches. As had slowly occurred in Germany over five years, the ostracism from public life forced many Jews to reevaluate their Jewish identities, bringing those who had never before supported the cause of Jewish nationalism now into the Zionist camp. For Austrian Jewry, this process occurred at a swifter pace.

In Berlin, however, the oppression had not yet accelerated. Arthur Ruppin, at that time a member of the Zionist Executive, visited the German capital in late March 1938. He recorded the following in his diary:

> It seems to me that many Jews in Germany have not yet fully grasped the seriousness of what has happened to them. There are still rich Jews who continue to live almost as before on their private incomes. As long as they are still able to buy their provisions at the nearest shopkeeper, they are oblivious of the misfortune. *They do not realize that there is no future for their children in Germany, either economically or spiritually,* and that they will be pariahs, at least for the next few decades, until the government may accept the few surviving Jews. Other Jews are in despair but see no way out. They are too intimately bound up with their present home and occupation, feel that they will not be any happier elsewhere—in spite of all the dangers threatening—and are too inflexible to emigrate. The process of pauperization is proceeding fast. In many average communities one-quarter or one-third of the Jews are already receiving assistance from the community. It must be said to the credit

[or oversight] of the government that at least no difference is drawn between Jews and Christians in the payment of unemployment relief. The Jews feel that they are helplessly at the mercy of a hostile power. The uncertainty about the future is harder for them to bear than past and present sufferings. (Emphasis in original.)[9]

Within two weeks of the Anschluss, the government announced the first significant piece of anti-Jewish legislation since the Nuremberg Laws, a decree calling for dissolution of the Jewish *Gemeinden*.[10] During the following months German authorities issued additional edicts against the Jewish community, demonstrating an increasingly active Jewish policy culminating in the forced expulsion of Polish nationals in October 1938, which indirectly resulted in the extreme violence of November 10–11. After the Austrian collapse, Youth Aliyah representatives in Berlin attempted to contact Vienna, but communications in general remained difficult and speaking with Jewish offices was nearly impossible. In fact, Nazi authorities prohibited Jewish officials from the Altreich from visiting Austria. Zionist leaders therefore dispatched Schattner, a Palestinian national, to Vienna.[11] Of the total Jewish population in Austria, Zionists represented a minority. The assimilationist element in Jewish Vienna was far stronger than elsewhere and had been operating for generations. Only in response to the Anschluss did the native, authentic Viennese Jews begin to turn in large numbers to Zionism. As one writer has noted of this period, "Hitler was creating more Zionists in Vienna [than] Herzl had probably ever hoped to do."[12] Their genuine dedication to the Zionist idea is clearly debatable, but the fact that many individuals wanted to leave Austria and viewed Palestine as at least an acceptable, if not preferable, destination is not in doubt.

Szold received requests to institute an Austrian Youth Aliyah immediately following the Anschluss, and Hadassah raised pledges of twenty thousand dollars for this purpose.[13] As Youth Aliyah represented a special category of immigration to Palestine, and the political status of Austria in the eyes of the Mandatory government was unclear, Zionist organizations could not allot youth certificates to Austrian Jews until the Palestine authorities granted permission. Once the annexation of Austria was accepted there was no need, from the British perspective, to earmark specific certificates for Austrian Youth Aliyah, for officially the emigrants would be arriving from Germany. The Jewish Agency had to determine how many youth certificates would be given to Austria as opposed to those for the Altreich. Zionist activists in Vienna established an entity similar to the Jüdische Jugendhilfe, responsible for choosing and training potential Youth Aliyah candidates. During the summer of 1938 an office was officially opened under the name Beratungsstelle der Jugendalijah (Youth Aliyah Advisory Office), comprised of representatives from different communal bodies and varied ideological positions.[14]

In Berlin the Jugendhilfe hoped to oversee the entire Germany-based operation, including Austria, and immediately suggested establishing a *hachsharah* camp for Austrian youth, either on the outskirts of Vienna or in Bavaria, under the supervision of the Berlin office.[15] In Vienna itself, on the other hand, those interested in promoting Youth Aliyah were less concerned with preserving a centralized bureaucracy than with actually setting the process in motion. Initially two commissions were established: one through the Zionistische Vereinigung (Zionist Association) and the Keren Hayesod responsible for solving the financial issues; the second composed of representatives of the Zionist and pioneer youth groups that would oversee the technical and pedagogical requirements.[16] Yet the future of all Jewish organizations remained unclear until Eichmann reopened the communal institutions in early May. Even though the Jüdische Jugendhilfe in Berlin had decided to make some certificates available for Austrian youth immediately after the Anschluss, and to send application forms, contracts, and so on to Vienna, there was no recognized administration until May.[17]

Apparently the concerns in Berlin regarding proper selection were shared, albeit less strenuously, by the individuals organizing Youth Aliyah from Vienna. Registration numbered in the hundreds in the first few days, many of whom, from the Zionist perspective, did not represent ideal candidates for Palestine. The Vienna Hechaluz office complained that "assimilated youth come to us, who have never been organized in any Zionist association. There is no *Hachscharah* and no general retraining. It is clear that an agricultural *Hachscharah* in Austria itself will scarcely be possible, we can now only offer vocational [*handwerklichen*] courses."[18] These newcomers would have to compete with veterans of the Zionist youth movements for the coveted certificates. Not only the ideological backgrounds of the applicants but also the poor prospects for proper training in Austria caused Zionist leaders to worry. Organizers in Vienna anticipated accommodating more than 750 teenagers and, through a program combining instruction with sport and recreation, attempted "to preserve some semblance of normalcy in the life of the young."[19]

The same desperation had not yet reached Berlin, and Youth Aliyah's policy there remained the same. Each spring, as a new wave of students completed their schooling, concerned Jewish leaders in Germany raised questions regarding young Jews' future prospects.[20] In March 1938 Youth Aliyah's message had not changed, stressing that Palestine offered an opportunity for both economic and spiritual fulfillment obviously lacking in Germany. The Jugendhilfe, in early 1938, still presented its various educational activities as *Berufsausbildung*.[21] Additionally, some Jewish schools, which had not previously expressed strong support for Zionism (despite the Reichsvertretung's educational program), organized and prepared groups for Aliyah within the framework of after-school programs.[22]

Though the general mood of German Jewry following the annexation of Austria became increasingly anxious, Youth Aliyah provided some hope to buoy the community's spirits. In response to the Anschluss, the British colonial minister, William Ormsby-Gore, declared a policy of unlimited immigration to Palestine for youth and students, from April to September 1938, provided that acceptance and support at an educational institution could be insured.[23] Realistically, this offer translated to an increased youth immigration schedule of 884 for the period April to October 1938. Young Jews already selected for immigration, particularly Orthodox groups that had received many of these certificates, welcomed this announcement. On the other hand, the creation of a separate Youth Aliyah department in Austria resulted, at least initially, in a conflict for the prized permits between the Jugendhilfe and the Vienna office.[24]

During the summer of 1938 Kurt Goldmann assumed the helm of the Jugendhilfe in Berlin. Goldmann had been a regional leader for Habonim in Cologne during 1937, and with his move to Berlin the Jugendhilfe began to take many of the roles previously filled by youth movements. This shift further exemplifies the decline of the *Bünde* in general as effective educational institutions. In fact the inadequate number of certificates issued resulted in greater focus upon the services the Jugendhilfe could provide to the oppressed Jews in Germany rather than focusing exclusively on immigration.

As a welfare institution Youth Aliyah aided young Jews already emotionally scarred by the experience of living under Nazi control. No doubt social workers and teachers were ill equipped and unprepared to handle the damage already being inflicted upon young Jews living under ongoing oppressive conditions, foreshadowing the circumstances that would confront such professionals after the war. In individual cases, the awesome power of the state bearing down on helpless Jews could result in grave psychological consequences. Youth Aliyah leaders noted that often children would feel responsible for the fate of their parents: fathers inexplicably imprisoned on accusations of transgressing economic or racial laws; parents taken to concentration camps on claims of political activity; mothers deported without their children. Since any communication—by mail, telephone, or in face-to-face conversation—remained quite dangerous, many children were extremely reticent to discuss these matters, even within the confines of *hachsharah*. When young emigrants arrived for training from small towns, *madrichim* had to overcome a severe degree of paranoia before trust was established and the children would speak freely.[25] This problem became increasingly apparent to those working with young refugees during the war and afterward.

Louis, for instance, was born and raised in the Hessian village of Kesselbach. Prior to 1938 he had no knowledge of Youth Aliyah, but relatives in the United States had collected money to enable the six boys and girls in various branches of the family in Germany to go to Palestine via Youth Aliyah. A relative in Hamburg, whom Louis had never met, contacted him and instructed him to go to *hachsharah*. Louis had never before been away from Kesselbach. Since the Christian children in his town avoided him and there were no other young Jews, Louis had not even spoken to anyone his own age for the past three years. Thus the camp experience was essential for Louis to redevelop basic social skills. Of course he had difficulty adapting, as he was totally unfamiliar with the culture of the Zionist youth groups and he spoke and dressed differently from the boys from the city. But his rural background served him well when the group began agricultural training. Louis found his niche and immigrated to Palestine in early 1938, but still bearing the psychological scars of these difficult times.[26]

In Austria, however, conditions had become so severe that the benefits of *hachsharah* could not always be utilized. As early as June 1, at least one Youth Aliyah staffer in Jerusalem recognized the urgent need to act, for emotional as well as physical rescue. As a memorandum stated, "it is now of the utmost importance to remove as many girls and boys as possible from Austria before their morale is broken by their experience there."[27] The first Youth Aliyah group departed from Austria without the requisite four weeks in a preparatory camp. In order to minimize the risk of accepting a group of youths in this manner, the Jugendhilfe decided that a successful cohort without the usual preparation could be comprised only of teens who had previous experience in youth groups. Hans Gaertner, who directed a Jewish school in Berlin, confirmed the distinction between young Jews who had prior exposure to Zionism and those who did not. "The less active children and those that had not been members of youth organizations were by far less determined to leave their parents; they had many doubts to overcome and they suffered very much at the moment of departure."[28]

Regardless of political orientation, the most urgent consideration to all interested parties was initiating the process of moving the children from Austria to Palestine. Robert Weltsch, editor of the *Jüdische Rundschau*, recognized the emotional impact of beginning an Austrian Youth Aliyah, even on a small scale, as soon as possible, even if the financial circumstances were less than desirable.[29] Weltsch understood that, as in Germany, Youth Aliyah could serve as a rallying point within the oppressed Jewish community.

Yet even in Austria, not all parents equated the Jews' precarious situation with an imperative to send their children to safety. Ruth Kluger recalled an episode with her mother. "Once when she and I were at the Jewish Community Center, a young man asked us whether she would consider sending me by myself with a children's transport to Palestine. It was a last chance he said. . . . My heart pounded, for I would dearly have loved to leave Vienna, even if [it] meant betraying my mother. But she didn't ask me and didn't even look at me as she answered in an even voice: 'No. A child and its mother belong together.' . . . I have never forgot that brief glimpse of another life."[30]

Letters exchanged between Vienna and Jerusalem during the summer of 1938 prove that the *yishuv* still failed to comprehend Austrian Jewry's utter hopelessness. The director of the largest Jewish school in Vienna wrote that he continually received letters from Palestine demonstrating that the population remained unaware of the efficiency with which the Nazis were undertaking the "liquidation of Austrian Jewry."[31] The Jewish Agency did in fact request additional immigration certificates in response to the Anschluss, yet this action lacked the sense of immediacy exhibited in Vienna. For example, nine hundred "emergency" labor certificates were requested from the Mandatory government, of which only one hundred would be specially marked for Austrian emigrants.[32]

By early July 1938 the first Youth Aliyah groups left Vienna for Palestine. Since conditions in Austria were even less stable and some in the community equated emigration with rescue, the question of selection took on a significance that would soon appear in Berlin as well. This problem can be seen from two perspectives. First, the distribution dilemma questioned whether an applicant's Zionist background should be taken into consideration, and if so what factors would be given primary importance. Second, were those responsible for Youth Aliyah in Austria prepared to apply the same selective criteria as had already been put into practice by the Berlin office? The first issue exemplified a more general question of who should receive priority in terms of immigration, while the second focused on commitment to Youth Aliyah's specific educational goals. In this sense Austrian Youth Aliyah shared the difficulties faced by the Zionist movement as a whole during this crisis. This issue also demonstrated the different attitudes expressed by those working in the capitals of Nazi Europe as opposed to the Zionist leadership in Palestine. In other words, if one equates immigration to Palestine with "rescue" from Europe, then the question of who should immigrate is really the same as who should be saved. On the other hand, if one equates immigration to Palestine as working to build up the Jewish homeland, then the question is rather who can best serve the needs of Zionism in Palestine.

Whereas in Germany the initial motive for emigration seems to have been the search for better prospects for building a life than would be available to a Jew living in the Third Reich, the Jewish leadership in Austria seems to have been more prescient in assessing the future facing a Jew living under Nazism.[33] While the representatives of the Zionist movement in Palestine, including the *shlichim* in Vienna, demanded a highly selective process, the Viennese communal leadership argued for saving those whose individual needs were most pressing. For example, preference should be given to youths whose fathers had been put in concentration camps or who had been arrested themselves, regardless of their suitability for life in Palestine.[34] In contrast, Kurt Goldmann in Berlin argued as late as the summer of 1939 that Youth Aliyah must not concede its commitment to selective immigration, even when confronted with similarly tragic cases.

As the outbreak of hostilities over the fate of Czechoslovakia grew imminent in mid-1938, the Zionistische Zentralverband in Prague contacted the Zionist executive in Jerusalem and related the deteriorating conditions faced by Jews, particularly in Sudeten areas with sizable ethnic German populations. German nationalist activities resulted in an influx of Jewish youth to the Zionist movement. Palestine regulations allowed only limited emigration from Czechoslovakia to the youth village Ben-Shemen, which had the right to distribute immigration permits according to its own wishes.[35] During the spring of 1938, only two youth groups, Techelet-Lavan and Makkabi Hazair, became involved with these efforts, and the movement received little public support. Only following the Munich accords did the opportunity for bringing Czech youth to the various "open" agricultural settlements arise, at which point the Jews in Czechoslovakia began to take greater interest.[36] Following the September agreement, non-Germans from the Sudetenland swarmed into Prague, Brno, and other cities. Additional refugees followed after Poland seized the Tseschen region in October and Hungary annexed parts of Slovakia and Ruthenia in November. For Jews, this migration represented a dash for freedom. Prague Zionists established a Jüdische Jugendhilfe, which instituted training programs including Hebrew courses, camps, and schools.[37]

Now functioning from three organizational centers, Youth Aliyah leaders from Germany, Austria, and Czechoslovakia established a joint council, the Irgun der drei Landesorganisationen. This governing board maintained responsibility for allotting certificates granted in Jerusalem to Jewish youth in Grossdeutschland (greater Germany) as well as among refugees in other countries.[38] As pressure to find avenues of emigration grew, the training opportunities offered by Youth Aliyah became increasingly important, even for young Jews who would not immediately receive entry permits for Palestine. As Josephthal described it, the benefits were most significant in boosting morale and providing a sense of purpose and social belonging rather than just the development of practical skills: "We see in our Youth Aliya . . . that in general the youth groups show very little in the way of actual training, that their important function was only to set people on the right path, the path of work, of possible fellowship and community."[39]

During this period, the number of colonies in Palestine volunteering for and receiving approval to participate in Youth Aliyah continued to grow. However, many of the settlements hoped to take in young Jews from Poland, another country where the government's anti-Semitic posture had become more oppressive. Many kibbutzim viewed the pioneers from Poland more favorably, and indeed a high proportion of the Jewish teenagers in Germany selected for Youth Aliyah hailed from families that had migrated from eastern Europe during or after World War I. Yet the Mandatory government's earlier stipulation remained intact, and it would only grant Youth Aliyah certificates for emigrants from Nazi-controlled lands.[40] Youth Aliyah was able to bring in a few young *chaluzim* from Poland and Romania, but only to "closed" educational institutions, such as Ben-Shemen and other schools that could distribute their own certificates.

Not only did German Jewry face heightened discrimination during this time, but Jews also had to contend with the ambivalence of foreign governments. The Evian conference in early July, convened by Franklin Roosevelt to address the growing refugee crisis, demonstrated that most countries remained unwilling to change their immigration policies. The failure of Evian, combined with Hitler's diplomatic success at Munich in September, undoubtedly strengthened the Nazi leaders' confidence that more radical policies could be pursued without significant political consequences, as became clear that fall.

In accordance with a law announced in March 1938, on October 15 the Polish government required all Polish nationals to validate passports issued by consulates abroad with a special stamp by October 30 or lose their citizenship status, including the right of reentry into Poland. The law clearly targeted the seventy thousand Polish Jews living in greater Germany, many of whom had been settled in Germany for a full generation. The German government responded in late October by rounding up eighteen thousand Polish Jews and delivering them to the Polish border prior to the deadline. Authorities in Warsaw refused to grant entry to most of the refugees, who were forced to remain in makeshift camps on the no-man's-land between Germany and Poland.[41] The largest group found themselves homeless in the border town of Zbąsyń, on the main rail line between Berlin and Warsaw.

A Jewish girl who had been living in Düsseldorf, which her father had called home since 1910, recalled that one evening friends visited her family to say that compulsory arrests of Jews in Germany were going to occur; her father was distraught and could not sleep. At midnight he noticed that in the opposite house her uncle had been forced to leave his apartment. The local police knocked on their door at 3:00 A.M. and demanded passports and all property, suggesting they take clothes and some food. They did not know where they were going or for how long— and no answers were forthcoming. Before leaving the apartment they were handed a slip of paper giving them twenty-four hours to leave Germany.

They were taken to the local police station and then to police headquarters, at which point the family was separated. The girl and her mother were taken to a women's division, where sixteen women plus a baby carriage were crammed into a cell meant for three people. They waited there from 4:00 A.M. to 4:00 P.M. At that point trucks arrived and took them to the train station. Crowds of people were there—men, women, and children—packed into cars already overflowing. It was Friday evening when the train pulled out to an unknown destination. They traveled until 8:00 A.M. the next day and came finally to Zbąszyń.

Near the crossing they saw long lines of Jews struggling with suitcases— many pieces of luggage were abandoned—forced by Germans to march. The refugees were brought to an old stable. There was a thin layer of straw in the stalls for sleeping. There was initially nothing to eat. That evening it began to rain but everyone had to be registered, so they stood in line for many hours. "I saw scenes that I can only remember with horror. A woman losing her mind, men crying, screaming, complaining. Inside was unbearable—the air was suffocating." The following day a truck arrived from the Jews of Posen, with bread and butter, as well as soap, "which when distributed also created frightful scenes. The men tore the bread out of the hands of the people in the trucks, scuffled and men . . . who the previous day had still been well educated and cultivated, attacked the truck with stones and prevented it from leaving the courtyard—also preventing people coming from the train station with bread—these were things that one could never forget."

But always she thought that soon she would return to Germany, that the Polish government would negotiate, and that people could not be forced to live this way. "The hygienic conditions were indescribable—

one could just forget about brushing one's teeth. Continually we hoped for a return to Germany, I also hoped for a return to school—for me it was all so unbelievable that I had even taken my schoolbooks with me to the police station."[42]

As Polish-German negotiations failed to resolve the crisis, Jewish organizations in Poland and elsewhere bore the cost of caring for these refugees. Among the deportees were many Jewish children. In some cases the Gestapo actually removed children from Jewish orphanages and transported them to the border. For the younger victims, retraining for emigration was viewed as a high priority by the relief organizations.[43] Those who had belonged to youth groups in Germany tried to organize soon after the deportation. As one account put it, "On Friday we were expelled from Germany and on Saturday we arrived in Zbąszyń. Already on Monday the first meeting was held there of the pioneering youth. Everywhere there were notices: 'To all members of the [youth] group, meeting at 4 o'clock.'"[44] Zionist groups prepared for life in Palestine and danced and sang amid the misery of no-man's-land.

Since Polish Jews comprised a significant element within Youth Aliyah groups, among the evacuees were a number who had registered prior to deportation. Some had already completed their preparation in Germany or were forcibly removed from *hachsharah*.[45] Youth Aliyah dispatched *madrichim* and *shlichim* to organize those refugees already enrolled in the program as well as potential new candidates from among the more than a hundred children brought to Poland without their parents. These leaders established a training center near the Zbąszyń refugee camp. Relatives in Palestine, particularly siblings and cousins who had been brought by Youth Aliyah, petitioned Szold's office to help family members trapped in no-man's-land.[46]

In most cases in which young Jews had already received immigration certificates for Palestine, Youth Aliyah was able to secure their release from Zbąszyń and return to Germany, provided the children leave Germany soon after. One boy from the Rhineland had already arranged the necessary paperwork for leaving Germany with his Youth Aliyah group, which was scheduled to depart the very week he was deported to Poland. His passport was in order, his trunk packed, and his railroad and steamship ticket reserved. He begged the police to let him remain in Germany for the few remaining days before his departure but he was forced into the transport with his family. After ten frantic days at the Polish border the Palästina-Amt managed to secure his release and he traveled back to Berlin to pick up his tickets. His group had already left Germany, but he was able to make arrangements for getting to Palestine.[47]

Another boy from Berlin had a similarly frightening experience. He had been finishing his Youth Aliyah *hachsharah* when he was informed that the police had destroyed his home and deported his parents to Poland. He returned to a vacant apartment. That night a Christian neighbor knocked on the door threatening to burst in. The neighbor returned the next day with the police but the boy had gone to hide with an aunt. Though he had a certificate for Palestine and his trunk had been packed, the taxes had not been paid on his belongings. He left for the Mikveh Israel agricultural school without any money or even a change of clothes.[48] Not all the children who were subjected to deportation managed to find their way out so quickly.

For those young Jews who had not already received certificates before deportation, the path to freedom was much more arduous. Max and Ernst, for example, had registered with the Jugendhilfe prior to their expulsion in October 1938. They, along with two hundred other Youth Aliyah candidates in Zbąszyń, clung to the hope of immigrating to Eretz Israel to survive the hard and desperate months spent among the homeless thousands in no-man's-land. When Youth Aliyah finally arranged for these refugees to receive certificates, the group was sent to a training facility in Poland. In accordance with immigration regulations, the certificates were sent to Berlin.

In order for the two to join their Youth Aliyah group, they needed to return to Germany. Their passports were sent to Berlin where they were stamped with a visa for Palestine—the stamped passports were then returned to Poland—theoretically enabling Max and Ernst to return to Germany and join the transport. But by late August, Germany had broken off relations with Poland. The leader of a Youth Aliyah group that escaped to England just before the outbreak of World War II was given four certificates for Max, Ernst, and two others from Zbąszyń with the hope that the documents could be sent to Poland from England. But then the invasion began.

For almost ten weeks there was no word of the children. Max and Ernst, along with more than a hundred others registered with Youth Aliyah, were missing. In December 1939 the London Youth Aliyah office received a cable from Lithuania. Nearly two hundred teenagers, who had organized to train for immigration to Palestine, had traveled across Poland after the war broke out, mainly on foot, to the Lithuanian capital. Among them were Max and Ernst, and their certificates were dispatched to Kovno.[49]

During most of 1938 Youth Aliyah in Germany faced the double-pronged challenge of accelerating operations in order to confront continually changing circumstances and attempting to incorporate the Jews of Austria and eventually those from the Sudetenland within its operational scope. While this period witnessed an increase in Nazi persecution of German Jews and therefore additional pressure to emigrate, for Youth Aliyah it resulted in expanding the number of teenagers brought to Palestine and the continued extension of activities within the growing territory of the Third Reich.

Even before November, some Jews became radically pessimistic regarding the outlook in Germany and expressed their desire to accelerate emigration. Hilde David, on October 27, wrote the following to her colleagues in Jerusalem: "*Here* [in Berlin] it appears clear, that the liquidation of German and Austrian Jewry is proceeding rapidly."[50] As a result, the pressure on Youth Aliyah to provide some relief became exceptionally strong, and David suggested that a decisive move during the upcoming winter was essential. The most significant development in Jewish emigration, however, resulted from an unprecedented wave of anti-Jewish violence, signaling a radical turn in the Nazis' Jewish policy.

In early October 1938 the SS issued a secret directive calling for "a stepped-up operation against the Jews," in which Jews from Vienna would be forcibly expelled.[51] At that point even the *shlichim* in Vienna doubted the possibility of maintaining a strict commitment to their ideological positions. Ze'ev (Willy) Ritter recalled a message sent to Palestine by the Hechaluz *shaliach* in Vienna, Moshe Auerbach, that stated, "We have no room for educational activity as we thought. We must take care of the rescue of Jews."[52] While parents and children had already viewed the program in such terms, over the following months Youth Aliyah began to perceive itself as primarily a rescue as opposed to pedagogical operation.

On November 8, 1938, Herschel Grynszpan, a Jewish student from Germany whose family had been deported by Nazi police forces and who had been denied entry by Polish authorities at Zbąszyń, entered the

German embassy in Paris and, hoping to kill the ambassador, shot and wounded a midlevel bureaucrat. When Assistant Secretary Ernst vom Rath died as a result of this attack, Hitler and Goebbels seized the opportunity to unleash throughout greater Germany a wave of anti-Jewish violence reminiscent of the most brutal pogroms experienced by Jewish communities in tsarist Russia.[53] By the morning of November 10, nearly three hundred synagogues throughout greater Germany had been destroyed along with approximately seventy-five hundred Jewish-owned stores and businesses; more than twenty-five thousand Jews had been arrested and nearly one hundred murdered.[54]

These actions, named Kristallnacht by Nazi propagandists, in reference to the thousands of windows shattered during the rioting, represented the beginning of a new phase in the regime's approach to the Jewish question. Even the most optimistic Jews finally accepted the fact that little hope remained for Jewish survival in Germany. Accordingly, emigration, to practically all conceivable destinations by any means possible, attained an even more prominent position in the daily discourse of German Jewry.

For Youth Aliyah's staff in Berlin, the events of November 10 naturally altered their plans.[55] The Berlin office, as part of the Jewish community's governing institutions, was closed and sealed by the Gestapo, and communications with other countries even within the Reich were broken off. Many Jewish officials were imprisoned and their offices destroyed. The Jugendhilfe leadership questioned at first whether this action was directed against Zionism and in that way against the group's work (which was by no means impossible after the violent anti-Palestine attacks in the press) or whether closing the office was part of the general *Aktion*. When word came from Vienna that the branch there continued its work undisturbed, the Jugendhilfe hoped to secure the reopening of its office. Youth Aliyah was now bombarded with desperate pleas to evacuate children from Germany. In the interim, the staff worked in three different private homes. In spite of the difficulties, they did not want to leave the letters of the hopeless mothers unanswered and also wanted to make preparations for emergency drives.

When the offices reopened, the Jugendhilfe confronted an entirely new situation. As certificates for Palestine had not yet been received, a plan to settle the children in Holland and England was slowly taking shape. The settlement of a few thousand children in those countries was arranged, in addition to at least nine hundred Youth Aliyah certificates.

An important question to be addressed was that of selection. Leaders had to decide whether to consider every child, as all the children who came to them had either no home or no means of emigration, or whether to consider only suitability for Palestine as the necessary qualification. After a hard struggle the decision was reached to carry on with the usual form of preparation camps, the only difference being a shortened procedure, so as to enable a large number of candidates to prove their suitability.

The Reichsvertretung organized transportation for children between the ages of five and eighteen to England and Holland—these were the first *Kindertransporte*—and implemented this operation without a selection process. The explicit goal of the *Kindertransporte* was temporary refuge in the host countries, and the movement had no Zionist agenda. Yet the Jugendhilfe maintained that Palestine remained its candidates' final destination and that organizers should therefore consider suitability for reemigration. In their words:

> We did not want to be faced in 6 months or one year with the necessity of sending to Palestine children who had no relations whatsoever with Palestine and could not meet the physical and mental requirements of that country. We therefore came to the agreement with the Central office of the Reichsvertretung that a quarter of all the children who were sent to them would have to be selected by [the Jugendhilfe]. We hoped to have some time in which to make our choice. This was not granted to us however due to cogent technical reasons: It was necessary to get the children out of the country as quickly as possible.
>
> We therefore made our minds up to suggest only those children for settlement in England and Holland who were known to us through their work in the youth Movements or those who were known in the preparation camps of the Youth Aliyah, but we had no hope for a quick Aliyah owing to the very small number of certificates which were available. We therefore limited the age to 14 years.[56]

The Reichsvertretung, spurred by the urgency of the moment, did not adhere to the agreement. Among those children who were sent to the various countries were only a few who had been suggested by the Jugendhilfe.

Hundreds of people approached Youth Aliyah to discuss emigration possibilities, putting the organization under extreme pressure. These initial interviews consumed much time and demanded tremendous effort from an overburdened staff. Many fourteen- to seventeen-year-old boys were trying to avoid arrest by the Gestapo; others had orders to report three times daily to local police stations. Individuals working for the Jugendhilfe were not immune to the grave circumstances confronting German Jewry, but many of the workers faced personal difficulties. Even though operating with a full staff was imperative, changing personnel often was a necessity because some of the old workers were either forced to leave Germany or found a way to emigrate. Youth Aliyah could not protest against people leaving, as the organization could offer no security whatsoever. Inexplicably, it seemed, the preparatory camp Ruednitz near Berlin was untouched by the pogrom.[57] And the training farm at Schniebinchen was even guarded by the police because it had had a visit from drunken Nazi soldiers. At both places nothing had been destroyed and no one was arrested. On the other hand both camps near Hamburg were attacked, the leaders arrested, and the premises destroyed.[58]

After the pogrom, concerns also focused on finances:

Up to now the budget of the Jugendhilfe had been covered by means of the support given us by the Arbeitsgemeinschaft. It is certain that these payments will now stop. Collections (in Germany) have been discontinued completely, although collections of Sperrmark which are being made through our London office, are continuing. The payments which had been transferred to Palestine from the Jugendhilfe and which comprised contributions from parents or communities and the Reichsvertretung have also stopped since the communities are no longer in a position to make contributions. . . . Very soon all the means will be confiscated. A ruling will, therefore, have to be made whereby the Reichsvertretung will incorporate the Youth Aliyah into its Budget and pay all its expenses. . . . In spite of the difficulties described above we are endeavouring to continue our work in an orderly fashion. We believe that on the whole we have been fairly successful. How long we will be able to continue the work it is not possible to say.[59]

Though the Gestapo initially closed the Jugendhilfe's offices, the authorities did not officially dissolve the organization. In this respect, Youth Aliyah received exceptional treatment, since a significant repercussion of the November pogrom was a government decree to disband most Jewish associations, including youth groups. A group of Hitler Youth broke in to the offices of at least one Jewish youth group in Vienna and then beat up all the boys there. According to one account, "They did not leave till every boy was lying in a pool of blood, mercifully unconscious or less mercifully able to watch and feel what was happening."[60] Yet the Vienna Youth Aliyah office was permitted to continue its work relatively undisturbed by the authorities.[61]

As one of the few Jewish organizations permitted to function, the Jugendhilfe became adviser to hundreds of burgeoning young Zionists. From rural areas, terrified young Jews pleaded with Youth Aliyah for assistance.[62] Of approximately seven thousand Jewish youth between thirteen and seventeen in Vienna in late 1938, more than fifty-five hundred, nearly 80 percent of those in question, had registered for Youth Aliyah.[63] Many possessed no background in any youth organization. Even though urgency shortened the preparation many groups received, thereby reducing the effectiveness of the screening process, commitment to selectivity remained a high priority. Youth Aliyah still rejected at least 15 percent of applicants for medical reasons during 1939.[64] The medical supervisor for Youth Aliyah in Palestine, Fritz Noack, emphasized selection according to health in the interest of the candidates themselves, the other children, and Palestine as a whole.[65] The second consideration was emotional and educational preparedness and the potential contribution the candidates could make toward building up the land. As the historian Dina Porat has shown, selective immigration remained *yishuv* policy until 1942.[66]

The Beratungsstelle in Vienna was not deaf to the requests emanating from Jerusalem and attempted to ensure that those youths sent to Palestine were the best qualified. Yet the Youth Aliyah staff also expected to educate candidates unfamiliar with the Zionist message in order to attain a satisfactory level of preparation. The Beratungsstelle established its own *hachsharah* facilities and founded a Youth Aliyah School in Vienna, but the selection process was becoming more complicated, as the implications of rejection appeared increasingly severe.

Though of course the ultimate fate of those who remained under Nazi rule was unknown, applicants realized that failing selection meant continued exposure to Nazi cruelty. Goldmann reported on a case in April 1939 where a young Jew, recently released from a concentration camp, did not pass the screening process. Goldmann supported this particular decision with the statement that "as before, we maintain the opinion that Youth Aliyah is an educational movement, and not a philanthropic one, and we have structured our work in Germany accordingly, despite the circumstances of 1939."[67] Yet Goldmann and Szold were not immune to the real dangers facing young Jews during these chaotic months. In one instance Szold even pressured Berlin to make an exception for a fifteen-year-old boy then in Minsk, Poland, in danger of deportation to the Soviet Union. Szold justified her petition, sensing a different sort of danger: "I need you to prevent the result of a deportation to Russia. He would lose not only his Zionism, but rather also his Judaism. We would thus propose, that you arrange a spot for him in one of the youth groups [from Germany]."[68]

Even though the Jugendhilfe shortened the screening process, eventually to as little as eight days in order to accommodate greater numbers at the training centers, these *hachsharah* camps held great significance for young Jews. Following the November pogrom, when German Jewry faced the constant threat of unpredictable and violent anti-Jewish outbursts and when public sentiment grew demonstrably anti-Semitic, the schools, houses, and training centers organized by Youth Aliyah proved vital. Within a sea of terror and hatred, many young Jews found protection and solace in the insular community these institutions offered, referring to the camp at Schniebinchen for example as an "island of happiness."[69] In the words of one youth leader, these activities and the possibilities they represented had a "psychological value that can scarcely be put into words."[70]

Yet despite the refuge these establishments provided from the oppressive atmosphere, the ubiquitous force of the Gestapo was always present. For example, though the Nazis supported Youth Aliyah's goals, all noisy activity was forbidden, as was leaving campgrounds during evening hours. By this time the training centers faced additional pedagogical challenges as fewer and fewer immigration candidates had actually grown up within a Jewish youth group. Whereas previously the camps had served as a forum for expressing the shared Zionist culture of the youth groups, the new circumstances forced the pedagogical program to return to basic instruction, with a particular focus on the Hebrew language.[71]

Applications now arrived not only from impoverished Jews but also from wealthy families, many of whom had previously expected either to weather the storm of Nazi rule or eventually to find refuge, along with their capital, in the West. These parents often turned to Youth Aliyah in the hopes of finding care for their children for two years. During that period the parents hoped to have facilitated their own emigration and economic security, at which point they would send for their children to join them, ideally in America. When such plans were known, the Jugendhilfe rejected the candidates, even though they could cover costs and more and more trainees relied on public support.[72] Undoubtedly Youth Aliyah and immigration to Palestine in general were viewed as effective means for reaching more desirable destinations such as the United States or England, and many emigrants had such motives, though never admitted publicly. All the while, communal funds in Germany grew increasingly scarce, due largely to the government's imposition of a $400 million (1 billion Reichsmark) fine on the entire Jewish community to cover the expenses incurred during the November pogrom. At the same time, the regime effectively cut off Youth Aliyah's ability to transfer funds to Palestine.[73] As Germany's financial ministry grew reluctant to provide foreign exchange, the Palestine clearinghouse office in Berlin permitted transfers only in exceptional cases. In these instances trainees had to pay their own fees, and parents had to demonstrate to German authorities that they had fulfilled all outstanding financial obligations in Germany.[74]

Szold suggested that the Berlin office adopt a more pragmatic approach with respect to Youth Aliyah's finances. She concurred with Goldmann that Youth Aliyah was "largely" an educational (as opposed to philanthropic) movement. Yet she emphasized that lack of financial stability threatened to bring the process to a halt.[75] For Szold at least, economic considerations could justify, at times, the recognition of the philanthropic aspects of Youth Aliyah. In other words, the larger need to secure the viability of the greater project, be it Youth Aliyah in particular or the Zionist enterprise as a whole, demanded flexible application of ideology.

The urgency for initiating more ambitious emigration projects derived not only from the uncertainty regarding the future but also from the disruptions within Jewish life. In view of the arrests that accompanied the November riots, as well as the deportation of Polish Jews in October, German Jewry faced the difficult task of providing material and spiritual care for large numbers of youths whose parents could no longer perform that function. To complicate matters, the German government dissolved Jewish welfare institutions that had previously provided child care, such as orphanages. In many such cases Youth Aliyah, often through its Mittleren-Hachscharah camps, could provide some measure of security. The Jugendhilfe increased the number of individuals MiHa could accommodate and also hoped to incorporate these cases into Youth Aliyah groups after three to six months of training.[76]

As war in Europe loomed on the horizon by late 1938 and immediate transfer to Palestine seemed unlikely, Youth Aliyah attempted to arrange for applicants to find shelter in England.[77] Great Britain's offer of refuge in response to the pogrom resulted in the evacuation of nearly ten thousand threatened children before September 1939; more than seventy-four hundred of these young refugees were Jewish, and Youth Aliyah provided much of the organizational machinery and technical expertise required to realize this mass emigration.[78] Although the Jugendhilfe helped coordinate the *Kindertransporte*, this rescue operation and earlier youth emigration were quite distinct. These differences highlight the urgency brought about by the pogrom. The selection process played a less prominent role, and in many cases new standards were applied as determined by the organizing bodies in England. The guarantors in Great Britain, who pledged to house the refugees, valued different qualities than the Jugendhilfe. They preferred younger children, and the majority of foster parents stipulated girls between the ages of seven to ten. Additionally, specific requests often included a predilection for fairer skin tone. In contrast to Youth Aliyah, which reflected the general labor Zionist preference for males, girls represented the majority on the transports to England.[79] The mood attending the departure from Germany was another difference. Even though many parents experienced trepidation when transports departed for Palestine, the overall atmosphere among the youths had generally been celebratory. A much more somber tone characterized the groups leaving Germany in the wake of the No-vember pogrom, with children and parents weeping and shouting. When the first group of two hundred youths bound for England pulled out of the Berlin train station, parents dispersed silently, not wishing to draw any attention from the German public.[80]

Following the pogrom, as Jews frantically searched for means to es-cape, many parents now willingly sent their children unaccompanied to find refuge in other lands. In early 1939 Youth Aliyah expanded its pro-gram and prepared to accept children below the age of fourteen. The two-year training formula previously established could not sufficiently provide for the needs of this Children's Aliyah, as it was called. A plan was prepared in Palestine calling for families in the *yishuv* to adopt young Jews from Germany along the lines of the foster program insti-tuted to care for refugee children in England. Requests for a Children's Aliyah emanated from Germany soon after the November pogrom, sug-gesting that the Jewish Agency provide funds immediately to establish "several large educational institutions" and secure permission from the Palestine government to allow several thousand children to enter for adoption.[81]

Owing to financial and technical difficulties, Szold initially refused to accept this additional responsibility.[82] Yet the pleas from Germany and the desperate times eventually compelled her to accept. Though a sepa-rate office of the Jewish Agency's Social Service department would handle care and placement of the children, all communications with families and organizations in Europe would fall under the aegis of Youth Aliyah. The Jugendhilfe agreed to select school-age children to partici-pate in this program.[83]

In addition to supporting these initiatives with younger children and the *Kindertransporte*, Youth Aliyah faced new challenges. Following the creation of the *Protektorat* and a Nazi satellite state in Slovakia, Youth Aliyah's central office in Berlin became increasingly concerned with dis-tributing youth certificates among the various lands under German con-trol. The *Irgun* established in September 1938 to promote cooperation between different Youth Aliyah centers expanded its role to accommo-date the new map of Europe. After German troops were "invited" into the newly independent Slovak state, a Youth Aliyah office opened in Bratislava. The *Irgun* attempted to calculate each region's relative re-quirements, based on the number of Jews in the appropriate age categories.[84] As one might expect, this issue created competition between the various centers. Chaim Hoffman from Prague, for example, agreed with estimates of each country's overall Jewish population. But he claimed that in former Czechoslovakia, where emigration was just beginning, the age distribution within the Jewish community differed from that in the Altreich, justifying a greater percentage of youth certificates for Prague and Bratislava than proposed by leaders in Berlin.[85]

In late May 1939 Freier reported the need for ten thousand certificates to be distributed to Jewish youth living under Nazi rule. She claimed that the Jewish youth leaders throughout central Europe had declared that immigration to Eretz Israel represented the only possible rescue for thousands of young Jews. According to Freier, Jewish youth possessed an intense determination to realize *aliyah*, their "final hope."[86] Some leaders in Palestine had already conceived similar grandiose immigration plans in November 1938, but the Mandatory government refused to change its policies.[87] In fact the Palestine immigration authorities would not even relax their regulations for dependants of immigrants arriving on A1 (capitalist) certificates. According to the quota schedule, immigrants in the capitalist category could not claim dependents over the age of fourteen. Even parents with financial means to immigrate on their own beseeched Youth Aliyah to provide a way to bring their teenage children with them.[88] Such cases show the less common scenario in which parents faced the dilemma of leaving their children behind rather than the reverse. In one instance where two children fell under such circumstances and the father requested youth certificates for both, the Jugendhilfe would only accept one because the second child was not a Zionist.[89]

Grateful as Zionist leaders were for the temporary shelter other lands provided, these havens created social and educational difficulties, which Youth Aliyah had hoped to avoid. The 350 children in Sweden were mostly placed with non-Jewish families. Holland, which had accepted more than 1,500 young Jews, accommodated them largely in temporary camps. Even England, which by May had taken in more than 4,500, was subject to harsh criticism for failing to provide a Jewish environment. Youth Aliyah representatives feared that the young refugees would be quickly attracted to the non-Jewish lifestyle, and educational work would confront extreme difficulties.[90] Indeed these difficulties exemplified many of the same problems, viewed as inherent to diaspora Judaism, which Youth Aliyah was expected to solve. In this respect and in the context of Zionist political propaganda, one can understand David Ben-Gurion's December 1938 remark that "if all Jewish children could be saved from Germany by being transferred to England, whereas only half of them could be saved if transferred to *Eretz Israel,* [I] would choose the second alternative, since the problem . . . was not only one concerning the children, but a historical issue of the Jewish people."[91]

Nevertheless, when existing Palestine certificates remained insufficient, the Jugendhilfe continued sending groups to other countries, particularly Denmark, England, Holland, and Sweden. In contrast to the humanitarian projects sponsored in immediate response to the events of November 1938, which had no long-term goals, Schattner developed this reliance on other countries as *Transit-Hachscharah* stations to remove groups as rapidly as possible from Germany until Palestine certificates became available.[92] Charitable organizations sheltered young refugees after the November pogrom, but these operations did not always respond to young Jews' spiritual, religious, or educational needs. The *hachsharah* centers Schattner promoted sought to fill any such void and respond to the additional pedagogical challenge of forging Jewish and Zionist identification. By 1939 Youth Aliyah had established training centers in Denmark, England, France, Holland, Italy, Sweden, Switzerland, and Yugoslavia.[93]

This excerpt from a letter sent by Joseph Baratz to Szold indicates both the challenges inherent in the use of transit centers and the painful reality that immigration activists routinely confronted.

> I am delayed for a time in London. . . . During this time I have had the opportunity to see the German children. . . . The same children that go to the Land [of Israel]. Same faces, same clothes, same large suitcases. Of course, they were not received equally. Reporters and photographers, magnificent automobiles and wealthy women came to see the "unfortunate children" (*yeladim miskenim*) on the same day. Innumerable boxes of chocolates and sweets were sent to them. I do not discount at all the feeling of compassion that appears among the people here, I only wanted to describe the difference. But that is not the main point. The main fundamental difference is internal.
>
> What did we say to our youth, [when] we first received them in

the dining hall of the school in Daganiah? . . . What an awakening, and how many hopes did these children awaken within us?

And what is there to say here to the children regarding their future? What can we do with them here? They are scattered to families. To which families? What is their future? This is the difference! . . . I knew that among all these children was one who had a brother in Daganiah. I had heard special things about him. I went, therefore, to visit him. At lunchtime, the director of the camp announced that Mr. B[aratz] from *Eretz Israel* wants to see the children with relatives in Palestine. 20 children came to me. They asked questions, wrote letters, and sent greetings. To my question of whether they wanted to travel to Palestine, only 9 answered in the affirmative. The rest either did not want to or had doubts. The reason—In England they have been set up in wealthy homes, and perhaps there will be some opportunity to save or help their parents.

These words demonstrate the children's perceptions of refugee life. Certainly most of those evacuated to England were not placed in wealthy homes, and the material comforts they enjoyed would have varied little compared to life in Palestine, especially as war engulfed the continent less than a year later. Baratz continued,

Lastly came to me the boy with the Daganiah brother. . . . "I want to go to Palestine, I will not remain here!" I explained to him the difficulties but he went on, "I want to go to Palestine." . . . He cries, refuses to eat, hides himself when people come to choose children, "I want to go to Palestine!" The counselors are very worried, they are particularly worried that such a child would actually run away from the camp. When he conversed with me, and I gave him details on his brother he was very pleased and relaxed. At the end of our discussion he hugged me and asked . . . "when I will be in *Eretz Israel* will I be able to get my father out of the detention camp?" . . . His eyes filled with tears, it was difficult to talk and he waited for my answer. . . . What could I say to him. A boy of 14. . . . We must enable him to immigrate, he is exemplary in his way, all of the counselors note. Could you do something to arrange his immigration? . . . I do not believe that here [in England] the matter will work out.[94]

The new circumstances in Germany led the Jugendhilfe to focus on preparing and arranging groups for direct immigration to Palestine and for transport to transit countries. In other words, the organization had finally evolved into a pure rescue operation. In early May, in order to accelerate the rate at which young Jews could be removed from Germany, the Jugendhilfe instituted a new intermediate *hachsharah* called *Hachsharat Hanoar* (youth preparation), which would be shorter in duration than the conventional Mittleren-Hachscharah. The prior years of living under Nazi restrictions had created a setback in general knowledge and education, demanding a more thorough academic training. Since many children had no homes to which they could return, the *Hachsharat Hanoar* would supervise trainees and provide some security before departure. In 1939 the Jugendhilfe required every candidate for Palestine to attend the Youth Aliyah School before admission to either preparatory camps or *Hachsharat Hanoar.*[95] This step proved necessary since the authorities had banned the individual youth groups, which had previously provided essential social and educational programs.

The role of the youth groups had changed since Youth Aliyah had first started its work. As Schattner later wrote, "At the beginning of [Youth Aliyah] the youth movements still had all their strength and were able to provide their members with Jewish and Zionist education, but the fact had changed after five years. The oppression, the arrests, the emigration of leaders—weakened the strength of the youth movements, and they were no longer able to educate their members. From this perspective as well, Youth Aliyah was compelled to take upon itself responsibility for training its members."[96]

Madrichim also faced the challenge of undoing six years of education under a Nazi regime. Prior to the terror of the November pogrom, a significant proportion of Jewish students had remained in state schools, and this experience promoted a servile attitude and commitment to the leadership principle, as well as self-hatred among many of these young Jews.[97]

The number of individual cases requiring immediate attention taxed the staff's energies. Young Jews with fathers, mothers, or brothers taken into custody who managed to reach the Jugendhilfe offices during the afternoon needed placement in a group by evening.[98] Youth Aliyah accepted the role of guardian in such cases where no adult family member could assume responsibility. Nonetheless the infrastructure Youth Aliyah had created proved insufficient to handle the tremendous demands upon it during 1939. The Berlin community alleviated some of this pressure by establishing an emigration school (*Auswanderungsschule*), which included a special Palestine section. Outside the capital as well, Youth Aliyah cooperated with Jewish schools to organize ninth school years focused on immigration to Palestine.[99]

Even though youth certificates were formally exempt from any numerical limitation, the Jewish Agency concluded that the Palestine government "appeared to have some fixed maximum figure which it was reluctant to exceed."[100] The Mandatory authorities still required that funds be secured and living quarters receive official approval before allotting additional certificates, thus Szold hoped to realize a proportionately significant increase, even though the final figures would fall far short of the immediate demand.[101] The excitement that accompanied the announcement of unrestricted youth immigration in 1938 gave way to a more realistic attitude and a more practical approach to emigration a year later.

The Mandatory government strictly adhered to the legal requirements for Youth Aliyah, especially regarding candidates' ages. As happened on a number of occasions during previous years, a minor bureaucratic delay could mean the invalidation of an immigration permit, even as war loomed on the horizon. In early 1939, for example, a girl named Lotte had already been approved for Youth Aliyah, yet that June she was still in France awaiting a certificate. Lotte had completed a year of *hachsharah* in Cologne and two years of domestic work in Paris. By March 1939 her visa for France had expired and French immigration authorities only allowed Lotte to remain because Youth Aliyah had guaranteed her certificate for Palestine, which had already been sent to Berlin and was awaiting transfer to Paris. However, she was born in April 1922. In June 1939, when the certificate arrived, she had passed her seventeenth birthday and was no longer eligible for Youth Aliyah.[102] In July, as the continent moved toward war, the French government ordered Lotte to leave France as her permit had expired and had already been renewed several times.[103]

As German Jews grasped at any possible avenue of escape, the urgent circumstances affected even the supposedly unanimous support for youth emigration. On July 24 the director of the Palästina-Amt noted the community's conflicting needs. "We have in Germany dozens (or more) of people, who are actually in danger, demanded to turn in identity papers, etc., whereas children are generally not immediately endangered. Under these circumstances, is it just to make available so high a percentage of certificates for youths? . . . I can only say that I completely despair, as I work daily with endangered people, long-time Zionists, with relatives in Palestine, etc."[104]

According to Hans Beyth, however, from the perspective of building up Jewish Palestine young people still represented the best material for the task.[105] If the period following the November pogrom can be characterized as the beginning of rescue operations, most Zionist leaders in Palestine nevertheless refused to deviate from the commitment to selective immigration. In fact correspondence between Jerusalem and Berlin during the first half of 1939 still reflected a rejection rate around 25 percent based on physical or psychological criteria.[106]

In many cases enormous time and effort were put into getting young Jews recognized and registered only to be rejected for medical reasons. One can imagine the bitter frustration and disappointment on the part of the lobbying relatives in Palestine, England, or elsewhere, when hearing the news that their sibling, niece, nephew, or friend had been rejected. The argument often followed this pattern: "But I know him—He is healthy and perfect for Palestine." In one case, an uncle traveled from Cyprus to Palestine for a half-hour interview with Szold to petition on behalf of his nephews in Vienna. Other examples abound of siblings who had already immigrated with Youth Aliyah pleading with Szold or Beyth to bring their brothers and sisters from Europe.[107]

But exceptions did occur. In the case of Ursula, Youth Aliyah's physician rejected her, arguing that severe myopia would make physical labor difficult for her. Szold seconded this decision in a telegram to Berlin.[108] The Jugendhilfe immediately appealed with the comment, "[Ursula] is the best girl in the group." The Jerusalem office reconsidered and accepted the girl conditionally, provided they could receive the full two-year's maintenance in Palestine currency prior to her arrival.[109]

Recent historical criticism charges the *yishuv* leadership, after World War II, with maintaining prejudicial attitudes when confronting the challenge of absorbing the surviving remnants of European Jewry. Indeed this perspective may also have guided Zionist leaders during the 1930s.[110] Regarding Youth Aliyah, though, no evidence suggests that *yishuv* leaders did not sincerely press the government for additional certificates. The documents merely demonstrate a reluctance to circumvent official policy, lest the authorities further restrict immigration reserved for students. During early 1939, in fact, when individuals were rejected during the selection process, Youth Aliyah was recommending that parents find an alternate way of getting their children out of Germany, even if the destination was not the land of Israel.[111]

As Szold wrote to Goldmann, this new attitude among the Jewish public in Palestine stressed removal from Germany regardless of whether the young refugees could expect a structured educational program to await them. Szold, however, absolutely refused to support this position. She maintained that true rescue work comprised more than physical salvation and formulated her position in the following sentence: "Rescue as many as possible, but not at the expense of their education."[112]

During the chaotic period surrounding the outbreak of hostilities, Youth Aliyah groups continued to play a prominent role in the frenetic attempts by German Jewry to flee. The Palestine government had announced a youth immigration schedule of 1,051 for the six-month period beginning April 1939. By late August this quota had not yet been filled. Twenty-four hours before the outbreak of war, without obtaining proper documentation, a Youth Aliyah transport bound for England crossed the Dutch border. Another large group of trainees arrived in Denmark the same day World War II began. According to the Youth Aliyah department in Jerusalem, eventually all the young Jews scheduled to immigrate with these certificates found their way to Eretz Israel, the last group arriving in May 1940.[113]

Between November 1938 and September 1939, Youth Aliyah managed to bring almost as many young Jews to Palestine as it had during the previous five years combined. Despite these statistical accomplishments, Goldmann stressed that "the importance of [Youth Aliyah] was not in its practical value, but rather its strong psychological influence to continue working, even under difficult conditions." The emphasis on Youth Aliyah's educational aspects allowed the Jugendhilfe to maintain its vibrancy during this trying period and prevented the activity from becoming mechanical and meaningless in nature.[114]

The ensuing years confronted European Jewry with even more arduous circumstances and represented another stage in the history of Youth Aliyah. Yet in many respects the work completed during this formative prewar time foreshadowed the period of augmented Youth Aliyah activity after World War II. Specifically, the struggle to find common ground among disparate factions and to determine Youth Aliyah's role within broader Zionist activity continually challenged the organization's ability to effectively serve the needs of young Jewish emigrants.

Fig. 1. Youth Aliyah trainees leave Berlin for Palestine in 1936. Photo by Herbert Sonnenfeld, courtesy of the Jewish Museum Berlin.

Fig. 2. A crowd of parents and friends send off a Youth Aliyah group from Berlin in 1936. Photo by Herbert Sonnenfeld, courtesy of the Jewish Museum Berlin.

Fig. 3. In Berlin, Martin Buber and Ernst Simon teach Bible to youth group leaders, 1935. Photo by Herbert Sonnenfeld, courtesy of the Jewish Museum Berlin.

Fig. 4. Students conduct a science experiment in Hebrew at the Youth Aliyah School, Berlin, 1936. Photo by Herbert Sonnenfeld, courtesy of the Jewish Museum Berlin.

Fig. 5. Youth Aliyah children dance the hora onboard a ship as it approaches the shores of Palestine, 1937. Photo by Herbert Sonnenfeld, courtesy of the Jewish Museum Berlin.

Fig. 6. Henrietta Szold in 1933. Courtesy of the Jewish Museum of Maryland, JMM 1992.242.7.

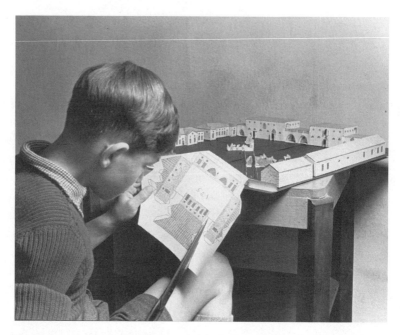

Fig. 7. A student in Berlin builds a model of a Jewish settlement in Palestine, 1935. Photo by Herbert Sonnenfeld, courtesy of the Jewish Museum Berlin.

Fig. 8. Students participate in vocational training in workshop of Theodore-Herzl-Schul, Berlin, 1935. Photo by Herbert Sonnenfeld, courtesy of the Jewish Museum Berlin.

Fig. 9. Children dance the hora during free time at Rüdnitz, 1935. Photo by Herbert Sonnenfeld, courtesy of the Jewish Museum Berlin.

Fig. 10. Students in the *hachsharah* camp at Rüdnitz march to work in the fields, 1935. Photo by Herbert Sonnenfeld, courtesy of the Jewish Museum Berlin.

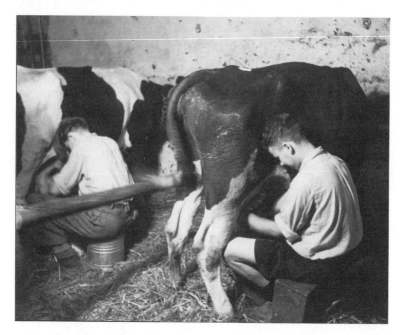

Fig. 11. Youth Aliyah learn to milk cows at Schniebinchen *hachsharah* camp, 1938. Photo by Herbert Sonnenfeld, courtesy of the Jewish Museum Berlin.

Fig. 12. Students attend a biology lecture in Hebrew at the Youth Aliyah School, Berlin, 1936. Photo by Herbert Sonnenfeld, courtesy of the Jewish Museum Berlin.

5
Conflicts and Resolutions

From Youth Aliyah's inception, the participation of Orthodox Jews received special consideration and posed unique challenges to the program's unity and its ideological integrity. The organization committed itself to the immigration of observant Jews within the Youth Aliyah framework, yet realizing this goal proved troublesome. Of approximately five thousand teenagers brought to Palestine by Youth Aliyah before World War II, only around eight hundred entered under Orthodox auspices. Even though these figures reflected the lack of Orthodox facilities in Palestine, rather than an ideological bias, the discrepancy exacerbated existing tensions between religious leaders and the agencies responsible for Youth Aliyah. This particular aspect of Youth Aliyah's work demonstrates not only the fragile nature of Zionist unity but also the distinction between good intentions and the practical realities of relocating young Jews to Palestine.

As early as the summer of 1932, Pinchas Rosenblüth of the Orthodox pioneering federation in Berlin contacted Recha Freier regarding the nascent Youth Aliyah project. Rosenblüth recommended transferring a group of observant youths from Germany to Hapoel Hamizrachi (religious Zionist workers' party) settlements in Palestine.[1] Though none of the leading figures in Berlin or Jerusalem denied the need for including Orthodox groups in theory, the actual application of this ideal proved a persistent problem throughout the period preceding World War II and thereafter.

In July 1933 the Jugendhilfe established a special department to handle Orthodox youth, while in Palestine Orthodox leaders founded the Committee for the Preparation of Religious Youth from Germany in Eretz Israel.[2] These bodies ensured that observant teenagers received proper representation in terms of both certificates and funds. Furthermore, Orthodox delegates supervised the educational programming and religious observance at separate facilities instituted specifically for religious pioneers. From the beginning, however, a problem became apparent that would continue to plague Youth Aliyah: the lack of Orthodox colonies sufficiently prepared to accept groups of young Jews from Germany. Aside from Rodges (now Kibbutz Yavneh), no other collective settlements offered this opportunity.[3]

That August, the committee proposed alternative locations, such as a Mizrachi girls' school in Jerusalem, and the construction of new institutions for the benefit of Orthodox youth. Consequently, Freier remarked that the Orthodox groups had already begun to shift Youth Aliyah's emphasis from its original intentions. Instead of bringing young Jews to kibbutzim, which implied commitment to a specific social and educational ideology, religious leaders merely sought any physical accommodations.[4]

Toward the end of the year, the Jugendhilfe began receiving complaints from religious leaders in Palestine that certificates were being distributed unfairly.[5] In the political context of 1930s Palestine, religious Zionists may have viewed Youth Aliyah as a means to bolster their presence in the *yishuv*. To be sure, the urgent entreaties penned by religious leaders did not equate Youth Aliyah with rescue at this early stage. They did not demand that young Orthodox Jews be removed from Germany to Palestine, regardless of the host settlements' political affiliations. Religious Zionists, though willing to work with socialist leaders in a common cause, criticized the influence wielded by the left, and suspected that labor Zionists, particularly in the agricultural settlements, consciously conspired to suppress Orthodox Judaism in Eretz Israel.[6]

Nevertheless, the movement for religious Youth Aliyah found support in nonsectarian philanthropic circles, notably London's Women's Appeal Committee, an important group within the Central British Fund.[7] This organization's proposed budget for 1934 included the necessary capital investment in Rodges, significantly more costly than the erection of new barracks at Ein-Harod. The committee's plan also called for settling a hundred Orthodox boys in urban locations to receive vocational training, as well as placing forty girls in a Mizrachi boarding school in Jerusalem.

Since kibbutzim were the most cost-effective means of training Youth Aliyah students, the expenses for observant youths in Palestine ran significantly higher than the financial requirements for young immigrants on nonreligious settlements.[8]

In December 1933 Szold noted the importance of determining an acceptable quota for observant youth, so Youth Aliyah and Orthodox representatives stipulated that the Jugendhilfe would allocate 25 percent of its certificates for "religious" youth. Whether this figure accurately represented the proportion of young Jews desiring placement on observant settlements is difficult to determine, and most estimates would provide a ratio closer to 15 percent as representative. The Jugendhilfe felt compelled to establish a quota, and thereby ensure Mizrachi leaders' support for Youth Aliyah in order to present the appearance of unity.[9]

The term "religious," however, as it referred to German Jewry, escapes simple definition and certainly did not always conform to common Mizrachi attitudes toward Jewish practice. The varied levels of religious observance present within German Jewry often led to confusion when placing the youths in Palestine. Orthodox representatives in Palestine argued that the desire to settle in Eretz Israel characterized young Orthodox Jews in Germany more strongly than nonreligious youth. Yet religious identification in this instance referred to "young Jews who want to keep Sabbath and holidays, eat kosher meat, etc."[10] In Germany, however, this terminology could be applied to many young Jews whose religious upbringing was Liberal rather than Orthodox.[11] A large segment of German Jewry (as in the United States during the same period) maintained some degree of commitment to *kashruth* (dietary laws), Sabbath observance, and synagogue attendance. Certainly many Zionists remained committed to Jewish traditions but did not personally identify with complete observance of Jewish law in accordance with Orthodox practice. In fact, descriptions of the preparatory camps run by the Jüdische Jugendhilfe, organized by left-wing Zionists, reflect dedication to some elements of religious tradition. The Youth Aliyah School in Berlin, for example, also included a weekly *kabbalat-shabbat* (Friday evening prayer service) celebration in its schedule.[12] In describing the school's curriculum one student noted, "Nor has the purely Jewish aspect been neglected. With a young rabbi, we study Tenach [Bible] twice a week."[13] Such programming does not reflect a concession to Orthodox interests but rather demonstrates the less polarized character of German Judaism.

Whereas in the land of Israel the opposite of religious was secular, in Germany the opposite of Orthodox was Liberal, decidedly different from pure secularism.

The composition of the youth group Makkabi Hazair exemplified this trend. This movement, established in Germany after the Nazis' rise to power, espoused an ideology centered on personal *aliyah*. Its creed did not demand adherence to any specific religious orientation.[14] Makkabi Hazair requested special consideration for religious teenagers within its membership who wished to participate in Youth Aliyah. According to the group's leaders, placing these individuals on nonreligious colonies, where in fact its members generally did settle, would cause hundreds of young Jews to stray from Jewish law. Yet they also refused to join the Orthodox pioneering groups. Though rejecting the dogmatic approach to *halachah* (Jewish law) represented by groups such as Bachad or Agudat Israel, these young Jews nevertheless affirmed a commitment to Torah study and Judaic traditions as integral elements of their Jewish identities.[15] Similarly, the Orthodox youth groups had no interest in sharing their certificate quota with young Jews not fully committed to their lifestyle.

Thus the application of the Hebrew term *dati*, religious, did not correlate well to the German Jewish environment, where "religious" did not necessarily mean Orthodox. These definitions proved problematic for many young emigrants from Germany unable to find a religious environment corresponding to their personal beliefs. The religious infrastructure of the *yishuv* gave no voice to non-Orthodox Jewish practice. As Conservative and Reform Judaism only became visible in Israeli life in the late twentieth century, the challenges that confronted Liberal Jews from Germany during the 1930s are not surprising. Young German Jews who adhered to non-Orthodox Judaism experienced difficulty accommodating to the highly polarized outlook toward religion present in Palestine, and the institutions that took in Youth Aliyah trainees did not reflect the religious sensitivities of Germany's Liberal Jews. This problem is perhaps best illustrated not by transfer requests to Orthodox establishments but rather where young immigrants, who had registered as religious, asked to be relocated from observant to secular colonies.[16]

Even before the first certificates were approved, Orthodox circles argued that of the initial 500 youth certificates allocated to German Jewry they deserved 125. This figure reflected almost half the permits allotted to the Jüdische Jugendhilfe. The figure of 500 included 230 certificates distributed to the youth village Ben-Shemen and the children's home Ahawah, which, according to the agreement reached in Berlin, were not subject to the quota. Orthodox leaders were not satisfied with 25 percent of Jugendhilfe certificates and sought a share of the Ben-Shemen allotment as well, even though the village was deemed religiously unacceptable. Orthodox circles repeatedly alleged unfair treatment, frustrating Szold, who claimed that she allocated a disproportionate amount of time attempting to accommodate Orthodox interests.[17]

The 25 percent quota, however, referred to certificates, not funding. While at first glance the difference seems technical, it proved significant. One reason that observant circles pressed for high representation was their contention that the need for Youth Aliyah was greatest among Orthodox youth. The reasons given for this claim were (1) because of religious obligations (for example, observance of Sabbath and dietary laws), economic prospects for religious youth were worse; (2) possibilities for immigration to other countries were therefore also more difficult for religious Jews; and (3) the Orthodox community had fewer resources available to support itself in general.[18]

Szold validated these claims, adding that despite her commitment to equitable distribution of opportunities and funds for all, she would be inclined to favor observant over nonobservant youth, as a result of the particular economic circumstances in Germany.[19] Therefore, though she originally supported a scheme in which, even for Orthodox youths, 50 percent of the costs for each Youth Aliyah candidate would be covered by public funds and 50 percent by parents, Szold later reinterpreted this plan. She argued that the 50 percent rule should be applied to the Jüdische Jugendhilfe as a whole but that the religious quota should not be stringently subjected to this rule.[20] In other words, for Orthodox Youth Aliyah, the Jugendhilfe would be prepared to accept a larger proportion of candidates lacking private means of support.

The evidence, however, demonstrates that factors other than concern over Orthodox Jewry's deteriorating economic situation led to this generous attitude. Constant threats from Orthodox circles to initiate separate fund-raising campaigns helped persuade the Arbeitsgemeinschaft to reevaluate its position vis-à-vis observant groups. As Youth Aliyah already labored under the handicap of coordinating its efforts with the Keren Hayesod, and the Zionist movement as a whole struggled to maintain unity in the face of constant fighting among political factions, threats of separate appeals received great attention.[21] When pressing for financial compromise, the committee for religious Youth Aliyah wrote, "We want to avoid a special priority and special collections for religious youth, but right now, we see no other way!" Szold responded, "If the religious circles carry out their threat of instituting a separate collection, they may not succeed in benefiting themselves, but they will certainly succeed in harming the general collection. . . . I am convinced that the threat of a separate collection will be carried out unless concessions are made."[22] Orthodox circles exerted strong influence, despite their weaker representation within the Jewish population.

Quite often the battle lines were ideological, rather than practical. From Youth Aliyah's inception, highly influential non-Zionist Orthodox rabbis in Germany complained that the organization wanted to bring young Jews to nonreligious settlements against their parents' wishes.[23] Among observant Jews in Germany, some were Zionist, some were sympathetic to work in Palestine, and others rejected most Zionist enterprises. Georg Landauer remarked that Agudat Israel did not even support Mizrachi settlements in Palestine, and therefore its criticism of nonreligious Zionists should be viewed in that light. In fact, the Jugendhilfe continually addressed the question of children being sent to nonreligious institutions in Palestine seemingly against their parents' wishes. In April 1934 Simonson reiterated to parents that certain colonies in Palestine did not provide for traditional Orthodox practice and sought reassurance from parents and applicants that they understood this situation. To further prevent any misconceptions concerning the nature of various kibbutzim and moshavim in Palestine, the Jugendhilfe tried working with religious leaders in order to clarify these issues.[24] Such explanations were deemed necessary to avoid cases where a parent, upon learning that a specific kibbutz did not observe Jewish law, demanded the child's transfer to an observant settlement. In 1934, for example, some Orthodox representatives claimed that a number of young immigrants at Ein-Harod desired relocation to Rodges; investigation revealed that only one girl had asked to transfer, solely at her brother's behest.[25]

Yet even when the applicants' religious proclivities had been known in Berlin, difficulties during the absorption process remained unavoidable. The group brought to Givat Brenner in early 1935 best exemplified this problem. One-third of this group wrote to Szold that they were indeed religious but not Orthodox. As such they had no desire to be placed on a *dati* settlement in Palestine but rather demanded the right to follow their own beliefs and practices within the framework of a non-religious settlement.[26] Young Jews belonging to the same youth group in Germany, comrades sharing similar ideological perspectives, could find themselves in conflict over religion following their immigration to Palestine. Thus the faith-based identification within a liberal society, independent of national identity, best formulated by the CV as *deutscher Staatsbürger jüdischen Glaubens* (German citizens of the Jewish faith), became problematic in a community where religion and nationality overlapped considerably. This conflict demonstrates a difference between theoretical diaspora Zionism and actual absorption into the *yishuv*'s political framework.

In fact, the choice of what type of settlement to join generally resulted from the ideological inclinations of the various *Bünde* with which youths were associated in Germany. The political affiliation of the young immigrants rather than the parents' religious sensitivities usually determined the child's destination. Parents remained free to complain, and Youth Aliyah strove to avoid conflicts of this nature, but administrators in Palestine and Germany concluded that the movement would have to respect the personal decisions of individuals deemed mature enough to participate in the immigration program.[27]

Orthodox leaders' claims that the 25 percent quota of Jugendhilfe certificates remained undersubscribed appeared to be their most substantial criticism. In truth, especially during the first year of Youth Aliyah, non-religious settlements received significantly more German-Jewish youth groups than did Orthodox institutions. By July 1935, of the twelve participating kibbutzim, only one, Rodges, accepted observant groups. Of 612 teenagers brought to Palestine by Youth Aliyah, 109 were supervised in accordance with Jewish law, and many of these trainees lived in urban environments.[28] This fraction amounts to 18 percent, below the agreed upon allocation. In an interesting twist, considering the emphasis on selection, the disparity between religious Youth Aliyah and the established quota did not necessarily reflect the suitability of candidates for Palestine. As one observer commented, especially regarding Hebrew-speaking ability, Orthodox trainees seemed academically more prepared than most other groups.[29] In fact, the imbalance resulted from both the ideological aims of Youth Aliyah and the realities of Jewish Palestine during the 1930s.

To bring Jewish youth to collective farming settlements in Palestine remained Youth Aliyah's goal. Despite the Zionist rhetoric of bringing urban settlers to the countryside and thus transforming them into productive citizens imbued with the ideals of social equality embodied by kibbutz life, pragmatic needs demanded that Youth Aliyah focus on rural settlement.[30] The bureau in Jerusalem devised a budget whereby trainees raised on collective agricultural colonies could be cared for at a cost of $152 per year. Training costs at urban facilities ran significantly higher. Thus both ideology and economics determined that German Jewish youth undergo training on collective farms.

Therein lay the difficulty for the proponents of religious Youth Aliyah. Ideologically there was little conflict, as long as the settlements accepting the Orthodox youth promoted a *dati* lifestyle and would provide a proper religious as well as agricultural education. However, in 1934, only Rodges, which accepted a group of fifty-six trainees that year, fit these criteria. Conversely, the secular Zionist groups relied on a large number of established kibbutzim, and eventually moshavim, in particular the growing number of settlements in the Jezreel Valley. Mindful of its commitment to provide Orthodox Jewry with one-fourth of the certificates distributed by the Jugendhilfe, Youth Aliyah explored alternative sites. Reluctantly, Szold consented to settling Orthodox youth in urban areas, and providing domestic or technical training, as opposed to agricultural instruction.[31] However, placing groups in urban environments raised educational and social problems for which Youth Aliyah was unprepared, and maintaining groups in these settings created expenses not encountered at farming settlements.

Therefore, 1935 saw a reduced flow of observant youths into Palestine via Youth Aliyah. At the same time, the offices in Berlin and Jerusalem recognized the urgency of finding suitable places for these trainees and gave this issue high priority.[32] However, many Orthodox leaders, especially those not personally familiar with the situation in Palestine, failed to recognize the rationale and reacted rather sharply to the basic fact that the number of Orthodox emigrants among youth from Germany declined. During the period between the Nineteenth and Twentieth Zionist Congresses, 1935–37, when Youth Aliyah in general experienced tremendous growth (from 612 trainees in Palestine to more than 1,650), Orthodox youth could only claim a modest increase, from 109 to 171.[33] Obviously with the fraction barely tipping the 10 percent figure, Youth Aliyah had failed to fill the religious quota.

Both Szold and Youth Aliyah leaders in Berlin sought to lay the blame, if blame could be ascribed, on the shoulders of Orthodoxy at large for failing to establish effective roots in the soil of Palestine. These excerpts typified Szold's attitude: "The real explanation of our difficulty is this: The Youth Aliyah became possible in its present form only because the Kewutzot gave us the possibility of maintaining, educating, and adjusting young people to agricultural pursuits at a minimum expenditure of funds, and the religious elements in Jewry had not provided Kewutzot." Similarly Szold wrote, "The difficulty . . . lies not in the attitude of the Arbeitsgemeinschaft towards religious children and youth, but in the fact that the Jewish religious classes have not prepared for the Hitler emergency even in the measure in which the a-religious Jews have."[34] No doubt some individuals associated with the youth immigration did not view the matter of accommodating Orthodox circles as one of terrible urgency. In general, however, concern was great, but solutions were lacking. Even the educator Ernst Simon, an early sponsor of religious Youth Aliyah in Palestine, conceded that insufficient possibilities for observant youth immigration resulted from the decades-long reluctance of Orthodox Jewry, in all its shades, to contribute effectively to building up the Jewish national home.[35]

Orthodox leaders in Palestine also failed to promote a spirit of cooperation between religious and nonreligious leaders within Youth Aliyah. In early 1936 Chief Rabbi Isaac Herzog of Palestine wrote the following to Chief Rabbi Joseph Hertz of England: "I maintain that even in the absence of an intimation in that direction on the part of their parents, it would be our bound and sacred duty to do everything in our power with the view of ensuring their religious education and upbringing. This duty is all the more binding now that, as Rabbi Dr. Hoffman of Frankfurt has informed us, more than 50% of the parents have expressly stipulated that their children shall be reared up religiously."[36] The chief rabbinate of Jaffa and Tel Aviv even criticized Szold for allowing any child from Germany, even with parental consent, to be raised under the auspices of nonreligious institutions in Palestine. The Arbeitsgemeinschaft's supporters throughout the world tried to dissuade public figures such as Herzog and Hertz from openly criticizing Youth Aliyah in hopes of preventing any adverse effects in international fund-raising.[37]

In Germany, however, as circumstances grew increasingly desperate, the very real paucity of immigration sites in Eretz Israel for observant youths failed to satisfy the demands of Orthodox parents and children. In their desperation these families did not necessarily affirm Youth Aliyah's social and educational ideals. Parents constantly requested that Orthodox youth be sent for instruction in manual trades, an avenue not limited by the lack of observant farming settlements. Many even dismissed the social ethos of Youth Aliyah by arguing that a tradesman held a higher status than an agricultural laborer.[38]

Two possibilities existed for solving this dilemma. Most apparent was the option of rapidly placing Youth Aliyah groups for vocational training in the cities, as was done initially. Orthodox circles in Germany favored this alternative. Many parents in Germany actually wanted their children to receive technical rather than agricultural training, for a trade would leave the young immigrants better prepared to earn a living. (This attitude was also evident among nonreligious circles, but was most prevalent among the Orthodox.) Szold and her associates tried to stand by their conception of Youth Aliyah's mission, claiming that the organization was not instituted for the purpose of vocational training.[39] The second prospect was to construct new agricultural institutions appropriate for the absorption and education of Orthodox youth. The Jerusalem office favored creating an establishment along the lines of Ben-Shemen capable of accommodating large numbers of young immigrants. Youth Aliyah eventually realized this proposal with the construction of the village Kfar Noar Dati near Kfar Hasidim. However, the cost of this undertaking remained prohibitive, resulting in a long delay before completion. The total capital investment required to construct this facility amounted to more than one hundred thousand dollars.[40]

Recognizing the need for extra subsidies to create sufficient settlement opportunities for observant pioneers, the Arbeitsgemeinschaft grappled with the dilemma of how to allocate those funds. Did the commitment to grant 25 percent of the youth certificates to Orthodox immigrants warrant allotting additional portions of its budget to create the necessary infrastructure? How could the organization justify taking funds that could support twice the number of nonreligious youths in order to construct this youth village?

In mid-1935 the Arbeitsgemeinschaft approved a special appeal for funds earmarked for Kfar Noar Dati, up to fifteen thousand dollars to be deposited in a separate account. If collections fell short, Youth Aliyah would budget up to ten thousand dollars for the project. The Arbeitsgemeinschaft rather than the religious committee would retain overall responsibility for this campaign. In order to prevent competition between the regular Youth Aliyah campaign and the drive to support Kfar Noar Dati, special collections outside of Germany or Palestine would require prior approval from the Arbeitsgemeinschaft.[41] In Germany, appeals for the Orthodox youth village succeeded. In some communities support equaled the general Youth Aliyah contributions. The Arbeitsgemeinschaft's willingness to budget considerable funds for Kfar Noar Dati derived in large part from a desire to prevent Mizrachi from undertaking independent appeals.[42]

Though an Orthodox youth village was planned as early as 1934, only after the Anschluss did Kfar Noar Dati see its first allotment of fifty-eight certificates. In fact only during 1938–39 did Orthodox youth once again receive their full allocation of 25 percent.[43] Financial considerations did not prejudicially prevent or block religious Youth Aliyah. The organization demonstrated a willingness to provide a greater proportion of public funds than the quota would warrant for Orthodox youth. Additionally Youth Aliyah agreed to spend more to maintain Orthodox youths in Palestine than it allocated to support nonreligious trainees. Szold wrote in April 1936 that meeting the needs of observant youth cost at least 25 percent more than the provision made at secular settlements. For every group of Orthodox youth, including Rodges, Youth Aliyah was forced to budget more money per trainee than in nonreligious sites.[44] As religious parents did not contribute more to support their children, and since Orthodox trainees were more likely to receive financial assistance, Youth Aliyah in fact did allocate more money per capita to accommodate them.

Even after the war began religious disposition remained an issue. The following excerpt is taken from a letter dated September 1939 from Hadassah's Marion Greenberg to Michaelis-Stern.

Mrs. [Rose] Jacobs has now received a letter from Dr. Ascher dated September 11th, informing her that the children have been refused by your office *only two weeks ago*. Dr. Ascher quotes from your letter to him, in which you give as your reason for the rejection of the children the fact that you had no *religious certificates* at your disposal. It is true that Dr. Ascher, in answer to the question as to special groups did state a preference for Rodges and Ahawa. He must have done so, however, in May or in June. A prompt reply from you would have made it possible for him to have communicated with you again. He did write to you saying that the situation was so desperate that he would take any available certificates for the children, but his letter was delayed as a result, it would seem, of your own tardy response. The question is an extremely serious one. In the first place the children are superlatively trained for Palestine, and as you have been informed, they are threatened with expulsion from Switzerland which would involve their return to Germany.[45] (Emphasis in original.)

The religious question during the early years of Youth Aliyah mirrors the paradoxical position of the Orthodox Jewry regarding the development of Palestine during this time. Most Orthodox Jews in Germany and elsewhere did not support the Zionist enterprise, as the movement's political agenda seemed to conflict with a focus on religious belief and practice, and secular Jews dominated the leadership roles. Yet Orthodox leaders wielded sufficient power to influence public officials and receive concessions, mainly financial, beyond their numerical strength within the Jewish community, both in Germany and Palestine. On the other hand, Orthodox Jewry's weak representation in Palestine, specifically in the agricultural sector, prevented religious youth from participating in Youth Aliyah in accordance with the quota allotted them.

Clearly, attempts at including young Jews from all sectors of German Jewry in the youth immigration program did not always succeed. Prior to 1938 significant elements of the German Jewish community remained dubious regarding Youth Aliyah's ultimate success, and others criticized the organization's monopoly on youth certificates. Furthermore, the Arbeitsgemeinschaft's thriving fund-raising operations created tensions between Youth Aliyah and other Zionist charities.

Henrietta Szold herself criticized the Jugendhilfe's propaganda as overromanticizing life in Palestine. Young immigrants generally expected an immigration experience focused on hiking and traveling in accordance with the tradition of the German *Wanderbünde* as opposed to the reality of pioneer life, which demanded sweat and toil. These complaints, while present to a small degree in early 1935, increased over time, as more and more young Jews with little or no prior exposure to Zionism joined Youth Aliyah.[46] According to Szold, the people running the schools and training centers in Germany did not sufficiently downplay this romantic conception of Palestine, resulting in unnecessary difficulties for the new immigrants. Why would the Jugendhilfe want to give this false impression? If its organizational aims differed from the absorption concerns of Szold's department in the Jewish Agency, this approach makes perfect sense. In other words, the Jugendhilfe's immediate concerns were registering as many young people for Youth Aliyah as possible and increasing support among the Jewish public in Germany, not ensuring a smooth immigration process.

Szold further chastised the Berlin leadership for the presence of conflicting political attitudes within Youth Aliyah groups. Some students had requested transfer from their host community in Palestine to one more in tune with their particular outlook. In Szold's mind Youth Aliyah needed to avoid importing ideological conflicts into a land where political conflict defined daily life.[47] The settlements themselves regarded this issue as a very serious problem and protested when groups originally destined for one location were routed to another. Apparently political divisiveness within groups had not been a significant issue during the selection and training period in Germany, or if the Jugendhilfe was aware of any such problems it chose to ignore them. Similar difficulties also arose concerning religious observance. In all likelihood such conflicts remained hidden in Germany because of the overarching concern with selection and actual emigration, along with the solidarity forged by a common goal. Many enrollees in Youth Aliyah deliberately avoided ideological confrontation in order to leave Germany at the earliest possible date.

But the much acclaimed unity of purpose among all youth groups represented by the Jugendhilfe faded under the pressure of limited youth certificates and points of settlement in Palestine. This problem came to the fore early, even among Zionist groups, and eventually became more serious. In February 1934 the leaders of Hashomer Hazair, one of the smaller Zionist movements in Germany, complained of inadequate representation within Youth Aliyah. Since the group contributed to the Jugendhilfe's propaganda efforts, its leaders demanded significant participation in the immigration program. Specifically, they expected not only that Hashomer Hazair receive certificates but also that the organization's young members be sent to Hashomer Hazair kibbutzim in Palestine.[48]

Criticism also came from within the German Jewish establishment. Youth Aliyah had not convinced all the leading personalities and institutions of organized German Jewry that the program deserved support. Significantly, the Jüdischer Frauenbund (Jewish Women's League), an organization whose name was synonymous with social welfare and child care among German Jews, initially refused to endorse the project. Marion Kaplan's history of the JFB clearly places the organization within a specific socioeconomic environment that helps explain its reluctance to support Youth Aliyah.[49] The league's founder and dominant personality, Bertha Pappenheim, proved decisive in this regard. Despite the growing number of Zionists in the JFB, Pappenheim pressed the organization to devote all its energies to preserving the integrity of the family unit, as long as the prospect for continued communal existence in Germany remained. A program geared toward separating children from their parents did not reflect this ideal. Pappenheim sharply criticized Youth Aliyah in 1933, derisively calling the program a "*Kinderexport*," and claimed that mothers who sent children on such a journey were evading their parental responsibilities.[50] Committed to the perception that under Nazi rule there was still a place for Jews in Germany, Pappenheim fought this plan vigorously.[51]

The JFB criticized the departure of unmarried young women for distant lands and would not counsel parents to permit their daughters to follow such a course. Rather the bourgeois ideals of the JFB encouraged girls to remain with the family in Germany and saw the risky adventure of emigration as the male's prerogative. In fact the JFB was initially distressed that many of the young women trained under its auspices in the vocation of home economics left Germany as soon as possible, and the organization only moderated its position during 1935.[52] But did these attitudes regarding emigration of girls differ greatly from the Zionist perspective that Youth Aliyah embodied?

Any list of prominent individuals and organizations responsible for the realization of Youth Aliyah reveals that women played a highly significant role in bringing so many thousands of young Jews from Germany to Palestine. Certainly there were men who performed important functions, but in fact women undertook the overwhelming majority of creative, philanthropic, and administrative work. On the other hand less than 40 percent of the youth certificates went to girls.

Why were women so conspicuous in this welfare/immigration/rescue activity? If women dominated the leadership roles in Youth Aliyah, why were so many more boys than girls brought from Germany to Palestine? Do the figures merely reflect the reality of a male-dominated movement, despite the Zionist myth of gender equality? In fact the answers are interrelated.

The role that gender played in the youth immigration program, both in terms of the women who ran the organization and the children who participated in it, is best understood as a function of the social orientation of most German Jews. The prominence that women held in organizing Youth Aliyah, not only in Germany but throughout the world, stems from (middle-class) Jewish women's traditional involvement in social work and child care activities. Marion Kaplan noted that while Jewish men were hit particularly hard by both the Depression and the rise of Nazism, the unique circumstances of the 1930s opened up many opportunities in social service and pedagogy for Jewish women.[53] Equally significant is the fact that Youth Aliyah's success or failure was directly dependent on its ability to raise money. Many charitable foundations, particularly in Jewish circles, were largely dependent on the services of talented women, a trend well established during the Weimar period.[54]

Perhaps in Zionist circles, which were less established within mainstream German Jewry during the Weimar period, this connection was less clear, but certainly by the early 1930s WIZO had made an impact in Europe, and Hadassah was on its way to becoming the most successful Zionist philanthropy in the United States.[55] Whether they recognized the fact initially, the women who ran Youth Aliyah in Germany also benefited from the Nazis' general willingness to allow them to work unfettered, both because they were female, and thus did not pose a serious threat according to Nazi thinking, and because they were acting to remove Jews from Germany.

No doubt a major factor as to why so many women's organizations supported and sponsored Youth Aliyah was the emotional appeal of the project. Slogans such as "save the children" or "care for the homeless" imbued the youth immigration program with a certain maternal quality. Ensuring the survival of so many teenagers with seemingly nowhere else to turn was viewed as an extension of a woman's traditional responsibility of caring for hearth and home. That these protective instincts did not necessarily result in equal regard for the daughters of German Jewry was a function of both the perceived needs of the Jewish national home and the preconceptions of most German Jewish families regarding emigration.

Some of the people promoting Youth Aliyah, however, did criticize the prevalence of young men. Yocheved Bat-Rachel emphasized that she was sent as a *shlichah* to Germany specifically because there was no female representation and in order to increase the number of girls recruited for *aliyah*.[56] And in 1936 Georg Josephthal wrote that "we still have only a small number of girls in our constituency. . . . There is a need to invest special resources in order to bring them into the movement. . . . The percentage of girls in hachsharah is no greater than 23 percent, which is an untenable situation."[57]

The Jewish Agency's selective immigration policies gave preference to individuals perceived as essential to Palestine's economic and industrial productivity. At least one writer has suggested that women were actually considered an "element" whose *aliyah* should be restricted.[58] Even during the 1930s most certificates went to unmarried males in their twenties. The workers' certificates the Jewish Agency set aside for German *olim* in late 1932 were distributed in the following manner: 65 for *chaluzim* (male), 25 for *chaluzoth* (female). Twenty-three additional certificates were available for certain categories of artisans, also male.[59] By 1934 many more certificates were available for German *olim*, but the percentage earmarked for young women was even smaller—of 884 certificates issued during the first half of 1934: blank certificates for males, 18–25 years old: 625; artisan (*Handwerker*) certificates for males 18–25: 145; blank certificates for males 35–45: 24; blank certificates for young females: 90.[60] While a 10 percent allotment from Jerusalem was certainly extreme (90 out of 884), the general preference for males not only reflected a labor Zionist chauvinism but also coincided with prevailing German Jewish attitudes toward emigration.

While young women certainly suffered economically from the Depression, lack of work was viewed as a man's issue, the traditional breadwinners and potential husbands and fathers. For example, in mid-1932 the Berlin *Gemeinde*'s welfare office held special advisory seminars for young men, but not young women, on the verge of completing their compulsory schooling.[61] Germany's initial attempts at alleviating the job crisis were almost all geared toward finding work for men, and female Jewish professionals suffered disproportionately under the Nazis compared to Jewish men.[62]

Despite the success achieved by Germany's left-wing political parties during the 1920s, the dominant social ideology was conservative, which viewed woman's proper place as the home, responsible for the three traditional Ks—*Kinder* (children), *Küchen* (cooking), and *Kirche* (church). This outlook, certainly reinforced by the reactionary Nazi regime, also characterized much of mainstream middle-class German Jewry. The lack of jobs during the Great Depression was generally seen as a problem for men rather than women.

Not only were young males perceived to be in more immediate need of economic opportunities, but after Hitler's regime came to power, men were in greater physical danger than women. Nazis generally did not assault young women as frequently or violently as they would Jewish men, though certain aspects of Nazi anti-Jewish policy clearly targeted women.[63] This bias probably resulted from a combination of some strange notion of chivalry, despite Nazi racial theory, which charged all Jews as subversive and dangerous, and a genocidal approach that generally targeted men first, in order to eliminate a possible military threat. Jewish women were certainly subject to deportation and ultimately targeted for extermination, but prior to World War II, concentration camps were generally reserved for men, who were only released from prisons and concentration camps on condition that they leave Germany within the next few weeks. Youth Aliyah at times tried to accelerate the emigration process for young Jews in danger and almost always such cases involved young Jewish males.

Even though the kibbutzim in Palestine typically preferred groups with more boys, Youth Aliyah in general, from early on, tried to find other means of accommodating female immigrants. Before the first group was sent to Ein-Harod, WIZO had proposed absorbing 112 girls from Germany in its various training institutions in Palestine.[64] Similarly the Mizrachi School in Jerusalem and the training farm in Talpiot were set aside exclusively for girls. Of course one of the reasons Youth Aliyah used these facilities was a belief that the education and vocational training young women demanded varied greatly from the instruction required by young men. Not only men, but most women, certainly middle-class

German Jewish women, acknowledged a distinct difference between the pedagogical needs of and societal expectations for the "fairer" sex.

Even after the Nazis came to power, the *Jüdische Rundschau,* when addressing relocation to Palestine, noted that far fewer economic opportunities existed for women than for men. The greatest need was for (male) manual laborers.[65] In the sociologist Deborah Bernstein's words, "[since] women found it far more difficult to find employment than men, they immigrated to Palestine primarily as the dependents of male immigrants, who were expected to find employment more easily and thus provide for their womenfolk."[66] Particularly in urban areas single women had trouble finding work, though by early 1935, the news from Palestine showed that young women were being successfully absorbed in the agricultural sector.[67] Of course the measure of such success is relative. Despite socialist rhetoric regarding gender equality in communal settlements, most women in kibbutzim were generally relegated to traditional women's work, the cooking, cleaning, laundry, and child care, in addition to helping with the farm work. Nevertheless there was still greater demand for their labor in these settlements than in the cities.

The Jugendhilfe's institutions in Germany did little to alter these conceptions. Curricula of the Youth Aliyah School in Berlin, as reported (favorably) by the Jüdische Frauenbund, distinguished between vocational education for boys and girls. Whereas young men received instruction in wood- and metalwork, young women received training in home economics and sewing.[68] Though these skills were needed in Palestine, the segregation according to gender seems to counter the socialist ethos on which most kibbutzim were founded. In fact the emphasis on domestic skills agrees with the accepted middle-class division of labor that characterized German Jewry from the late nineteenth century through the Weimar era, which steered Jewish girls toward "social housekeeping" careers.[69] Not surprisingly the preparatory requirements for young males and females prior to *aliyah* were perceived to be quite distinct. A January 1935 report on Youth Aliyah's *hachsharah* activities notes, "the boys are trained in all the various branches of farming, fruit and vegetable growing, tree-cultivation, gardening, bee-keeping, cow-keeping, horse-breeding, and sheep rearing, locksmith and blacksmith work, shoe-making, etc. The girls are trained in housekeeping, nursing, laundry work, gardening, and also branches of farm work, such as bee-keeping, dairy work, etc."[70] The enrollment was also heavily skewed toward boys.[71]

Marion Kaplan suggests that the gender breakdown for Youth Aliyah was 60 percent boys and 40 percent girls "because of what its leaders considered the division of labor on the collective farms."[72] In general the percentage for those girls taken to kibbutzim and moshavim stood closer to 30 percent. But the unequal representation derives not solely from the demands that emanated from settlements in Eretz Israel. Most German Jewish families were reluctant to view Palestine as a whole, and kibbutzim in particular, as acceptable future homes for their daughters. In fact there is no evidence suggesting that Youth Aliyah's leaders either in Jerusalem or Berlin enacted a strict quota based on sex. There was never a need to do so.

Whether Kaplan's assertion that "women wanted to leave Germany well before their men" is correct, no doubt the claim that fewer women actually left is accurate. This fact conforms to conventional emigration patterns whereby young men were sent off on their own to start a life in the hopes of arranging to bring other family members out of Germany at a later date. In Kaplan's words, "Bourgeois parents worried about a daughter traveling alone, believing boys would be safer. Families assumed that sons needed to establish economic futures for themselves, whereas daughters would marry."[73] Girls were more often expected to remain and assist the family at home, even to the point of contributing financially to their brothers' emigrations.

Arguably Youth Aliyah enabled a higher proportion of girls to immigrate to Palestine than the *yishuv* ordinarily permitted with its general allotment of workers' certificates. Only 20 percent of permits went to young women, and for girls from Germany the percentage was at times even lower.[74] Other than marrying a potential *oleh*, which is how the overwhelming majority of women came to Palestine, youth immigration seems to have been the most successful way for young women to make *aliyah*.[75] In fact a German girl who had not yet reached age seventeen and registered with the Jugendhilfe had a much better chance of reaching Palestine than an older single woman. In a letter to Berlin in mid-1934, responding to a request to secure a labor permit for a Youth Aliyah candidate who had since passed her seventeenth birthday, Szold wrote, "There is not a single labor certificate available for girls at present."[76]

Comparatively, the gender gap for Youth Aliyah does not seem as unbalanced as it might at first glance.

Youth Aliyah's demographics reflect two complementary factors. First, the labor movement in Palestine, which was indeed dominated by male figures, supported immigration in general weighted toward single young men, perceived as more valuable in reclaiming the land, and thus Youth Aliyah did not differ from traditional pioneer immigration. Second, perhaps as a reflection of this attitude combined with their own perceptions of gender roles, German Jews registered more boys than girls for Youth Aliyah. This pattern prevailed particularly among families that had previously been middle or upper-middle class, which could no longer employ domestic help.

More progressive attitudes toward including young women in Youth Aliyah could be found among active female leaders within the Zionist labor movement, such as the women dispatched as *shlichot* to Germany, who professed the need to recruit more girls for youth immigration. This position however reflected a small minority, and most German women seemed to share the conservative attitude of the JFB.

Youth Aliyah attempted to penetrate the Frauenbund, which it recognized as an important potential source of support. In the summer of 1934, the JFB newsletter detailed the success of the first Youth Aliyah group in Palestine and outlined the movement's general goals and activities. Given Pappenheim's considerable influence, one can imagine the reluctance with which the editorial staff agreed to print the short article, albeit with the preface, "The Jüdische Jugendhilfe . . . requested that we take up the following article," thereby disclaiming outright support for the message.[77] Notwithstanding their revered leader's outright opposition, the JFB membership grew more receptive, reflecting the growing appeal of Zionism in general and Youth Aliyah in particular within mainstream German Jewish society.

In late 1935 the Jüdischer Frauenbund still maintained reservations about fully endorsing Youth Aliyah and working actively to realize its aims. Ottilie Schönewald, a Zionist who represented the JFB at the Youth Aliyah conference that September, reported favorably on the gathering in Amsterdam. She argued that the positive exchange of ideas, strongly supported by the powerful presence of Szold, convinced her of the importance of Youth Aliyah. Yet the JFB would only resolve that all local chapters promote *religious* Youth Aliyah. Though Schönewald argued that this step should be viewed merely as a beginning, the leadership of the JFB was demonstrably reluctant to provide an unequivocal endorsement of Youth Aliyah at that time.[78] Indeed the Frauenbund contacted the Arbeitsgemeinschaft in December 1935 pledging its support for fund-raising drives, but only promising to campaign for Orthodox Youth Aliyah.[79]

This reserved attitude is not merely an example of the JFB's traditionally cool outlook toward Zionism as a whole. In fact by September of 1935 the organization had certainly warmed to the prospect that Palestine could serve the needs of many young Jews. An article in the league's journal at that time stressed that Jewish schools should emphasize the importance of building a connection between the students and Jewish Palestine. This positive nationalistic affiliation, in contrast to the Nazi government's determination to exclude Jews from German nationalist movements, gave a psychological lift to Jewish students in Germany and also provided essential preparation for those who would eventually immigrate to Palestine.[80] Therefore it was Youth Aliyah in particular, and not the general program of Jewish immigration to Palestine, that was still controversial to the Frauenbund leadership. In fact, Pappenheim had helped many friends and acquaintances immigrate to Palestine. Yet even as she was confined to her sickbed during the summer of 1936, the immigration of Jewish children to Palestine continued to worry her; she loathed the idea of the separation of families. "Just think," she told her close friend Hannah Karminski, "of the children over there alone, and of the parents. What they have to put up with!"[81]

Perhaps Pappenheim's death in 1936 removed a strong source of conflict and played a role in warming the relations between the Frauenbund and the Arbeitsgemeinschaft, or maybe it was the continued deterioration of conditions in Germany. Whatever the cause, from late 1936 onward the JFB's official position toward Youth Aliyah became increasingly supportive, even promoting opportunities for young women. A JFB report from 1938 criticized a welfare office that had subsidized training for only ten girls as opposed to seventy-two boys. The JFB pledged its sewing circles in various locations to produce outfits and equipment needed by Youth Aliyah immigrants.[82] At this point, the JFB's strongest interest had become promoting feasible emigration opportunities for girls and young women. According to Kaplan, the league thereby hoped to compensate for a distinct failure on the part of Jewish parents as well as communal bodies to provide adequate preimmigration training for girls.[83] Between March and September 1938 almost every issue of the league's journal included strong endorsements of Youth Aliyah as an important means of helping solve the crisis of Jewish youth.[84]

Perhaps another reason the Frauenbund initially refused to support youth immigration was the understanding that Youth Aliyah was affiliated with a specifically socialist brand of Zionism. Indeed there is some logic to this assumption, and it explains why the initial endorsement was reserved for religious youth.

Certainly Youth Aliyah seemed to favor labor Zionism over other ideological positions. The overwhelming majority of Youth Aliyah staff and *madrichim* emerged from youth groups affiliated with Hechalutz. In contrast to the goal of inclusiveness expressed by Szold, both right-wing Revisionist Zionist and Orthodox Agudat Israel youth remained excluded from Youth Aliyah. And even through Revisionists clearly defined themselves as antisocialist, they nevertheless expected some youth certificates. In the fall of 1935 the idea of sending an entire Revisionist group was rejected. Regarding Agudah youth, Schattner believed that neither the Jugendhilfe nor the Arbeitsgemeinschaft should support the formation of a Youth Aliyah group that might influence German children against the official Zionist organization.[85] In both cases, Youth Aliyah stressed that individuals and groups participating in the program shared some basic precepts regarding the primacy of labor Zionism in building up Palestine. Yet the movement could not afford to reject these groups publicly, since this might undermine fund-raising. In addition, the Arbeitsgemeinschaft did not wish to exacerbate the increasing tension between Agudat Israel and the Zionist movement resulting from the former's establishment of its own emigration facilities.[86]

Youth Aliyah was concerned that Agudat Israel would exploit the phrase "Religious Youth Aliyah," a tool already employed by the Jugendhilfe, in order to finance a separate immigration plan.[87] The Agudah was an outspokenly anti-Zionist group whose committee for youth immigration was founded with the cooperation of the assimilationist RjF. Moreover, Orthodox leaders had occasionally engaged in negative propaganda against Youth Aliyah. For example, in July 1935 Rabbi Moses Unna of Mannheim protested against the "awful religious conditions" in Ben Shemen and other settlements.[88] The Arbeitsgemeinschaft hoped that an accord with Agudat Israel would prevent further slanderous publicity.

Youth Aliyah leaders hoped somehow to include Agudah youth within the work of the Arbeitsgemeinschaft, and thereby prevent the appearance of disunity.

Only upon reaching a suitable accommodation could organized groups of Agudah youth be brought to Palestine via Youth Aliyah. Schattner enumerated the following conditions under which the Arbeitsgemeinschaft would be willing to enter into an agreement with the Agudah: (1) that the Agudah not collect "for religious Youth Aliyah" (the Arbeitsgemeinschaft already used this slogan) but rather for "Agudah"; (2) that the Agudah collect only in those circles of its own members or among individuals expressly permitted by the Arbeitsgemeinschaft; and (3) that the Agudah avoid any propaganda, in word or in print, for which its members were responsible, against the Arbeitsgemeinschaft and its constituent components.[89] The joint activity only truly began in November 1938, at which point a group of twenty Agudah youths received permits to join a settlement near Kfar Saba.[90]

Youth Aliyah was similarly compelled to deal with the issue of Revisionist participation. Szold noted in late 1935 that no Revisionist settlements in Palestine could possibly train a group of young Jews according to the criteria she had formulated—the Revisionist presence in Palestine was almost exclusively urban. Revisionists rejected collectivism and the kibbutz ideal, favoring a more capitalist perspective, but that stance left them poorly positioned to bring in young members via Youth Aliyah. In Berlin, Josephthal argued that Revisionist youth would not be rejected out of hand but would be included provided they forswore their ideology. This stipulation arose out of concern for preserving the Jugendhilfe's social and pedagogical ideals. Josephthal claimed that the right-wing Zionist youth group Herzliah was examined in this respect and found unacceptable. Herzliah was founded in Germany after the government dissolved the national branch of the Revisionist youth movement Betar. From the Jugendhilfe's perspective, organized groups of Revisionist youth were not desirable, regardless of Palestine's ability to absorb them. This situation reflected the antipathy between labor Zionists and Revisionists during these years.[91]

When the Staatszionistische Organisation, which represented German Revisionists in the ZVfD, formally complained in May 1936 about their exclusion from Youth Aliyah, the Jugendhilfe had to consider carefully its response to the accusation of impropriety. The Revisionists argued not merely that groups composed exclusively of their youth were excluded but that young Revisionists who applied to participate through religious Youth Aliyah were effectively barred from immigration as well.[92] Prior to the November pogrom, according to a Revisionist source, from a pool of more than a thousand Betar youths in Germany only two immigrated to Palestine via Youth Aliyah.[93]

By February 1937 the Jugendhilfe had tactically managed to delay including Revisionists for so long that even Szold, who harbored little positive sentiment for the right-wing movement, claimed that the Jugendhilfe should reexamine the possibilities for Revisionist Youth Aliyah and "that this time the issue should be met fairly and squarely."[94] Szold obviously recognized complications in including Revisionists within other groups, particularly in terms of fostering a sense of community within the group. She noted a case in point: "the individual Betar member who came with the Group to the Ludwig Tietz School at Yagur has already become the subject of unpleasant discussion. The tendency of the discussion seems to be to ask him to leave the group."[95] Szold faced criticism from two directions in Palestine: Revisionist leaders demanding satisfaction and complaints "from a Kewuzah here and a Group there that individual Revisionists are in the Groups and are asserting themselves 'ideologically.'"[96]

To prevent further disruptions within settlements in Palestine and to placate the Staatszionisten in Germany, the Jugendhilfe entreated Szold's office to approve suitable host communities for Revisionist teens.[97] According to Szold's requirements, however, acceptable settlements needed to be modern, hygienic, and financially stable. Additionally, Youth Aliyah preferred to send immigrants to communities large enough so that the group of young trainees would not present an unbearable financial burden. Since most Revisionists in Palestine settled in urban areas, Szold and Beyth were hard-pressed to find potential host communities for young Betarim. For example, Revisionists suggested sites in Naharia and Yessod Hamaalah, that were immediately dismissed as either too small or underdeveloped. Hans Beyth also examined a larger community in Rosh Pinah, but initially rejected this location since there was no economic basis for the group other than labor outside the settlement.[98]

Revisionist leaders suggested settling Betar youth in an urban setting and affiliating with a traditional educational institution, such as the Technicum in Haifa. Szold rejected this idea on the grounds that Youth

Aliyah could not oversee the group's educational and social development, and Youth Aliyah did not have the authority to grant admission to prestigious educational institutions. Experiments in bringing Youth Aliyah to a city environment, previously attempted to solve the difficulty in placing religious youth, had been deemed unsuccessful.[99] In late 1937 Szold requested certificates for Revisionist youth, although only in March 1939 did a group of nineteen finally arrive at Rosh Pinah. In August 1939 Szold wrote with dismay that the group had only been expanded to include twenty boys and two girls.[100] This delay between the initial request and eventual immigration demonstrates Revisionism's weak position within both German Zionism and the *yishuv*'s political apparatus.[101] Especially at a time when immigration clearly meant rescue from imminent danger, Revisionists were unable to acquire the prized certificates for their children. Since they did not believe in collective settlements, they could not realistically expect to benefit from a movement geared toward settling young immigrants on kibbutzim.

The competition between Zionist parties for Youth Aliyah certificates was perhaps best demonstrated in Austria following the Anschluss. The ideological positions assumed by organized Jewish youth reflected the varied political outlooks present among Austrian Zionists. As in Germany, there were groups committed to varying degrees of socialist Zionism, groups affiliated with the centrist "general" Zionists, and Revisionists. This pluralism within Austrian Zionism complicated the task facing those individuals committed to organizing Youth Aliyah, who overwhelmingly held personal convictions of a left-wing political orientation.[102]

On June 8, 1938, a meeting was held in Vienna to discuss the following three subjects: "(1) How to proceed with the selection of youth (a) with preparatory training (b) without preparatory training. (2) How to organize the youth that came from *various* youth groups. (3) The participation of un-organized youth."[103] Ideally the individual groups that would be sent to Palestine would be "closed" groups; that is, all the participants would come from the same political/ideological background. Upon the establishment of appropriate preparatory facilities, one-third of the candidates were to be taken from the "un-organized" youth. In these cases, the *madrich* assigned to each group would select the candidates. For all groups immigrating without preparation, a specific key for determining the allotment of certificates would be employed. For example, one cohort of 65 certificates would be divided as follows, "15 un-organized, 20 B-[general Zionist] and *Staatsjugend* [Revisionist] and 30 from the *Chewer Hakwuzoth, Kibbuz Hameuchad* and *Kibbuz Arzi.*"[104] These figures, when compared with the difficulties faced by Revisionists in Germany, reflect the movement's stronger representation in Austria.

Despite the determination to apportion certificates according to a strict plan, the distribution among competing groups remained a serious problem. Only two days after these decisions were made, the Austrian *Hechaluz* criticized the rapidly growing nonpioneering Zionist youth (affiliated with the centrist general Zionists), grouped together as *Hanoar Hazioni,* and the Revisionist youth for their inferior commitment to educational ideals. The language used to refer to these groups gives a taste of a rivalry that was not only ideologically motivated but also class-oriented. The *Hechaluz* office called them "spoiled children of Zionist lawyers and doctors . . . [who] in the last few weeks enrolled in the *Noar Hazioni.*"[105] The letter requested a separate allotment (outside of the distribution plan) for one closed group of forty to be sent to one of "our" communal settlements. The general Zionists, effectively represented in the adult Zionistischer Landesverband, responded to such claims for preferential treatment with their own demands based on enrollment figures as the largest Jewish youth group in Austria. Considering its numerical strength and professed commitment to Zionism, the organization requested distribution of certificates accordingly.[106]

In Vienna the overwhelming majority of the first allotment of 350 Youth Aliyah places was earmarked for the more *chaluzisch* groups. This distribution was based primarily on the political/religious outlook of the settlements in Palestine that were prepared to receive Youth Aliyah candidates, yet it undermined the cooperative spirit with which the Beratungsstelle in Vienna had been organized.[107] Only by threatening to turn the Austrian Youth Aliyah certificates over to Berlin did Landauer convince the various groups in Vienna to accept the decisions made in Jerusalem.[108]

Not to be outdone by the religious and general Zionists, Revisionists did not hesitate to register complaints of unfair treatment regarding distribution. In a letter to Szold, the leadership of the youth group Barak pressed its own claims as the strongest Jewish youth group in Austria.[109] The Revisionists also protested the division of certificates according to conditions in Palestine because much financial support for the program came from Jewish sources unallied to any political camp within the Zionist movement, Jews who contributed without preference for saving a specific "part" of endangered Zionist youth.[110] This discrepancy in fact reflected a common element of Zionist fund-raising. Though they tapped into resources throughout the Jewish world, allocation was generally determined according to the political strength of the Zionist parties in Palestine. These debates show not only political confrontation but also a sense of despair that had engulfed the youth groups. How else to understand former Betar members basically begging to be included in a program administered by their political opponents? Of course such conflicts also suggest that these young refugees may have been victims of the political antagonism of their parents' generation, attitudes perhaps not shared by the children. By late 1938, when emigration was viewed as equivalent to rescue, such disputes could not be resolved to everyone's satisfaction, and in the end the socialist groups did receive a greater share of certificates.

Arguments among the rival youth groups and political parties were not new and were hardly unexpected. However, though perhaps predictable, Youth Aliyah's leaders were surprised to find themselves in conflict with other philanthropic agencies, both in Germany and internationally. Considering the dire financial straits of German Jewry, fund-raising competition was fierce as community chests were stretched to their limits. In October 1936, for example, two Youth Aliyah fund-raisers encountered difficulties in planning the upcoming appeal in Bavaria. They had to negotiate with the Munich *Gemeinde* and agree to delay collecting for Youth Aliyah until the communal *Winterhilfe* (winter aid) appeal had been introduced.[111]

More striking was the fact that the Arbeitsgemeinschaft undertook its appeals outside the framework of traditional Zionist philanthropies. Since Youth Aliyah always followed Keren Hayesod campaigns, the Arbeitsgemeinschaft's task of begging contributions from an impoverished community became even more formidable.[112] In late 1935 Eva Stern had already reported on the tight competition for charitable donations within Germany. The *Winterhilfe* project in particular, which paralleled a nationwide campaign directed by Nazi welfare agencies, inhibited all the Palestine-oriented collections, as many German Jews worked hard to contribute to the needs of their own communities.[113] This difficulty was not only limited to activity in Germany; Stern and Arthur Hantke, director of Keren Hayesod in Jerusalem, negotiated over potential conflicts between Youth Aliyah and Keren Hayesod activities in many countries. Reflecting an antagonism that dated back to the early 1920s, Hadassah leaders complained that conflicts with the Keren Hayesod endangered their work on behalf of Youth Aliyah.[114]

In early 1934, to prevent internal Zionist conflict, Keren Hayesod had pressured Youth Aliyah to limit collections to $28,000, corresponding to 10 percent of Keren Hayesod income in Germany during that year. Youth Aliyah refused to renew this contract for 1935. The Arbeitsgemeinschaft maintained that its needs were growing, that it was entitled to more funds, and that it would be able to raise substantially greater contributions than the limits set in 1934. In fact, during 1935 appeals in Germany generated more than $60,000. For 1936 the Arbeitsgemeinschaft anticipated raising as much as $92,000. The proceeds would directly benefit Jews in Germany by covering Youth Aliyah's extensive administrative costs in addition to the expenses of running preparatory camps and schools in Germany; and $4,030 would be transferred monthly to Palestine via Ha'avara.[115]

Keren Hayesod, however, once again requested that Youth Aliyah limit its intake to no more than 10 percent of the sum the larger organization would raise, far less than the Arbeitsgemeinschaft's anticipated needs. Keren Hayesod stressed that maintaining the flow of charity toward traditional Zionist enterprises necessitated limiting contributions to Youth Aliyah. According to Keren Hayesod officials, representatives on fund-raising missions in Germany often received the reply, "We already gave for Youth Aliyah." On the other hand, in early 1935 Friedl Levy reported from Thuringia that her campaign for the Arbeitsgemeinschaft encountered great difficulties as most people had already contributed to other charities.[116] According to representatives in the field, both Keren Hayesod and Keren Kayemet Leyisrael could effectively block other appeals in certain locations.[117] The fact that the Keren Hayesod remained concerned about the challenge to its fund-raising capabilities demonstrates that the Arbeitsgemeinschaft often succeeded in the face of such obstacles.

An agreement reached in January 1936 permitted Youth Aliyah to collect $60,000 during the course of the Jewish year 5696 (1935–36). Should the Keren Hayesod raise $360,000 by June 1936, the Arbeitsgemeinschaft would be allowed an additional sum of $20,000.[118] This new agreement demonstrated the growing importance of Youth Aliyah, as it received allocations significantly greater than the 10 percent stipulated in the 1934 contract.

Youth Aliyah's leadership remained convinced that its appeals succeeded for the following two reasons: Their specific propaganda activities often interested Jewish circles that had previously remained distant from Zionist causes to contribute to Youth Aliyah. Individuals who contributed to both Youth Aliyah and Keren Hayesod invariably donated larger sums, in total, than they would have made available to Keren Hayesod alone.[119] Moreover, the extra contributions raised by Youth Aliyah appeals resulted in funds earmarked specifically for projects relating to the settlement of German Jews in Palestine, an endeavor that most German Jews favored. Responding to the Nuremberg Laws, Arthur Rau said the role of Youth Aliyah could not be underestimated. In his words there was "no doubt that [Youth Aliyah] won wider circles of [German] Jewry for Zionism, and that Youth Aliyah even enjoyed the goodwill of non-Jewish official bodies."[120]

Despite the difficulties of working around the Keren Hayesod drives, the Arbeitsgemeinschaft succeeded in raising approximately $110,000 during the 1936–37 fiscal year, not including payments made by parents or local community support.[121] According to Stern, already looking toward the 1937–38 budget, the Zionist establishment, though supportive, still could not clarify how to best incorporate Youth Aliyah into the larger fund-raising process. Stern argued that this conflict relegated Youth Aliyah to a position solely reliant on Sperrmark contributions.[122]

Negotiations regarding an agreement for the 1937–38 year began following the Jewish New Year in September 1937. When, in late October, a contract had not yet been produced, the Arbeitsgemeinschaft threatened to embark on an independent campaign. Within two weeks the organizations concluded a formal agreement entitling Youth Aliyah to raise the unprecedented sum of $120,000 in Germany.[123] Youth Aliyah had indisputably become an essential element in fund-raising and propaganda for the Zionist cause in Germany.

The conflicts of interest between Keren Hayesod and Youth Aliyah do not reflect any lack of enthusiasm on the part of the Zionist establishment for youth immigration. In truth the seriousness with which the Jewish Agency addressed this aspect of immigration is evident from the fact that the first item on the budgetary proposal presented to the Central British Fund for German Jewry in 1933 was a $106,000 allocation for youth immigration, including capital investments for new construction. This appropriation represented the largest single budgetary item aside from land purchase through the Keren Kayemet Leyisrael.[124] Yet this distribution, along with subsequent allocations for Youth Aliyah, is misleading. Despite the large sums that appeared on official budgets, these moneys were not allotted from a preexisting source. Youth Aliyah, in order to meet its expenses in both Germany and Palestine, raised its funding independently. Initially all the traditional philanthropic bodies that helped facilitate immigration to Palestine refused to finance Youth Aliyah. Shalom Adler-Rudel, who served on the Arbeitsgemeinschaft's board of directors, viewed the situation as paradoxical, in which "Youth Aliyah, occasionally acclaimed at congresses as a very important and new contribution for the up-building of Palestine, was for many years a kind of illegitimate child for whom none was willing to undertake any alimentation."[125]

The obvious question is: why was Youth Aliyah dependent on only its own resources? Why did the Jewish Agency refuse to foot the bill? This attitude reflects the utilitarian terms through which some Zionists perceived youth immigration. Rather than delving into the *yishuv*'s material resources, even those allocated for German *olim*, in order to promote the emigration of young Jews from Germany, Youth Aliyah could be used as a public relations device to increase the flow of philanthropic donations to the Zionist project in Palestine. Youth Aliyah's effectiveness as a propaganda tool for the benefit of German Jewry is perhaps best expressed in a letter from Landauer, a constant supporter of youth immigration, to the American Zionist leader Louis Lipsky.

> The Youth Aliyah is a very important and beautiful task, but by no means the most important and most urgent. For our duty to incorporate and settle German Jews in Palestine, there are considerably more important and more urgent jobs. It is, according to [existing] financial possibilities, a completely utopian assumption, that in the foreseeable future it would be possible, to transfer the Jewish children of Germany, or even a considerable part thereof, to Palestine and train them there. If we can succeed in bringing over a couple of hundred children each year, without including that as our primary task, that is certainly good and wonderful; but it is truly ri-

diculous when the attempt is continually made to proclaim Youth Aliyah as the most important and most urgent task. As a watchword and propaganda tool the notion of Youth Aliyah and the transfer of Jewish children out of Germany is very useful, since this idea appeals directly to the Jewish heart. But if we do not want to create difficulties for the success of our larger task, we should be aware that the use of this phrase does not inevitably result in funds earmarked for this specific aim.[126]

Landauer feared that Youth Aliyah would so greatly overshadow other Zionist projects, specifically those focused on large-scale adult emigration from Germany, that traditional fund-raising operations would suffer. On the other hand, Youth Aliyah could be, and eventually was, used effectively to bring in previously untapped resources in support of Zionism and rebuilding the land of Israel.

In the final analysis the unique circumstances of Jewish life under Nazi rule determined which of the conflicts in which Youth Aliyah found itself embroiled would be satisfactorily resolved and which would not. In terms of the distribution of certificates among the various youth groups, the stakes were ultimately too high to achieve any agreement satisfactory to the nonsocialist and religious parties. German Jews initially opposed to the general aims of Youth Aliyah had no choice in the end but to support any program that could remove young Jews from Germany.

Epilogue

On the night of November 8, 1938, Margit went to sleep in the Frankfurt orphanage as usual, but she was woken up by terrible shouts and banging on doors. The door was broken open as Nazis stormed the building, destroying everything. She heard shouts of "fire" and when she finally left the house could see the synagogue burning across the street. All the orphans had someone in the town with whom they could find shelter. Margit stayed with relatives for three weeks. The children from the orphanage and some others were then called together and told they would be going to Holland. They were in a group of nineteen—ages seven to fifteen—and very confused.

The children spent six weeks quarantined in Amsterdam, receiving food from the local Jewish sanatarium. Margit recalled that although the food was not good, "we did not mind, as we felt happy enough to have escaped from the hell. We were also given the clothes we needed. As we were the first group of refugee children to come to Holland, we were a source of wonder to the Dutch." They were soon moved to a Christian orphanage at Hoboghen. While at the orphanage they heard about a "Beth Chalutzim" that was preparing children for life in Palestine. Margit registered for *hachsharah* and went to the house in Amsterdam. They soon learned that Holland had been granted thirty-eight Youth Aliyah certificates for German refugees, thirty-six of which were allocated to the Beth Hehalutz. Those selected rejoiced; those who were not, were depressed and taken to another home, near Rotterdam. Margit was among those not initially selected. The residents at this home became very close to the surrounding farmers and villagers. When war broke out their friends in Amsterdam who had been chosen for *aliyah* joined them. When Margit received word that she had also received a certificate, she was elated, but the war made the prospect of emigration unlikely. The situation remained unchanged until November 1939, when they were told to make preparations and be ready to leave for Palestine at a moment's notice. She finally received her certificate and immigrated to Palestine in February 1940.[1]

The outbreak of war in September 1939 severely restricted the possibilities for emigration in general and Youth Aliyah in particular. Transporting people to Palestine from lands controlled by the Third Reich, a country officially an enemy of the British Empire, grew increasingly difficult. Nevertheless, Youth Aliyah continued directing Jewish youth to Palestine via transit countries and occasionally through illegal immigration, until Hitler's armies overran these areas. In general, Jewish youth in transit fared only as well as the other Jews in the countries where they found themselves. More than three hundred Youth Aliyah candidates along with most of the country's Jews were shuttled from Denmark to Sweden and thereby rescued, but the young Jews training in Holland generally shared the tragic fate of Dutch Jewry, except for those evacuated by early 1941.

During the war years, Youth Aliyah focused its attention mainly on trainees and graduates already in Palestine. The movement also took responsibility for absorbing any unaccompanied young refugees who managed to reach the land of Israel; most notable in this respect was a group of more than six hundred young Jews from Poland who fled eastward after the German invasion and traveled overland eventually reaching Teheran, from where they were transported to Palestine.[2] In addition to the psychological stress of their experiences, some of the children had gone years without any direct adult supervision, not to mention any formal education. The attempt to integrate these children, who had experienced unheard-of trauma during their long journey, foreshadowed the complicated task that would confront Youth Aliyah as it handled large numbers of young Holocaust survivors during the late 1940s.

Even for those who survived without physical hardship, the war experience would forever shape their identities. For the thousands of children brought to England before the war, many of them very young, the end of hostilities and the revelation of Jewish destruction in Europe raised serious questions regarding their futures. Zionist leaders hoped to transport the children to Palestine, either to live with relatives or as independent groups. Many of these young Jews, having become acclimated over six years, barely knew their estranged families, had scarcely a common language in which to communicate with them, and felt little compulsion to uproot themselves a second time and readjust to new surroundings. For most, the time in England, often living with Christian foster families, had not created a bond with Zionism and Palestine. Yet the fact that some children were the sole survivors from their families imposed not only a grave psychological burden but often a sense of responsibility and obligation to those who had perished.[3]

After World War II, Youth Aliyah expanded its activity to bring in young refugees from throughout Europe and helped organize youth groups and educational institutions for teenagers in the displaced person camps. Youth Aliyah in fact facilitated the arrival of one-fourth of the total immigration to Palestine between 1945 and May 1948.[4] With the advent of large-scale Jewish emigration from Arab lands in the early 1950s, particularly from North African countries, Youth Aliyah extended its mission to these communities as well. Though preparatory work in the diaspora continued, Youth Aliyah had become almost exclusively concerned with the complex pedagogical and sociological issues related to absorbing young Jews into the new State of Israel.

During its decades-long work with children and teenagers from a wide range of backgrounds, most often trying to help them overcome tremendous loss and psychological trauma, Youth Aliyah benefited greatly from its early experience with young refugees from Germany. Though quantitatively Youth Aliyah handled many more cases after 1948, and certainly the trials that many young Jews endured during the Holocaust created intense emotional scars, the years prior to and during World War II allowed Youth Aliyah to develop methods for coping with these difficult issues that would appear with increasing frequency in later years.

Young Jews dispatched to safety by their parents before 1939 already shouldered the burden of survivor guilt, even before their parents' ultimate fate was determined and years before psychologists in the United States recognized the severity of this phenomenon. A boy from rural Austria wrote the following in late 1938: "By December 21st my father must leave Vienna. He is a young man still, 49 years old—where shall he go? Before I left, the Gemeinde in Vienna was paying rent for the family.

Now I don't even know my parents' address. Still we should not complain for the family is at least together and so many families have been torn apart. My friend is here in Palestine, his mother in Sweden—so far apart!"[5] Many children, especially after November 1938, and even more so after the war broke out, felt responsible for bringing the rest of their families out of Europe. The children knew all too well that whatever difficulties they faced in adapting to their new surroundings could not compare to the dangers confronting those who remained behind.

Inside Germany the beginning of World War II did not signal the end of Youth Aliyah's activity. Occupying an entire floor of the Zionist offices at 10 Meinekestrasse, the Jugendhilfe continued assisting young Jews to prepare for eventual immigration to Palestine. The two largest youth groups, Makkabi Hazair and Habonim, as well as Bachad, functioned during the first years of the war. All the *Bünde* coordinated activities through the Jugendhilfe. In addition, until Jewish emigration was forbidden in October 1941, Youth Aliyah maintained its training facilities and schools, providing some measure of protection for those under its care.[6] During the summer of 1941 Recha Freier left Europe for Palestine, bringing with her more than 120 German-Jewish children who escaped by way of Yugoslavia. By war's end, Youth Aliyah had brought more than 11,000 young Jews from European lands to safety in Palestine.[7]

Critics have judged Youth Aliyah harshly for failing to consider the extreme gravity of the crisis confronting German Jewry by 1939, if not earlier, and refusing to explore any means, including illegal ones, to rescue Jews from German-controlled territory. According to Freier, Jewish Agency opposition to illegal emigration inhibited the survival of many Jews and her support of emigration by any means led to her official break with the Youth Aliyah organization.[8] Zionist leaders have also been charged with emphasizing selection, prioritizing the development of Palestine, specifically building up labor Zionism, over the survival of European Jewry. Though recent scholarship has focused on postwar Zionist policy regarding Jewish displaced persons in Europe, this critique is rooted in *yishuv* practice during the 1930s.[9]

Indeed Youth Aliyah's leadership, even those in Germany who experienced persecution firsthand, continued to stress selectivity and insisted on retaining the movement's educational mission. However, during 1938 and 1939, and in some cases even earlier, individuals in Germany based this policy on pragmatic considerations, specifically that the Palestine government limited the number of youth certificates allotted. Since immigration possibilities were restricted, practicality demanded that only those individuals most likely to succeed in Palestine should be approved. Yet Youth Aliyah did not abandon those children from Germany deemed unsuitable for immediate immigration.

Youth Aliyah in fact extended its activity and training programs to include thousands of young Jews, even though the leadership recognized that most would not be transferred to Palestine in the near future. Thus Youth Aliyah's work in Germany does not reflect the attitude of *yishuv* leaders who, according to Bela Vago, "agreed that, whereas the help lent to the German and Austrian Jews was an unquestioned Zionist duty, attention and effort should not be diverted from the central task—the creation of a National Home, which ultimately was to be the only solution of the Jewish question in Europe."[10] The unfortunate fact that most young Jews unable to leave Europe before 1939 perished during the Holocaust could not have been foreseen by Youth Aliyah's leaders, and little evidence suggests that they could have effected additional rescue projects from Germany without the collaboration of foreign governments. Given the benefit of hindsight, despite the thousands left behind, even Freier maintained that the decision to apply the selection principle was correct, since not every child was suitable for Palestine.

The history of Youth Aliyah also sheds some light on the often-criticized relationship between Zionist programs and National Socialist policy toward the Jews.[11] During the early years the Nazis clearly supported all projects promoting Jewish emigration, especially those sponsored by the Zionist movement. The Nazi determination to permit the expansion of agricultural training programs for young Jews destined for Palestine, an essential component for successful youth immigration and a decision seemingly contradictory to National Socialist ideals, demonstrates the government's favorable view of Youth Aliyah. Indeed the offices of the Jüdische Jugendhilfe and some of its training facilities operated until the fall of 1941. Youth Aliyah's personnel in Germany operated under the watchful eye of the Gestapo and the often arbitrary whim of Nazi officials responsible for Jewish policy.

Prior to 1948 no immigration program for Palestine could achieve any significant measure of success without the cooperation of the Mandatory authorities. Youth Aliyah's dependence on British policy is evident from the marginal success in Polish youth immigration. Before the outbreak of World War II, Youth Aliyah managed to bring in a total of 140 boys and girls from Poland, a state containing more than 3 million Jews and one where membership in Zionist youth groups numbered 70,000. Yet the Mandatory government did not extend youth permits to Poland, other than those used by closed institutions, such as Ben Shemen. *Yishuv* leaders were even wary of using these certificates for Polish youth, lest the immigration authorities impose further restrictions. An internal Youth Aliyah memorandum stated, "To the [closed] institutions of learning (e.g. Ben Shemen, Mikveh Israel . . .) there is no objection although it is [immigration minister Edwin Samuel's] personal feeling that the colonies should not be used for absorbing the youth other than from Germany and Austria. However, although the government does not say so officially, there is no doubt that the tendency toward expansion will cause the adoption of a quota for this category."[12] Failure in the case of Poland did not result from lack of effort by Zionist leaders but rather from British policy.

The number of youth certificates provided by the Palestine government appears most significant when compared with the overall emigration on the labor schedule from Germany. For the first half of 1934, when Youth Aliyah was allotted 350 certificates, a total of 884 blank worker's certificates were available to the Berlin Palästina-Amt, mainly for young males age between eighteen and thirty-five. Thus Youth Aliyah received almost half as many certificates as were available for "non-capitalist" German Jews of all ages.[13] By 1939 Youth Aliyah accounted for 26 percent of all Jews arriving in Palestine from the Third Reich.[14] Overall immigration to Palestine from Germany between 1933 and 1939, encompassing all categories and including Austria and Czechoslovakia, comes to 55,000. Youth Aliyah claimed responsibility for more than 5,400.[15] Even though Youth Aliyah accounted for bringing to Palestine around 10 percent of Jewish emigrants from Germany, Youth Aliyah raised close to 40 percent of the entire budget for the Jewish Agency's German Department between October 1933 and March 1939, and expenses for Youth Aliyah came to around 68 percent of the funds it brought in, leaving a large surplus for the use of German *aliyah* in general.[16]

As a tool for uniting Jews in common cause during the 1930s and beyond, Youth Aliyah effectively brought the message of Zionism to wider circles, both in Germany and elsewhere. Yet the movement's success as a propaganda tool should not obscure the fact that its history also

reflects the many divisions and constant competition that characterized the Zionist movement during this era. Youth Aliyah was one of
many factors contributing to the rising attraction to pioneer Zionism
among the younger generation of German Jews. For a Jewish teenager
in Germany, the prospect of Youth Aliyah represented many things—
excitement, adventure, camaraderie—including a viable future with legitimate economic and social integration in a uniquely Jewish environment. Undoubtedly these young emigrants' futures were also shaped by
the reality of leaving family and friends behind, many of whom did not
survive, but that impact was not readily apparent to most who left Germany during this period. Though the decision to leave one's family and
home was never taken lightly and was not always taken with great cer-
tainty, with few available options, the mere opportunity for these young
Jews to start anew in Palestine shone as a light in a very dark tunnel.

In early 1939 the Wagner-Rogers Bill was introduced in the U.S. Congress. This legislation would have allowed 20,000 refugee children from
Germany to enter America over a two-year period outside normal quota
restrictions. The bill was eventually dropped by its sponsors because of
the opposition it had generated in Congress and among certain segments of the U.S. population. Critics of the United States' policy view
this episode as both a lost opportunity and a demonstration of the
Roosevelt administration's hard-heartedness with respect to the Jewish
refugee crisis.[17]

Great significance is placed on the idea of children's rescue and survival. The plight of children who were victims of the Nazis is often men-
tioned, with emphasis on the 1.5 million Jewish children who perished.
The implication is that somehow the murder of the young was more
egregious, more compelling evidence of Nazi evil. If victims in general
were innocent, then the children were even more innocent, and they
symbolize a great potential that was quashed before having an opportunity to blossom. If the loss of so many young people represents a greater
tragedy, then certainly the rescue of youth, as perhaps an ultimate defiance of the Nazis, demands serious consideration and elucidates our understanding of responses to Nazi oppression.

While undoubtedly contributing to the development of the Jewish
homeland in Palestine, Youth Aliyah was created specifically to serve the
needs of German Jewry. While clearly subject to partisan conflict as well

as economic and political circumstances, Youth Aliyah nevertheless provided physical and spiritual sustenance to many thousands of young Jews, including those who did not find their way to the land of Israel. During a period that represented an end for so many, Youth Aliyah signified a new beginning.

Notes

INTRODUCTION

1. Saul Friedländer, *Nazi Germany and the Jews,* vol. 1, *the Years of Persecution, 1933–1939* (New York, 1997). Despite the appearance of new approaches, the main focus still remains on the Nazis, such as Christopher Browning's recent study, *The Origins of the Final Solution: The Evolution of Nazi Jewish Policy, September 1939– March 1942* (Lincoln, Neb., 2004). The volume of literature addressing the encounter between the Third Reich and the Jews continues to increase, though the issue of German Jewry's responses to the Nazi threat is not always identified. *Between Dignity and Despair: Jewish Life in Nazi Germany* (New York, 1998), by Marion Kaplan, while addressing Jewish life in Germany under Nazi rule, focuses primarily on the role of women. A number of titles have appeared quite recently addressing more specific cases of Jews responding to the Nazi challenge, such as Daniel B. Silver, *Refuge in Hell: How Berlin's Jewish Hospital Outlasted the Nazis* (Boston, 2003); *Vergessen kann man es nie—: Erinnerungen an Nazi-Deutschland,* ed. Klaus W. Tofahrn (Frankfurt, 2002); and Cynthia Crane, *Divided Lives: The Untold Stories of Jewish-Christian Women in Nazi Germany* (New York, 2000). Esriel Hildesheimer's analysis of the representative organization of German Jewry, *Jüdische Selbstverwaltung unter dem NS-Regime: Der Existenzkampf der Reichsvertretung und Reichsvereinigung der Juden in Deutschland* (Tübingen, 1994) is more informative with respect to communal response. Hildesheimer's study is further supported by the publication of relevant documents in Otto-Dov Kulka, *Deutsches Judentum unter dem Nationalsozialismus, I: Dokumente zur Geschichte der Reichsvertretung der deutschen Juden, 1933–1939* (Tübingen, 1997). Hagit Lavsky's *Before Catastrophe: The Distinctive Path of German Zionism* (Jerusalem, 1996), the final chapter of which deals with the Nazi era, is more pertinent, though it focuses on the German Zionist establishment.

2. A brief note on language. There is some difficulty discerning consistent use of the term "youth" (*Jugend*) both in the literature of the period and relevant scholarship. For Youth Aliyah, for example, the word refers to children between the ages of fourteen and seventeen. However, as it appears in both scholarly literature and

contemporary documents, the term can at times refer to those under the age of twenty-five, twenty-one, eighteen, and so on. Common usage, especially in terms of the German youth movement, often included all unmarried individuals under thirty. As they got older, unless actively involved as a group leader, most people would cast off identification as part of the younger generation. Though this book focuses on the fourteen–seventeen-year-olds who could qualify for Youth Aliyah, statements regarding the circumstances confronting youth in general often reflect a wider circle.

3. For example, Margaliot refers to the institution of Youth Aliyah as an important element in realizing emigration from Germany without expounding further than a few later references. Margaliot, "Teguvat Mosdoteyhah shel Yahadut Germanyah Natzional-Sotzialisti ba-Shanim 1933–1938," ed. and completed by Yehoyakim Cochavi, in *Toldot ha-Shoah: Germanyah,* ed. Avraham Margaliot and Yehoyakim Cochavi (Jerusalem, 1998), 94, 184, 210. Marion Kaplan's book *Between Dignity and Despair,* subtitled *Jewish Life in Nazi Germany,* mentions Youth Aliyah in terms of the greater number of boys than girls who participated, 117. Even Lavsky's work on German Zionism only gives a brief mention, *Before Catastrophe,* 242. Notable exceptions are found within two German sources: *Die jüdische Emigration aus Deutschland 1933–1941: Die Geschichte einer Austreibung* (Frankfurt am Main, 1985), 155–64; and Juliane Wetzel, "Auswanderung aus Deutschland," in *Die Juden in Deutschland 1933–1945: Leben unter nationalsozialistischer Herrschaft,* ed. Wolfgang Benz (Munich, 1988), 468–72.

4. Chanoch Reinhold, *No'ar Boneh Baito: Aliyat ha-No'ar ke-Tenu'ah Chinuchit* (Tel Aviv, 1953); Yoav Gelber, "Origins of Youth Aliyah," *Studies in Zionism* 9, no. 2 (1988); Raphael Gat, "Miph'al Aliyat Ha-No'ar 1933–1939," *Kathedra* 37 (1985): 149–76; Sandra Kadosh, "Ideology vs. Reality: Youth Aliyah and the Rescue of Jewish Children during the Holocaust Era, 1933–1945" (Ph.D. diss., Columbia University, 1995).

5. Tom Segev, *The Seventh Million: The Israelis and the Holocaust* (New York, 1993); on specific challenges facing emigrants from Germany, see 35–64.

6. Benny Morris, "Response of the Jewish Daily Press in Palestine to the Accession of Hitler, 1933," *YVS* 27 (1999): 397–98. The political split among Zionist leaders on this issue can also be seen in debates over Ben-Gurion's decision to accept reparation payments from West Germany for Jewish victims of Nazi Germany. Much has been written on the transfer agreement. See among others, Yfaat Weiss, "The Transfer Agreement and the Boycott Movement: A Jewish Dilemma on the Eve of the Holocaust," *YVS* 26 (1998): 129–71; Werner Feilchenfeld, Dolf Michaelis, and Ludwig Pinner, *Haavara-Transfer nach Palästina und Einwanderung Deutscher Juden 1933–1939* (Tübingen, 1972); Shaul Esh, "Ha-Ha'avara," in *Iyunim be-Cheker ha-Shoah ve-Yehadut Zemanenu* (Jerusalem, 1973), 33–106; Francis Nicosia, *The Third Reich and the Palestine Question* (Austin, Tex., 1985), 29–49; Niederland, *Yehudei Germanyah,* 101–6; and Yehuda Bauer, *Jews for Sale?* (New Haven, 1994), 5–27. For a more polemical account, see Edwin Black, *The Transfer Agreement* (New York, 1984).

7. Bauer, *Jews for Sale?* 27.

8. Most recently in this respect, see Browning, *The Origins of the Final Solution*, which explains emigration as favored Nazi policy even after the outbreak of World War II.

9. Bayerische politische Polizei, signed by Heydrich, January 14, 1934, IfZ Fa 119.

10. Document from Interior Ministry (signed by Klein) dated December 19, 1934, IfZ Fa 119.

11. Ibid., dated January 28, 1935, IfZ Fa 119.

12. "Nuremberg Law for the Protection of German Blood and German Honor," in *Documents on the Holocaust: Selected Sources on the Destruction of the Jews of Germany and Austria, Poland, and the Soviet Union*, ed. Yitzhak Arad, Yisrael Gutman, and Abraham Margaliot (Jerusalem, 1981), 78.

13. "Arbeitsbericht des Zentralausschusses," January 1–June 30, 1934, IfZ Fa 723/1, 79.

14. Reichsminister für Ernährung und Landwirtschaft to Gestapamt, Berlin, signed by Bäcke, February 26, 1934, "Gegen die beabsichtigte Regelung in der Frage der Umschulung von berufsfremden Juden zu Landwirten und Handwerkern haben ich in jeder Beziehung *erhebliche Bedenken*" (emphasis in original) YVA 051.0SO/82. Similar arguments by German farmers appear in an SS report from Cologne in March 1935, cited in Chaim Schatzker, *No'ar Yehudi be-Germanyah bein Yahadut le-Germaniut, 1870–1945* (Jerusalem, 1998), 295.

15. Reichsminister des Innern to Reichsminister für Ernährung und Landwirtschaft, June 13, 1934, YVA 051.0SO/82. Interesting is the use of the phrase "Deutschland lebenden Juden," implying exclusion from the *Volk*, rather than Deutscher Juden, even before the Nuremberg Laws that officially deprived German Jews of citizenship.

16. Reichsminister des Innern, report dated June 16, 1934, YVA 051.0SO/82.

17. *Central Zionist Archives, Jerusalem, 1933–39*, ed. Francis Nicosia, vol. 3 of *Archives of the Holocaust: An International Collection of Selected Documents*, Henry Friedlander and Sybil Milton, gen. eds. (New York and London, 1990), xxi.

18. Jacob Boas, "A Nazi Travels to Palestine," *History Today* 30 (January 1980): 33–38.

19. LIM [Leopold I. von Mildenstein], "Ein Nazi fährt nach Palästina," *Der Angriff*, October 2, 1934.

20. Nicosia cites an article written by Bernhard Lösener of the Ministry of the Interior published in November 1935. Nicosia, *The Third Reich*, 53. According to Nicosia, government and party officials did not seriously consider the success of Zionism's political aims before the debate over the Peel Partition Plan in 1937 (50, 159).

21. Document from Gestapo (signed by Brunner), February 20, 1935, IfZ Fa 119.

22. ICJOHP, interview with Eva Michaelis-Stern, November 26, 1981, 30–31. Claudia Koonz, "Courage and Choice among German-Jewish Women and Men," in *Die Juden im Nationalsozialistischen Deutschland: The Jews in Nazi Germany, 1933–1943*, ed. Arnold Paucker (Tübingen, 1986), 286, 289, noted that until the point deportations began, Jewish women were generally treated "chivalrously" in Nazi Ger-

many, and were more likely to travel throughout Germany unhindered than Jewish males.

23. Eric A. Johnson, *Nazi Terror: The Gestapo, Jews, and Ordinary Germans* (New York, 1999), 393.

24. Undated document by Eva Stern titled "Bericht," with handwritten notation, "Nach Lesen vernichten," CZA S75/506.

25. Martin Rosenblueth to Landauer, December 1, 1937; Hahn-Warburg to Landauer, December 18, 1937, CZA S75/506.

26. Eva Michaelis-Stern, "Errinerungen an die Anfänge der Jugendalijah in Deutschland," *Bulletin des Leo Baeck Instituts* 70 (1985): 61–62. Stern's recollections in this matter are confirmed by correspondence immediately following the events, CZA S75/506.

27. CZA S75/27.

28. Michaelis-Stern, "Erinnerungen," 61–63.

29. Levy-Stein had been active in WIZO prior to her work for Youth Aliyah. See *JR* (March 11, 1932): 103.

30. Rudolf Melitz, from Prague, to Beyth, December 27, 1937, CZA S75/506. This document also corroborates the previous examples.

31. Hahn-Warburg to Landauer, December 18, 1937, CZA S75/506. "Die Korrespondenz mit den verschiedenen Komitees und die Beantwortung der Briefe, die mit unserer Arbeit im Zusammenhang von Ausland kommen, ist ein ewiges Kopfzerbrechen."

32. See correspondence regarding "stamps," Beyth to Jüdische Jugendhilfe, May 18, 1936, and Kitzinger to Beyth, May 26, 1936, CZA S75/148.

33. Order cited in Karl Schleunes, *The Twisted Road to Auschwitz* (Chicago and Urbana, 1990), 227–28.

34. Undated report by Eva Michaelis-Stern (probably April 1938), CZA S75/506.

35. Friedländer, *Nazi Germany,* 244. Eichmann's reorganization scheme was a three-way division of responsibility among the Kultusgemeinde, the Zionistische Landesverband (National Zionist Association), and the Palästina-Amt (Palestine office), thus demonstrating his faith that the Zionists would best facilitate Jewish emigration.

36. Gerhard Botz, "The Jews of Vienna from the *Anschluss* to the Holocaust," in *Jews, Antisemitism, and Culture in Vienna,* ed. Ivar Oxaal, Michael Pollak, and Gerhard Botz (New York, 1987), 194; Schleunes, *Twisted Road,* 230; Friedländer, *Nazi Germany,* 242; Leni Yahil, *The Holocaust: The Fate of European Jewry, 1932–1945* (New York, 1990), 106.

37. David Cesarani, *Eichmann: His Life and Crimes* (London, 2004), 62–63. Heydrich's report at the infamous meeting called by Goering on November 12 noted that between March and November 1938, fifty thousand Austrian Jews had emigrated whereas only nineteen thousand had departed from the Altreich during that same period. Jonny Moser, "Die Katastrophe der Juden in Österreich 1938–1945— Ihre Voraussetzung und ihre Überwindung," in *Der Gelbe Stern in Österreich: Katalog und Einführung zu einer Dokumentation;* vol. 5 of *Studia Judaica Austriaca* (Eisenstadt: Roetzer, 1977), 124.

38. Eichmann to Gestapo, Vienna, April 5, 1939, YVA M38/194.

39. Ibid.

40. Testimony of Kurt Goldmann (Reuven Golan) YVA 01/204. Goldmann recalled that the liaison was named "Epstein." He was likely referring to Paul Eppstein, who represented a number of Jewish organizations. Ironically, Eppstein's commitment to the law led to his arrest by the Gestapo for failing to support illegal immigration to Palestine. Wolfgang Benz, *The Holocaust: A German Historian Examines the Genocide* (New York: Columbia, 1999), 115. See also Jizchak Schwersenz, *Die versteckte Gruppe: Ein jüdische Lehrer erinnert sich an Deutschland* (Berlin, 1988), 61–62.

41. ICJOHP, interview with Ra'anan (Rudolph) Melitz, June 15, 1965.

42. For a scholarly approach to this larger period, see the multivolume *German-Jewish History in Modern Times,* ed. Michael Meyer (New York, 1998). For a more popular chronicle, see Amos Elon, *The Pity of It All: A History of Jews in Germany, 1743–1933* (New York, 2002).

43. Ismar Schorsch, *Jewish Reactions to German Anti-Semitism, 1870–1914* (New York, 1972), 10.

44. Sarah Gordon, *Hitler, Germans, and "the Jewish Question"* (Princeton, 1984), 8. Schorsch gives a figure of 1.25 percent for 1871, *Jewish Reactions,* 13.

45. Gordon, *Hitler,* 8. Schorsch gives a birthrate for German Jews that was half that of the total German population for the period 1881 to 1909, *Jewish Reactions,* 13.

46. Gordon, *Hitler,* 9–10.

47. Jörg Wollenberg, "The Expropriation of the Rapacious Capital by Productive Capital," in *The German Public and the Persecution of the Jews, 1933–1945,* ed. Jörg Wollenberg (Atlantic Highlands, N.J., 1996), 120–22.

48. Peter Gay, *Weimar Culture: The Outsider as Insider* (New York, 1968).

49. Donald Niewyk, *The Jews in Weimar Germany* (Baton Rouge, 1980), 34–40.

50. Ibid., 43.

51. For a comprehensive analysis of this phenomenon, see Peter Pulzer, *The Rise of Political Anti-Semitism in Germany and Austria* (Cambridge, Mass., 1988).

52. Jehuda Reinharz, *Fatherland or Promised Land: The Dilemma of the German Jew, 1893–1914* (Ann Arbor, 1975), 37, 49.

53. Michael Brenner, *The Renaissance of Jewish Culture in Weimar Germany* (New Haven, 1996).

54. In local currency the required sum was one thousand Palestine pounds. The government did not initially place a quota on this category. Exceptions could be made for immigrants who were bringing less than the one thousand pounds to be included in category A provided they could prove other means of support.

55. Taken from the "Immigration Ordinance of the Palestine Government," August 1933, printed in the Jewish Agency for Palestine, *Report of the Executive of the Jewish Agency for Palestine submitted to the Fourth Meeting of the Council at Lucerne, September 4–5, 1935* (London, 1935), 68.

56. Quoted in Reinharz, *Fatherland,* 161.

57. Lavsky, *Before Catastrophe,* 90–93.

58. See Richard Evans, *The Coming of the Third Reich: A History* (London, 2003), for a history of the Weimar period that synthesizes the relevant historical research.

CHAPTER 1

1. Werner Mosse, ed., *Entscheidungsjahr, 1932* (Tübingen, 1966).

2. For historiography of late Weimar economic crisis, see Dieter Gessner, *Die Weimarer Republik* (Darmstadt, 2002), 80–87.

3. Alex Zukas, "Lazy, Apathetic, and Dangerous: The Social Construction of Unemployed Workers during the late Weimar Republic," *Contemporary European History* 10, no. 1 (March 2001): 28; Peter Stachura, "The Social and Welfare Implications of Youth Unemployment in Weimar Germany, 1929–1933," in *Unemployment and the Great Depression in Weimar Germany*, ed. Peter Stachura (New York, 1986), 125; Detlev Peukert, "The Lost Generation: Youth Unemployment at the End of the Weimar Republic" in *The German Unemployed: Experiences and Consequences of Mass Unemployment from the Weimar Republic to the Third Reich*, ed. Richard J. Evans and Dick Geary (New York, 1987), 177.

4. Peter Stachura, "Introduction: The Development of Unemployment in Modern German History," in *Unemployment and the Great Depression*, 12. On government responses to the Depression, see Ludger Grevelhörster, *Kleine Geschichte der Weimarer Republik 1918–1933: Ein Problemgeschichtlicher Überblick* (Münster, 2000), 134–81.

5. Elizabeth Harvey, "Youth Unemployment and the State: Public Policies towards Unemployed Youth in Hamburg during the World Economic Crisis," in *The German Unemployed*, 144–45.

6. Stachura, "Social and Welfare Implications," 135. He quoted Gertrud Bäumer.

7. Peukert, "The Lost Generation," 187; and Harvey, "Youth Unemployment and the State," 162.

8. Stachura, "Social and Welfare Implications," 122–25; Peukert, "The Lost Generation," 176.

9. Gerald Feldman, "Industrialists, Bankers, and the Problem of Unemployment in the Weimar Republic," *Central European History* 25 (1992): 78.

10. Hans Mommsen, "The Failure of the Weimar Republic and the Rise of Hitler," in *The Burden of German History: Essays for the Goethe Institute*, ed. Michael Laffan (London, 1988), 116.

11. The 1920 Nazi party program first defined Jews as foreigners who could not become citizens of the state, then demanded that the state dedicate itself to promoting the industry and livelihood of citizens only, and "if it is not possible to nourish the entire population of the state, foreign nationals [noncitizens of the state] must be excluded from the Reich." On the economic aspects of the party's anti-Semitism, see Avraham Barkai, *Vom Boykott zur "Entjudung": Der wirtschaftliche Existenzkampf der Juden im Dritten Reich, 1933–1943* (Frankfurt am Main, 1988), 18–21; also Lucy Dawidowicz, *The War against the Jews, 1933–1945* (New York, 1986), 16–17.

12. *JWuS* 3, Heft 5 (May 1932):1; Sibylle Morgenthaler recognized an organized Nazi boycott emerging in 1927, "Countering the Pre-1933 Nazi Boycott against the Jews," LBIY 36 (1991): 128–34.

13. Margaliot, "Teguvat Mosdoteyhah," 88.

14. Morgenthaler, "Countering the Pre-1933 Nazi Boycott," 130; Kurt Loewenstein, "Die innerjüdische Reaktion auf die Krise der deutschen Demokratie," in *Entscheidungsjahr, 1932*, 388; Ruth Röcher, *Die jüdische Schule im nationalsozialistischen Deutschland, 1933–1942* (Frankfurt am Main, 1992), 174.

15. Avraham Barkai, "Population Decline and Economic Stagnation," in *German-Jewish History in Modern Times*, 4:34–35, 39.

16. Donald L. Niewyk, "The Impact of Inflation and Depression on the German Jews." *LBIY* 28 (1983): 28.

17. Jonathan Friedman, *The Lion and the Star: Gentile-Jewish Relations in Three Hessian Communities, 1919–1945* (Lexington, Ky., 1998), 38.

18. Esra Bennathan, "Die Demographische und Wirtschaftliche Struktur der Juden," in *Entscheidungsjahr, 1932*, 125; and Wolf Gruner, "Die Reichshauptstadt und die Verfolgung der Berliner Juden 1933–1945," in *Jüdische Geschichte in Berlin*, ed. Reinhard Rürup (Berlin, 1995), 232.

19. Hertha Kraus, *Work Relief in Germany* (New York, 1934), 72–74; Oscar Weigert, *Administration of Placement and Unemployment Insurance in Germany* (New York, 1934), 139–40; Harvey, "Youth Unemployment," 159.

20. See report of social work in Berlin by Georg Lubinski in *JWuS* 3, Heft 4 (April 1932):140. See also *JR* (January 13 and January 17, 1933).

21. Case history recorded 1938, CZA S75/1071. Samuel came with a Youth Aliyah group to Tel Yosef in July 1934.

22. *JR* (January 12, 1932): 13, reported that Freier made a number of speeches in western Germany for the Verband jüdischer Frauen für Palästina-Arbeit in October 1931 and was responsible for forming new youth groups in Frankfurt am Main and Wiesbaden. Freier's husband was a rabbi in Berlin who was active in promoting Jewish schools.

23. Recha Freier, foreword in *Out of the Fire*, ed. Alan Sillitoe, collated by Meir Gottesman (London, 1979), 11–13.

24. ICJOHP, interview with Recha Freier, July 9, 1981. See, for example, postcard from Buber to Freier dated March 19, 1920, CZA A256/6.

25. *JR* (July 19, 1932): 1, (September 23, 1932), 367.

26. As Chanoch Rinnott, who brought the first Youth Aliyah group to Kibbutz Ein-Harod in 1934, recalled their encounters in Weimar era Berlin, "Recha was alert and high-spirited, very much attached to the needs of the household, but spiritually far away. In our talks she often let her imagination run free, and in many ways seemed to live in the clouds. Being a young boy, I drew back and kept my grip on reality as I saw it," Rinnott, "Looking Back on Youth Aliyah," in *Out of the Fire*, 15.

27. Freier later wrote that she had conceived of youth emigration from the diaspora to communal farming settlements in Palestine as early as 1931 but that the circumstances leading to practical application only arose when these young Jews approached her in 1932. Recha Freier, "Shelet Lavan Echad," in *Aliyat ha-No'ar: Korot ha-Miph'al* (Jerusalem, 1968), 109.

28. ICJOHP, interview with Izzi Eisner, Project 175 (10): May 21, 1981.

29. Recha Freier, *Let the Children Come* (London, 1961), 9. When Freier's state-

ments can be substantiated by other sources, these references are noted. When her retelling disagrees with others' memories, that too is considered. Using Freier's memoirs is problematic in some respects due in large part to her animosity toward Henrietta Szold and much of the Zionist establishment. Only later in her life, when she was awarded the Israel Prize for her achievements, did Freier believe she attained the recognition she deserved for pioneering Youth Aliyah.

30. Sharon Gillerman, "Between Public and Private: Family, Community, and Jewish Identity in Weimar Berlin" (Ph.D. diss., UCLA, 1996), 180, 198; Gillerman, "The Crisis of the Jewish Family in Weimar Germany: Social Conditions and Cultural Representations," in *In Search of Jewish Community: Jewish Identities in Germany and Austria, 1918–1933,* ed. Michael Brenner and Derek Penslar (Bloomington, 1998), 194.

31. Glenn Sharfman, "The Jewish Youth Movement in Germany, 1900–1936: A Study in Ideology and Organization" (Ph.D. diss., University of North Carolina, 1989), 281.

32. "Jüdische Jugend und Wirtschaftskrise," *JR* (January 12, 1932): 12.

33. Giora Lotan [Georg Lubinski], "The Zentralwohlfahrtsstelle," *LBIY* 4 (1959): 194–95. On political differences, see Yehoyakim Cochavi, "Liberals and Zionists on the Eve of the National Socialist Seizure of Power," *LBIY* 39 (1994): 113–29, and Niewyk, *Jews in Weimar.* On efforts to establish a central organization for German Jews before 1933, see Esriel Hildesheimer, "Ha-Irgun ha-Merkazi shel Yehudei Germanyah ba-Shanim 1933 ad 1945: Ma'amado ba-Medinah u-va-Chevrah ha-Yehudit" (Ph.D. diss., Hebrew University of Jerusalem, 1982), 1–12; Jacob Toury, "Organizational Problems of German Jewry—Steps towards the Establishment of a Central Organization (1893–1920)," *LBIY* 13 (1968): 57–90; and Ahron Sandler, "The Struggle for Unification," *LBIY* 2 (1957): 76–84.

34. Freier, *Let the Children Come,* 10.

35. Chaim Schatzker, "The Jewish Youth Movements in Germany in the Holocaust Period: Youth in Confrontation with a New Reality," *LBIY* 32 (1987): 157.

36. *JR* (March 11, 1932) on speech Sereni gave on January 7, titled "Jüdische Jugend, jüdische Zukunft," 103. For history of Blau-Weiß and its relation to Jewish youth groups of the 1920s and 1930, see Bernhard Trefz, *Jugendbewegung und Juden in Deutschland: Eine historische Untersuchung mit besonderer Berücksichtigung des Deutsch-Jüdischen Wanderbundes "Kameraden"* (Frankfurt am Main, 1999); and Hannah Weiner, *No'ar Toses be-Eidah She'anenah: Tenu'ot ha-No'ar ha-Tzioniot ve-"Hechalutz" be-Germanyah* (Israel, 1996).

37. See letter from Georg Pappe to Eliezer Liebenstein, Ein Harod, March 9, 1932, and letter from Freier to Liebenstein, March 9, 1932, both in CZA A256/6. Pappe's letter calls Freier's plan one of great importance. Sereni, an Italian Jew by birth, was at this time a member of the kibbutz Givat Brenner, which had been established in 1930. Many of the settlement's founding members were German pioneers who had come to Palestine in 1928.

38. Doron Niederland, *Yehudei Germanyah—Mehagrim 'o Plitim? Iyun bi-D'fusei ha-Hagirah bein shtei Milchemot ha-Olam* (Jerusalem, 1996), 54–61.

39. Dirk Blasius, "Zwischen Rechtsvertrauen und Rechtszerstörung: Deutsche

Juden 1933–1935," in *Zerbrochene Geschichte: Leben und Selbstverständnis der Juden in Deutschland,* ed. Dirk Blasius and Dan Diner (Frankfurt am Main, 1991), 125.

40. Claudia Prestel, "'Youth in Need': Correctional Education and Family Breakdown in German Jewish Families," in *In Search of Jewish Community,* 205–6.

41. Georg Pappe, "P'nei ha-Dor," in *Sefer Aliyat Ha-No'ar,* ed. Bracha Habas (Jerusalem, 1941), 76; Arnold Paucker, "Das Berliner liberale jüdische Bürgertum im Centralverein deutscher Staatsbürger jüdischen Glaubens," in *Jüdische Geschichte in Berlin: Essays und Studien,* ed. Reinhard Rürup (Berlin, 1995), 226; Marion Kaplan, *Between Dignity and Despair,* 111.

42. ICJOHP, interview with Izzi Eisner.

43. Recha Freier, *Le-Korot Aliyat ha-No'ar, Reshumot* (Tel Aviv, 1947), 4:3. Nevertheless, as Werner Mosse wrote, "1932 should be perceived as a decisive year for the scholar looking backward, rather than extreme circumstances of which the historical actors were cognizant," "Vorwort," in *Entscheidungsjahr, 1932,* xii.

44. In 1939 the Youth Aliyah department of the Jewish Agency celebrated the fifth anniversary of Youth Aliyah. Freier protested the chronology, claiming that she had founded the movement in 1932. For decades Freier insisted that the Jewish Agency's dating deprived her of recognition as the originator of Youth Aliyah.

45. Text of speech by Eva Michaelis-Stern, March 14, 1984, before the Union for Israeli-German Understanding, CZA A440/box 2.

46. Alfred Landsberg, "Die besonderen Aufgaben des deutschen Zionismus: Zur Vorbereitung des Delegiertentag," *JR* (August 19, 1932): 317.

47. Willi Holzer, *Jüdische Schulen in Berlin: Am Beispiel der privaten Volksschule der jüdischen Gemeinde Rykestraße* (Berlin, 1992), 40–41. The school's aim was "zu einem nationalen Judentum zu erziehen mit einer starken gefühls- und verstandesmäßigen Bindung an Palästina und an das jüdische Aufbauwerk dort."

48. Recha Freier, "Die Anfänge der Jugendalijah," *JR* (July 5, 1935). Testimony of Selma Schiratzky, YVA 01/138; and Selma Schiratzky, "The Rykestrasse School in Berlin: A Jewish Elementary School during the Hitler Period," *LBIY* 5 (1960): 299–307.

49. Sharfman, "The Jewish Youth Movement in Germany," 176; Loewenstein, "Die innerjüdische Reaktion," 389.

50. Israel Tunis, "Zum jüdischen Berufsproblem," *JR* (July 12, 1932): 263.

51. "Kadimahdorf 1932," *JR* (June 17, 1932): 228.

52. "Vor Rosch Haschanah 5693, ein Aufruf der Jugend," *JR* (September 2, 1932): 338.

53. Gross, "Korot Aliyat Ha-No'ar," in *Sefer Aliyat Ha-No'ar,* 84.

54. See letter from Pappe to Liebenstein, March 9, 1932, noting Freier's fundraising efforts in Danzig. A256/6.

55. Landauer ultimately managed the Jerusalem office of the Central Bureau for the Settlement of German Jews in Palestine and had overall responsibility for the financial aspects of Youth Aliyah in Palestine.

56. Szold to Freier, July 3, 1935, CZA A125/93. Georg Landauer confirms this correspondence; see "Zur Jugendalijah und ihrer wahren Geschichte," in *Der Zionismus im Wandel: dreier Jahrzehnte* (Tel Aviv, 1957), 446–49.

57. "Verteilung der Zertifikate," *JR* (June 8, 1932).

58. *JR* (January 26, 1932): 34.

59. Gross, "Korot Aliyat Ha-No'ar," in *Sefer Aliyat Ha-No'ar*, 85. According to Recha Freier, this date represented the official beginning of Youth Aliyah as a program. The specific point at which Youth Aliyah began remained a point of contention between Freier and the Youth Aliyah department of the Jewish Agency. Freier maintained that dating the origin of the program to any later point would overlook her singular contribution. Her dispute was only resolved, through legal recourse, when Moshe Kol, then chair of the Youth Aliyah department, publicly declared, in a legal document, that Freier conceived and initiated the project. See court judgment dated April 13, 1954, CZA A256/4/5.

60. Freier to Berachjahu Azarjahu, June 2, 1932, CZA A256/2.

CHAPTER 2

1. Rinnot, "Looking Back on Youth Aliyah," 15–16.

2. Lavsky, *Before Catastrophe*, 247–52; Margaliot, "The Problem of the Rescue of German Jewry," 249; Abraham Edelheit, *The Yishuv in the Shadow of the Holocaust: Zionist Politics and Rescue Aliya, 1933–1939* (Boulder, Colo., 1996), 7–15; Friedländer, *Nazi Germany*, 61–65.

3. The social worker Edgar Freund noted that hundreds of young Jews gathered at the train station to bid farewell to the twelve, with the hope of soon following them, "Tatsache und Probleme der Jugend-Alijah," *JWuS* 7, Heft 2 (March 1937): 37.

4. Kadimah had originally formed in 1926 as an apolitical association, successor to the Bund jüdischer Pfadfinder, dedicated to pioneering and the general ideals of the German youth movement. The organization took a pro-Zionist position in 1930. Brith Haolim, which had formed in 1923, identified with socialist Zionism. The formation of the Werkleute in 1932 resulted from the politically neutral Kameraden's split into three groups representing three distinct ideological positions. Schwersenz, *Die versteckte Gruppe*, 37, and Yehoyakim Doron, *Ne'urim ba-Tenu'ah: Mekorot le-Toldot Tenu'ot ha-No'ar ha-Yehudiyot be-Germanyah 1909–1933* (Jerusalem, 1996), 16, 267–68.

5. Protocol for founding Jüdischen Jugendhilfe, e.V., dated February 5, 1933, CZA A256/2; Gross, "Korot Aliyat Ha-No'ar," in *Sefer Aliyat Ha-No'ar*, 85.

6. Jacob Boas, "Germany or Diaspora? German Jewry's Shifting Perceptions in the Nazi Era (1933–1938)," *LBIY* 27 (1982): 109–12.

7. See "Confidential Message from the Zionist Federation of Germany brought to London on March 26, 1933," which stated that "action against the Zionist Federation is expected to be taken any day," *Central Zionist Archives, Jerusalem, 1933–39*, 115.

8. Daniel Fraenkel, *Al Pi Tehom: ha-Mediniyut ha-Tsiyonit u-She'elat Yehudei Germanyah 1933–1938* (Jerusalem, 1994), 63. On the history of the Naumann Group, see Niewyk, *Jews in Weimar*, 165–78.

9. Francis Nicosia, "The End of Emancipation and the Illusion of Preferential Treatment: German Zionism, 1933–1938," *LBIY* 36 (1991):245–49.

10. Gross, "Korot Aliyat Ha-No'ar," in *Sefer Aliyat Ha-No'ar*, 85–86.

11. Jørgen Hæstrup, *Passage to Palestine: Young Jews in Denmark, 1932–1945* (Denmark, 1983), 18; Simonson, "Aych Hurchevah ha-Kevutzah ha-Rishonah," in *Sefer Aliyat Ha-No'ar*, 118.

12. Götz Aly and Susan Heim, "Forced Emigration, War, Deportation, and Holocaust," in *The Fate of the European Jews, 1939–1945: Continuity or Contingency?* ed. Jonathan Frankel (New York, 1997), 57.

13. Arno Klönne, *Jugend im Dritten Reich: Die Hitler-Jugend und ihrer Gegner* (Cologne, 2003), 298; Sharfman, "The Jewish Youth Movement," 382–84; Hetkamp, *Die jüdische Jugendbewegung in Deutschland von 1913–1933.* (Münster, 1994), 134–35; Chanoch Rinott, "Jüdische Jugendbewegung in Deutschland: Entstehung, Entwicklung und Ende (1912–1942)," *Neue Sammlung* 17 (1977): 77.

14. "Vereinigung chaluzischer Jugend," *JR* (February 21, 1933): 72. On Blau-Weiß at its zenith, see Weiner, *No-ar Toses*, 223–268.

15. *Ten Short Stories*, pamphlet printed by Hadassah in late November 1938, CZA S75/1106.

16. Lavsky, *Before Catastrophe*, 235–36. Schatzker, "The Jewish Youth Movements," 157, notes the increase in Hechaluz membership from four thousand to fifteen thousand.

17. "Jüdische Wirtschaftspolitik," *JR* (March 24, 1933): 116.

18. Eliyahu Abromowitz, "Na'ar Misaper," in *Sefer Aliyat ha-No'ar*, 120.

19. "What Happened Afterwards," in *Out of the Fire*, 53.

20. Ibid., 59–60.

21. Case history recorded June 2, 1938, CZA S75/775.

22. Habonim noar chaluzi Budesleitung to Henny Goldenblum, May 5, 1933, CZA A474/Box 1.

23. Shulamit Volkov, "German Jews between Fulfillment and Delusion: The Individual and the Community," in *In Search of Community*, 1.

24. On the German public's reaction to Nazi Jewish policy, see Robert Gellately, *Backing Hitler: Consent and Coercion in Nazi Germany* (New York, 2001).

25. Wollenberg, "Expropriation," 121. Evelyn Lacina, *Emigration, 1933–1945: Sozialhistorische Darstellung der deutschsprachigen Emigration und einiger ihrer Asylländer aufgrund ausgewählter zeitgenössischer Selbstzeugnisse* (Stuttgart, 1982), 53–55; Sebastian Haffner, *Defying Hitler: A Memoir* (New York, 2003), 140–178; see also Kershaw, *The Nazi Dictatorship: Problems and Perspectives of Interpretation* (London, 1985), 92. David Bankier, *The Germans and the Final Solution: Public Opinion under Nazism* (Oxford, 1992), 68–69.

26. Erich Leyens and Lotte Andor, *Years of Estrangement* (Evanston, Ill., 1996), 10.

27. A. Szanto, "Economic Aid in the Nazi Era: The Work of the Berlin Wirtschaftshilfe," *LBIY* 4 (1959): 208–10. Economic assistance came from the newly formed Zentralstelle für jüdische Wirtschaftshilfe; responsibility for immigration was divided among three organizations: the Palestine office, which only handled immigrants to that country; the Hilfsverein der deutschen Juden, responsible for immigration to European and other overseas countries; and the Hauptstelle für

jüdische Wanderfürsorge, whose purview was reemigration of eastern European nationals. See also Genschel, *Die Verdrängung der Juden,* 52–53.

28. Hans was the brother of Georg Lubinski, the director of the Arbeitsgemeinschaft; he had worked with Siegfried Lehmann during the 1920s running the youth home in Kovno, Lithuania, which would become the Ben-Shemen youth village.

29. Prestel, "'Youth in Need,'" 211; 215–16.

30. H. G. Reissner, "The Histories of 'Kaufhaus N. Israel' and of Wilfrid Israel," *LBIY* 3 (1958): 251.

31. Document dated May 30, 1933, titled "Satzungen der Arbeitsgemeinschaft für Kinder- und Jugendalija," CZA A440/Box 2.

32. On the founding of the Reichsvertretung, see Hildesheimer, *Jüdische Selbstverwaltung,* 17–27; Max Gruenewald, "The Beginning of the Reichsvertretung," *LBIY* 1 (1956): 57–67.

33. "Call to Jews of Germany by newly formed Reichsvertretung," dated September 21, 1933. LBIJ 555/1. On the desire of most Jews to remain in Germany, see Konrad Kwiet, "Gehen oder bleiben? Die deutschen Juden am Wendepunkt," in *Der Judenpogrom 1938: Von der "Reichskristallnacht" zum Völkermord,* ed. Walter H. Pehle (Frankfurt am Main, 1988), 132–33. William Rubinstein, *The Myth of Rescue: Why the Democracies Could Not Have Saved More Jews from the Nazis* (London and New York, 1997), 19–24, stresses this as the main reason most Jews did not leave Germany before November 1938.

34. Margaliot, "The Problem of the Rescue of German Jewry," 256–57.

35. *JR* (January 31, 1933): 44. From a speech given on January 22, titled "Die Wege der jüdischen Jugend."

36. A more detailed account of Lubinski's contribution to social work in Germany can be found in Oded Heilbronner, "Georg Lubinski: Ein Leben für die Sozialarbeit," in *Zedaka: Jüdische Sozialarbeit im Wandel der Zeit* (Frankfurt am Main, 1992), 129–34.

37. Georg Josephthal, "Die Berufsfrage der jüdischen Jugend," in *Gemeinschaftsarbeit der jüdischen Jugend* (Berlin, 1937), 41.

38. G. Warburg. *Six Years of Hitler: The Jews under the Nazi Regime* (London, 1939), 130–31.

39. Werner Angress, "Jüdische Jugend zwischen nationalsozialistischer Verfolgung und jüdischer Wiedergeburt," in *Die Juden im Nationalsozialistischen Deutschland,* 212.

40. Kaplan, *Between Dignity and Despair,* 98. Werner Angress, "Erfahrungen jüdischer Jugendlicher und Kinder mit der nichtjüdischen Umwelt, 1933–1945," in *Die Deutschen und die Judenverfolgung im Dritten Reich,* ed. Ursula Büttner (Hamburg, 1992), 93.

41. Rebekka Göpfert, *Der jüdische Kindertransport: von Deutschland nach England, 1938/39* (Frankfurt am Main, 1999), 37–38.

42. Kaplan, *Between Dignity and Despair,* 103. She gave the following statistics: in 1935 the number of Jewish schools had risen to 130; in 1936, to 160; and in 1937, to a peak of 167. Whereas in 1932 only 14 percent of Jewish children attended Jewish schools, in 1934 this number rose to 23 percent; in 1936, to 52 percent; and in 1937, to

approximately 60 percent. Notably, this proportion increased during a period when twenty to thirty thousand Jews left Germany annually.

43. Debórah Dwork, *Children with a Star: Jewish Youth in Nazi Europe* (New Haven, 1991), 22–23.

44. He cited a parallel to the challenge that confronted the Greeks in Turkey following World War I; Chaim Arlosoroff, *Mivchar Ketavim u-Firkei Chayim* (Jerusalem, 1958), 171.

45. Miriam Getter, *Chaim Arlosoroff: Biographia Politit* (Tel Aviv, 1977), 182.

46. "Was kann Palästina den deutschen Juden bieten?" *JR* (May 23, 1933): 214. As early as 1933, Arlosoroff recognized the distinction between an immigration program along the lines of Youth Aliyah and other schemes that offered only temporary refuge. In the Zionist lexicon the term *Nachtasyl,* meaning night shelter, was ideologically loaded. Though technically referring to a "temporary haven," it came to mean relocation in any territory other than Palestine. This attitude was evident in the debates surrounding the 1903 proposal, known as the Uganda Plan, supported by Herzl, to settle Jewish refugees from eastern Europe on land in British East Africa.

47. Norman Bentwich, *Ben-Shemen: A Children's Village in Israel* (Jerusalem, 1958), 28.

48. Arlosoroff, "Was kann Palästina" *JR* (May 23, 1933): 214.

49. Cited in Shlomo Bar-Gil, *Mechapsim Bayit Motz'im Moledet Aliyat Ha-No'ar be-Chinuch uve-Shikum Sh'erit Ha-Pleitah 1945–1955* (Jerusalem, 1999), 1.

50. Getter, for example, credits Arlosoroff with being "the first to raise the idea of a children's immigration to the land and their absorption in kibbutzim," *Chaim Arlosoroff: Biographia Politit,* 186. Some years later Freier reported that when she returned to Germany she discovered that Arlosoroff "strongly supported [her] plan," *Le-korot Aliyat Ha-No'ar,* 17.

51. Ilse Warburg noted that on May 1, 1933, her father-in-law, Otto Warburg, a representative of the Jewish Agency, told her that one of the most important elements to solving the German-Jewish problem was the removal of Jewish youth from Germany, Ilse Warburg, "Persönlicher Rückblick auf die Anfänge der Jugend-Alijah," manuscript written in February 1935, CZA S75/26. Yosef Shapiro, *Chaim Arlosoroff* (Tel Aviv, 1975), 268.

52. Reprinted as "Hatza'ah," in *Sefer Aliyat Ha-No'ar,* 196. Aharonovitz further noted, "It will be possible to obtain great sympathy throughout the world for this project and it will be possible to ensure the total cooperation of the governments of England and Palestine. . . . I believe with complete faith that the rescue of German Jewry from a national historical perspective—is first of all and most importantly, the rescue of the children of German Jewry" (96).

53. Eliyahu Biletzky, *Chaim Arlosoroff: Iyunim be-Mishnato ha-Yehudit* (Tel Aviv, 1966), 162.

54. J. Jacobs, Palestine government, to the Jewish Agency Executive, undated (most probably June or July 1933), CZA S75/24; Sima Arlosoroff, "Al Assor Echad" in C. Arlosoroff, *Mivchar Ketavim,* lv.

55. On the importance of *Bildung* as a value in its own right among German Jewry, see David Sorkin, *The Transformation of German Jewry* (New York, 1987), es-

pecially chapter 1 and the conclusion, and George Mosse, *German Jews beyond Judaism* (Bloomington and Cincinnati, 1985).

56. "Jugend- und Kinderalijah," *JR* (August 8, 1933): 406. One would hardly characterize this musical goal as an essential element of the pioneering lifestyle that dominated the kibbutzim.

57. Ruppin had advised Freier to be patient and to be confident that eventually her idea would find the necessary support; Freier, *Let the Children Come*, 30–31.

58. Landauer, "Über die Wege der Jugendalijah," in *Der Zionismus im Wandel*, 98–99.

59. *Stenographisches Protokoll der Verhandlungen des XVIII. Zionistenkongresses und der dritten Tagung des Council der Jewish Agency für Palästina, Prag, 21. August bis 4 September 1933* (Vienna, 1934), 188–89.

60. *Resolutions of the Eighteenth Zionist Congress, Prague, August 21 to September 3, 1933, with a Summary Report of the Proceedings* (London, 1934), 42.

61. Undated document (probably September 1933) titled "Proposals of the Jewish Agency for Palestine for the Settlement of German Jews in Palestine, Submitted to the Allocations Committee of the Central British Fund for German Jewry," CZA S75/35; S75/1.

62. Gross, "Korot Aliyat Ha-No'ar," in *Sefer Aliyat Ha-No'ar*, 87–88; Simonson, "Aych Hurchevah ha-Kevutzah ha-Rishonah," in *Sefer Aliyat Ha-No'ar*, 118.

63. Pinchas Rosenblüth, "Darcho shel ha-No'ar ha-Dati," in *Sefer Aliyat ha-No'ar*, 218.

64. "Proposals of the Jewish Agency for Palestine for the Settlement of German Jews in Palestine"; the actual figure was 340,000 Reichsmarks, CZA S75/1.

65. Gross, "Korot Aliyat Ha-No'ar," in *Sefer Aliyat Ha-No'ar*, 87–88.

66. "Mi-Yomano shel Eliyahu," in *Sefer Aliyat Ha-No'ar*, diary entry for October 6, 1933, 121.

67. Abromowitz, "Na'ar Misaper," in *Sefer Aliyat Ha-No'ar*, 121.

68. Ibid.

69. "Mi-Yomano shel Eliyahu," in *Sefer Aliyat Ha-No'ar*, diary entries for November 21 and December 4, 1933, 121–22.

70. "Jüdische Jugend in Palästina," *JR* (September 8, 1933): 495; "Kinderheim 'Ahawah' geht nach Palästina," *JR* (September 12, 1933): 512.

71. See Joachim Schlör, *Tel Aviv: From Dream to City* (London, 1999), 23–33.

72. On retraining, see "Probleme der Berufsumschichtung," *JR* (November 3, 1933): 751.

73. E. Stern, "Jugend Alijah: 500 Jugendliche aus Deutschland nach Palästina," *JR* (November 3, 1933): 751.

74. ICJOHP, interview with Eva Michaelis-Stern, November 26, 1981, 12–13.

75. This short biographical sketch is taken mainly from a questionnaire filled out by Eva Michaelis-Stern found in her files at the Central Zionist Archives, CZA A440/ Box 7. Additional biographical information can be found in Michaelis-Stern's ICJOHP, interview.

76. Stephen M. Poppel, *Zionism in Germany, 1897–1933: The Shaping of a Jewish Identity* (Philadelphia, 1977), 75, on post-WWI *hachscharah* in Germany: "between

1919 and 1930 almost 1,000 of these *chalutzim* left for Palestine, although 425 eventually returned."

77. *Bericht über die Erste Jugend-Alijah-Weltkonferenz, Amsterdam, 9–12 September 1935* (Berlin), 5–6.

78. Stern, "Jugend-Alijah," *JR* (November 3, 1933): 751.

79. Lucie Schachne, *Erziehung zum geistigen Widerstand* (Frankfurt am Main, 1986), 21.

80. Eva Stern, "Beginn der Jugend-Alija," in *Zur Eröffnung der Ludwig Tietz Lehrwerkstätte in Jagur*, ed. Friedrich Brodnitz (Berlin, 1937), 31–33.

81. Landauer, "Die Bedeutung Palästinas für die jüdische Gegenwart," *JWuS* 4, no. 3–4 (September–October 1933): 108–12.

82. S. Adler-Rudel, "Berufsumschichtung als Ausweg?" *JWuS* 4, no. 3–4 (September–October 1933): 112–13.

83. *Gemeinde-Zeitung für die israelitischen Gemeinden Württembergs*, October 1, 1933, 109.

84. Habonim noar chaluzi Budesleitung to Henny Goldenblum, May 5, 1933, CZA A474/Box 1.

85. On Szold's life and work see, among others, Nachum T. Gidal, *Henrietta Szold: A Documentation in Photos and Text* (New York, 1996); Ester Ziv Inbar, *Le-'olam Tiheyeh 'atsmecha: Sipurah shel Henrietta Szold* (Jerusalem, 1996); Joan Dash, *Summoned to Jerusalem: The Life of Henrietta Szold* (New York, 1979); Irving Fineman, *Woman of Valor: The Life of Henrietta Szold, 1860–1945* (New York, 1961); and Marvin Lowenthal, *Henrietta Szold, Life and Letters* (New York, 1942).

86. Gross, "Korot Aliyat ha-No'ar," in *Sefer Aliyat Ha-No'ar*, 89.

87. Notes taken by Henrietta Szold, November 6–12, 1933, CZA A125/82.

88. Resolution passed during negotiations between Arbeitsgemeinschaft and Miss Szold, November 7–10, 1933, CZA A256/2.

89. Ibid.

90. Edelheit, *Yishuv in the Shadow of the Holocaust*, 69; Hava (Wegman) Eshkoli, "Three Attitudes toward the Holocaust within Mapai, 1933–1945," *Studies in Zionism* 14, no. 1 (1993): 77–78. Both writers note that Ben-Gurion's attitude toward selectivity began to change only in late 1933.

91. Gross, "Korot Aliyat ha-No'ar," in *Sefer Aliyat Ha-No'ar*, 87; Lavsky, *Before Catastrophe*, 237. "Whereas genuine commitment had always been important to the Zionist Organization, it now faced the dilemma of maintaining high standards or opening its gates to all" (Lavsky, 237).

92. Ruppin to Weizmann, October 22, 1933, CZA S75/1.

93. Hans Lubinski, director of the Arbeitsgemeinschaft, and Arthur Rau, head of the Palästina-Amt, to the Jewish Agency, October 25, 1933, CZA S75/16.

94. Margaliot, "The Problem of the Rescue of German Jewry," 249–50.

95. F. Noack and S. Shapiro, "Ha-Sikkum ha-Rephu'i," in *Sefer Aliyat Ha-No'ar*, 327.

96. Barkai, *Vom Boykott zur "Entjudung,"* 111. Instituted to prevent the removal of German capital after the onset of the Great Depression, the tax originally applied only to assets over 200,000 Reichsmarks ($46,000); in May 1934 the flight tax was

levied on all assets of 50,000 Reichsmarks or more. Emigrants could not transfer remaining funds even after payment of the tax, but instead had to deposit their assets in special blocked accounts, which the government would exchange for foreign currency at increasingly reduced rates.

97. Dr. Kr (probably Kreutzberger) to the Reichswirtschaftsminister, Berlin, November 10, 1933, CZA S75/6.

98. Simonson to Landesfinanzamt, Devisenbewirtschaftungsstelle, Berlin, November 10, 1933, CZA S75/6.

99. See my introduction.

100. Simonson to Landauer, November 28, 1933, CZA S75/6.

101. Liebenstein to Department for Colonisation, November 28, 1933, S75/6.

102. J. Jacobs to Jewish Agency executive, undated, CZA S75/1; Gross, "Korot Aliyat Ha-No'ar," in *Sefer Aliyat Ha-No'ar*, 89.

103. Szold to Simonson, December 14, 1933, CZA S75/6.

104. Georg Pappe to Eliezer Liebenstein, March 9, 1932, CZA A256/6.

105. On French reaction to the refugee crisis, see Greg Burgess, "France and the German Refugee Crisis of 1933," *French History* 16, no. 2 (June 2002): 203–29.

106. ICJOHP, interview with Eva Michaelis-Stern, November 26, 1981.

107. Shalom Adler-Rudel, "Ten Years Youth Aliyah," CZA A140/203. See "Arbeitsbericht des Zentralausschusses der Deutschen Juden für Hilfe und Aufbau," April 1–December 31, 1933, IfZ Fa 723/1, 8–11. Almost as much of the publicly collected funding was used to send 2,182 people to Palestine as was used to repatriate nearly 17,000 Jews through the Hauptstelle für jüdische Wanderfürsorge.

108. Martin Rosenbluth, *Go Forth and Serve: Early Years and Public Life* (New York, 1961), 266–68, 273–75.

109. Simonson to Szold, January 17, 1934, CZA S75/6.

110. Stern and Schattner to Szold, January 25, 1934, CZA S75/16.

111. Rosenbluth, *Go Forth and Serve*, 274.

112. Jehuda Reinharz, "Hashomer Hazair in Nazi Germany," in *Die Juden in Nationalsozialistischen Deutschland*, 333–34.

113. Henrietta Szold, "Ha-Chevrah ha-Rishonah Ba'ah le-Ein-Harod," in *Sefer Aliyat ha-No'ar*, 117.

CHAPTER 3

1. *Youth Aliyah: A Review of Three Years' Achievement: Realizing an Idea*, ed. Eva Stern (Berlin, n.d.), 4.

2. Case history recorded in 1938, CZA S75/1071.

3. Niederland, *Yehudei Germanyah*, 35–37, citing the quarterly reports of the German government's emigration office, charts the relative increase or decrease in Jewish emigration from the Third Reich by quarter-year for the period 1933 to 1939. See also Herbert Strauss, "Jewish Emigration from Germany: Nazi Policies and Jewish Responses," *LBIY* 25 (1980): 326.

4. Simonson specifically highlighted their adaptability to succeed in a communal environment, to learn without external pressure, and to endure physical labor, "Jugend-Alijah: Der Weg der ersten Gruppe," *JR* (February 13, 1934): 4.

5. David Kramer, "Jewish Welfare Work," in *Die Juden im Nationalsozialistischen Deutschland*, 176; "Sterben die deutschen Juden aus?" *JR* (August 4, 1933).

6. Case history recorded June 6, 1938, CZA S75/774.

7. Case history recorded June 1, 1938, CZA S75/774.

8. For a statistical breakdown of immigration on the labor schedule by country of origin, see *Report of the Executive of the Jewish Agency for Palestine submitted to the Third Meeting of the Council at Prague, August 31–September 1, 1933* (London, 1933), 75, 81–83; *Report of the Executive of the Zionist Organisation Submitted to the Nineteenth Zionist Congress at Lucerne, August 20–30, 1935* (London, 1935), 276, 285; and *Report of the Executive of the Zionist Organisation and of the Jewish Agency for Palestine submitted to the Twenty-first Zionist Congress and the Sixth Session of the Council of the Jewish Agency at Geneva, August, 1939* (Jerusalem, 1939), 310.

9. *JR* (February 13, 1934): 4.

10. Eva Stern, *Jugend-Alijah* (Berlin, 1934), 3.

11. Ibid.

12. "45 Jugendliche reisen nach Palästina," *JR* (March 13, 1934): 10.

13. "45 Jugendliche auf dem Wege nach Palästina: Die Empfangsvorbereitungen," *JR* (February 27, 1934): 4.

14. Szold to Jüdische Jugendhilfe, March 15, 1934, CZA S75/6. Szold's argument apparently prevailed.

15. Ibid., March 13, 1934, CZA S75/6.

16. Schatzker, *No'ar Yehudi*, 291–92. He cites a complaint from the Jewish Agency's German Department in 1937, which claimed, among other points, that German emigrants arrived with diseases and defects. On selective immigration as policy, see Eshkoli, "Three Attitudes toward the Holocaust," 75–79. Dina Porat, *The Blue and Yellow Stars of David: The Zionist Leadership and the Holocaust, 1939–1945* (Cambridge, Mass., 1990), 245, claims that selectivity remained the policy of *yishuv* leaders until 1942.

17. Simonson to Szold and Landauer, April 5, 1934, CZA S75/6.

18. Schattner to Jewish Agency Executive, June 6, 1934, CZA S75/17.

19. "Arbeitsbericht des Zentralausschusses der Deutschen Juden für Hilfe und Aufbau," January 1, 1934–June 30, 1934, IfZ Fa 723/1, 6. This document provides the following breakdown of 884 certificates for the first half of 1934: blank certificates for males, 18–25 years, 625; artisan (*Handwerker*) certificates for males 18–25, 145; blank certificates for males 35–45, 24; certificates for young females, 90. The plurality of workers' certificates were sent to Polish *chaluzim*.

20. Figure cited in letter from Eliezer Liebenstein to Va'ad Hapo'el shel ha-Histadrut (Executive Committee of the Labor Federation), September 17, 1934, which speaks of 15,000 registered members—in 170 different branches, Archives of Kibbutz Ha-Me'uchad, Diaspora Group 7/33.

21. Simonson to Szold, May 18, 1934, CZA S75/6.

22. Josephthal came to Youth Aliyah with a background in the Jewish youth movement, having risen through the ranks of the apolitical Jüdischer Jugendbund, and professional Jewish social work. After Hitler's assumption of power, Josephthal was asked to direct social services for the young Jews of Munich and other commu-

nities in Bavaria, primarily preparing Jewish youth for emigration. Ben Halpern and Shalom Wurm, eds., *The Responsible Attitude: Life and Opinions of Giora Josephthal* (New York, 1966), 2–6.

23. Josephthal to Chanoch Reinhold, January 25, 1934, reprinted in *Livnot u-Lehibanot: Tenu'at "Habonim" be-Germanyah, 1920–1942* (Tel Aviv, 1990), 205.

24. Halpern and Wurm, *Responsible Attitude*, 7; Schatzker, *No'ar Yehudi*, 293.

25. Josephthal to Reinhold, July 12, 1934, CZA A344/10.

26. Ibid.

27. Freier, *Let the Children Come*, 42.

28. Habonim *shlichah* Yocheved Bat-Rachel referred to MiHa as a "revolutionary project" for its time, *Livnot u-Lehibanot*, 198.

29. Schatzker, *No'ar Yehudi*, 279, 297.

30. ICJOHP, interview with Yocheved Bat-Rachel, May 5, 1966.

31. Hans Gaertner, "Problems of Jewish Schools in Germany during the Hitler Regime," *LBIY* 1 (1956): 137. See also Rundschreiben des Schulabteilung der Reichsvertretung, March 16, 1936, LBIJ 557/2. For an analysis of the educational program of the ninth school year in Jewish schools, see Röcher, *Die Jüdische Schule*, 200–204.

32. "Aus Verhandlungen des Erziehungsausschusses 2. Oktober 1933," in Kulka, *Deutsches Judentum*, 95.

33. Reichsvertretung, Abteilung Berufsausbildung, to all district offices, June 20, 1935, reprinted in Kulka, *Deutsches Judentum*, 218.

34. Ilse Warburg, "Report on Conversation with the Arbeitsgemeinschaft held in Berlin, July, 1934," CZA S75/17.

35. Freier, *Let the Children Come*, 44.

36. "Diese Schule war weder Volks-noch höhere Schule. Sie war eher eine pädagogisch orientiert 'Zwischenstation' für enttäuschte Jugendliche," Röcher, *Die Jüdische Schule*, 198.

37. Ollendorf, quoted in Röcher, *Die Jüdische Schule*, 199.

38. "Kundgebung der neuen Reichsvertretung der deutschen Juden," and "Richtlinien zur Aufstellung von Lehrplänen für jüdische Volksschulen," in Kulka, *Deutsches Judentum*, 71–72, 114–15. See also Yfaat Weiss, *Schicksalsgemeinschaft im Wandel* (Hamburg, 1991), 97–98.

39. "Sorgen um jüdische Jugend," *Gemeindeblatt der Deutsch-Israelitischen Gemeinde zu Hamburg*, April 19, 1934, 4.

40. Poppel, *Zionism in Germany*, chapter 6.

41. Warburg, "Report on Conversation with the Arbeitsgemeinschaft held in Berlin, July, 1934," CZA S75/17.

42. "Arbeitsgemeinschaft für Kinder- u. Jugend-Alijah: Bericht über das erste Arbeitsjahr," *Informationsblätter im Auftrage des Zentralausschusses der deutschen Juden für Hilfe und Aufbau* 2, no. 6 (August 27, 1934): 74–75.

43. Szold, "Youth Immigration from Germany to Palestine," typewritten report, May 1934, CZA library call no. 39.062/Gimmel. She said that Youth Aliyah "called itself the Juedische Jugendhilfe . . . [and] might better have called itself the Juedische Jugendselbsthilfe."

44. For detailed exposition of this problem, see chapter 5.

45. ICJOHP, interview with Rudi Herz, December 14, 1966. In early 1934 Herz was sent by Hapoel Hamizrachi in Palestine to Germany to facilitate religious Youth Aliyah.

46. The leading figure of the Agudat Israel in Germany, Isaac Breuer, wrote in 1918 that Zionism was the most dangerous foe to challenge the Jewish people. The international Agudah was established as a direct response to Zionism, and among its founding figures were leaders from German Orthodoxy. Ya'akov Tzur, "Tenu'ot ha-No'ar ha-Dati'ot be-Germanyah ba-Shanim 1933–1939," in *Tenu'ot ha-No'ar ha-Tziyoni'ot ba-Shoah*, ed. Yehoyakim Cochavi (Haifa, 1989), 75, 81. The Agudah did not accept the leadership of the Reichsvertretung, which it viewed as a body subject to Zionist influence. See excerpt from *Der Israelit* dated September 18, 1933, reprinted in Kulka, *Deutsches Judentum*, 81.

47. On the early history of Esra, see Hetkamp, *Jüdische Jugendbewegung*, 44–46.

48. On change that occurred within Agudat Israel, see Tzur, "Tenu'ot ha-No'ar ha-Dati'ot," 75–76. Israel Oppenheim, *The Struggle of Jewish Youth for Productivization: The Zionist Youth Movement in Poland* (Boulder, Colo., 1989), 110, cited an Agudah youth leader in Poland who stressed that the land of Israel had become the only salvation in the eyes of those who had previously not wished to hear of it.

49. Article from March 30, 1933, cited in Herbert Freeden, *The Jewish Press in the Third Reich* (Providence, 1993), 63.

50. Stern to Landauer, July 14, 1934, CZA S75/17.

51. Warburg, "Report on Conversation with the Arbeitsgemeinschaft held in Berlin, July, 1934," CZA S75/17; Prestel, "'Youth in Need,'" 211–12.

52. "Arbeitsgemeinschaft," *Informationsblätter im Auftrage des Zentralausschusses der deutschen Juden für Hilfe und Aufbau* 2, no. 6 (August 27, 1934): 75.

53. See various documents reprinted in "Die Jugend-Alijah," in *Die jüdische Emigration aus Deutschland 1933–1941*, 160–62.

54. Kaplan, *Between Dignity and Despair*, 111–12.

55. Schattner to Landauer, July 11, 1935, regarding upcoming visit by Kreutzberger to the United States, CZA S75/34.

56. Hadassah's desire to participate in Youth Aliyah parallels fund-raising in other countries where women's organizations dominated appeals for Youth Aliyah.

57. Dash, *Summoned to Jerusalem*, 253.

58. Szold to Lola Hahn-Warburg, September 14, 1936, CZA S75/190.

59. Landauer to Rose Jacobs, August 27, 1935, YAA, 1/2.

60. Marion Greenberg to Hedwig Eppstein, April 5, 1938, YAA 1/4.

61. Lipsky to Hadassah, October 22, 1935, YAA 1/2.

62. "Contract with UPA," December 9, 1935, YAA 1/46.

63. Marion Greenberg to Judith Epstein, July 7, 1939, YAA 1/47.

64. "Arbeitsbericht des Zentralausschusses," January 1–June 30, 1934, IfZ Fa 723/1, 96.

65. Naomi Cohen, *American Jews and the Zionist Idea* (New York, 1975), 45.

66. Central Bureau, *Report to the Nineteenth Zionist Congress*, 5.

67. Ibid., 49.

68. Statistics printed in ibid., 83.

69. Rubishov's remarks appear in the *Nineteenth Zionist Congress and the Fourth Sitting of the Council of the Jewish Agency, Lucerne, August 20–September 6, 1935, Stenographic Report* (Tel Aviv, 1937), 173; Grossman's comments, 160–61. Grossman's State Zionist party provided the voice for Revisionist Zionism within the framework of the WZO following the establishment of the New Zionist Organization by Vladimir Jabotinsky in 1935.

70. "Offener Brief an Miss Szold," undated (likely August 1939), signed by Elchanan Eger, *Medina Ivrit*, CZA S75/298, CZA S75/858.

71. See speech by Eva Stern titled "Die Tätigkeit der Arbeitsgemeinschaft der Kinder- und Jugend-Alijah," in *Bericht über die Erste Jugend-Alijah-Weltkonferenz, Amsterdam 9–12 September 1935* (Berlin, n.d.), 6–7.

72. Minister of the Interior Adolf Wagner insisted that new legislative steps had to be taken due to the demands by a majority of the population for more anti-Jewish laws, Friedländer, *Nazi Germany and the Jews*, 140.

73. Ibid., 140–41. According to David Bankier, relying on his study of Gestapo reports, the impact of this legislation on Jews' decisions to emigrate remains debatable, "Jewish Society through Nazi Eyes, 1933–1936," *Holocaust and Genocide Studies* 6, no. 2 (1991,): 116. The statistical evidence, however, at least as an initial response, reflects a heightened desire to leave Germany.

74. Margaliot, "Teguvat Mosdoteyhah," 111. See also, "Teguvat ha-Tzibur ha-Yehudi be-Germanyah le-Chokei Nuremberg," *Kovetz Yad Vashem* 12 (1978): 55–76; "Excerpts from Hitler's Speech in the Reichstag," in *Documents on the Holocaust*, 81.

75. Sidney Bolkosky, *The Distorted Image: German Jewish Perceptions of Germans and Germany, 1918–1935* (New York, 1975), 175–76.

76. Kulka, *Deutsches Judentum*, 237.

77. Quoted in Margaliot, "Teguvat Mosdoteyhah," 142–43.

78. Jüdische Jugendhilfe circular, to Bezirkstellen für Berufsausbildung (undated, likely September or October 1935), CZA S75/50.

79. Case history recorded June 6, 1938, CZA S75/774.

80. Niederland, *Yehudei Germanyah*, 33, 35.

81. Central Bureau for the Settlement of German Jews in Palestine, *Report to the Twentieth Zionist Congress and to the Council of the Jewish Agency in Zurich* (Jerusalem, 1937). The report shows a youth immigration figure of 1,650 for 1935–37 compared to 612 for 1933–35.

82. Josephthal to Szold, January 23, 1936, CZA S75/116.

83. Gross, "1932–1937," in *Sefer Aliyat Ha-No'ar*, 94. In an attempt to ascertain the cause of the 1936 disturbances, Great Britain appointed the Peel Commission to study the issue. The commission submitted its findings in 1937 and recommended the separation of Palestine into autonomous Jewish and Arab regions.

84. Ibid., 95.

85. Jüdische Jugendhilfe Rundschreiben Nr. 4, March 23, 1936, CZA S75/144.

86. Yocheved Bat-Rachel, "Tachat ha-Magaf ha-Nazi," in *Sefer Aliyat Ha-No'ar*, 151–52.

87. David Kaelter, "Das jüdische Schulwerk in Deutschland nach 1933," *Bulletin des Leo Baeck Instituts* 2/3 (1958): 87; Margaliot, "Teguvat Mosdoteyhah" 112; Niederland, *Yehudei Germanyah*, 197–99, 208–21.

88. Bat-Rachel, "Tachat ha-Magaf," in *Sefer Aliyat Ha-No'ar*, 150; Schatzker, *No'ar Yehudi*, 277.

89. Case history, CZA S75/1071.

90. Rundschreiben des Schulabteilung der Reichsvertretung, March 16, 1936, LBIJ 557/2.

91. Undated handwritten notes by Recha Freier titled *batei-hechaluz* (Hebrew original), 1–2, CZA A256/4/5.

92. Ibid., 9–10, 12.

93. Arbeitsgemeinschaft *Postbericht,* May 4–6 and June 1–3, 1935, CZA S75/78.

94. Ibid., September 15, 1936, CZA S75/187.

95. Minutes of Jüdische Jugendhilfe meeting in Berlin, September 24, 1935, CZA S75/152. Szold expressed a similar attitude regarding a questionable case in 1936 writing, "if this girl causes any trouble she will be returned to Germany," Szold to Jüdische Jugendhilfe, April 27, 1936, CZA S75/146.

96. Undated report (likely December 1935) by Youth Aliyah, Jerusalem, copied to Jüdische Jugendhilfe, CZA S75/50.

97. Kitzinger to Beyth, January 6, 1936, CZA S75/289.

98. Edgar Freund to Szold, March 30, 1936, CZA S75/144.

99. Schatzker, *No'ar Yehudi*, 295; Röcher, *Die Jüdische Schule*, 136–37, 161–62.

100. Jüdische Jugendhilfe circular to Bezirkstellen für Berufsausbildung, December 9, 1935, CZA S75/50.

101. Berufsumschichtung und Berufsausbildung, found in, CZA S6/1907.

102. Grete Kitzinger, "Jugendalijah," *JWuS* 5, Heft 5 (September–October 1935): 165.

103. Ibid., 167.

104. Rahel Wischnitzer-Bernstein, "Der Film der Jugend-Alijah," excerpt from *Jüdischen Gemeindeblatt,* May 31, 1936, p. 20, appended to Arbeitsgemeinschaft *Postbericht,* June 5, 1936, CZA S75/188.

105. A simple translation of this title does not suffice as it can be read at a number of levels. A basic translation could be *Departure of Youth,* demonstrating the departure from Germany; additionally *Aufbruch* can mean "start," emphasizing the new beginning of a life in Palestine. Yet the word also connotes a literal "breaking out," which can be understood as young pioneers breaking free from the chains of traditional diaspora existence and working for a renaissance of Jewish life in the land of Israel.

106. Wischnitzer-Bernstein, CZA S75/188. See also "Veranstaltung der Kinder- und Jugend-Alijah," *CV-Zeitung,* May 27, 1936.

107. Letters dated November 4, 1935, March 19 and 24, 1936, summarized in document titled "Youth Aliyah in Letters," CZA A440/Box 2.

108. Letter signed by Stern and Hahn-Warburg, September 1936, CZA S75/190.

109. Gross, "1932–1937," in *Sefer Aliyat Ha-No'ar*, 96.

110. See *JWuS* 5, Heft 5 (September–October 1935).

111. Georg Josephthal, "Die Berufsfrage der jüdischen Jugend," in *Gemeinschafts-arbeit der jüdischen Jugend,* 43.

112. See "A Description by Franz and Ruth Ollendorf of the Youth Aliyah School in Berlin," in Freier, *Let the Children Come,* 95. According to Yocheved Bat-Rachel, Youth Aliyah often assisted children of mixed marriages, *Ba-Nativ she-Halachti,* 160.

113. Adelyn Bonin, *Allegiances* (Santa Barbara, 1993), 36–42.

114. Ibid., 43.

115. Ibid., 50; Bat-Rachel, "Tachat ha-Magaf," in *Sefer Aliyat Ha-No'ar,* 149.

116. Hans Beyth to Jüdische Jugendhilfe, November 5, 1936, CZA S75/145.

117. Szold to Kitzinger, September 29, 1937, CZA S75/298. Szold wrote that she was approached in this regard by the Mizrachi member of the Jewish Agency Executive, Rabbi Fischman. "I told Rav Fischman that we had already begun our inquiries, what our method of choice of candidates was in view of the form of our questionnaires and that in many cases the religious proclivities of given boys and girls are hidden because the fear is harbored that unless they took the first opportunity presented for coming to Palestine, they might be deprived of the privilege. To [the Jugendhilfe], however, I must say that unless in any cases in which a doubt arises a member of the Religious Committee is present when the question is put regarding religious proclivities, nothing avails to demonstrate our fairness in the matter . . . the desire to secure the privilege of emigration may outweigh all other considerations."

118. Ibid.

119. Beyth to Jüdische Jugendhilfe, December 24, 1935, CZA S75/50. Rejection of Orthodox institutions also arose as a result of the ambiguous term "religious." Whereas devout Liberal Jews in Germany might reject the nonreligious tendencies of most kibbutzim, they would nevertheless feel uncomfortable in an Orthodox institution, which was really the only religious option available in Palestine.

120. Henrietta Szold, *Five Years of Youth Immigration into Palestine, 1934–1939* (Jerusalem, 1939), 35. "The circumstance that the supply of religious places in Palestine falls below the demand in Germany has influenced parents and their children to conceal the desire for the traditional Jewish life. They fear that they may lose the chance of redemption. Religious young people thus find themselves in radical surroundings, the subsequent removal from which presents almost insurmountable obstacles."

121. See chapter 5.

122. "Ha-Hachsharah ha-Tze'irah be-Schniebinchen," *Alim* 25 Nisan 5700 (May 3, 1940), quoted in *Livnot u-Lehibanot.* 201.

123. Bat-Rachel, *Ba-Nativ she-Halachti,* 182.

124. Bat-Rachel, "Tachat ha-Magaf," in *Sefer Aliyat Ha-No'ar,* 151–52.

125. Bat-Rachel, *Ba-Nativ she-Halachti,* 144–45, 183, 189.

126. Letter from Lea to her friend Hannah, April 10, 1936, included in "Youth Aliyah in Letters," CZA A440/Box 2.

127. Szold to Arbeitsgemeinschaft, May 19, 1936, CZA S75/189.

128. Szold to Kitzinger, July 5, 1937, CZA S75/296.

129. Bat-Rachel, *Ba-Nativ she-Halachti*, 144–50.

130. "Hehalutz in Germany from 1933 to 1938," in Halpern and Wurm, *The Responsible Attitude*, 96.

131. Central Bureau for the Settlement of German Jews in Palestine, *Report to the Twenty-first Zionist Congress and to the Council of the Jewish Agency for Palestine in Geneva* (Jerusalem, 1939), 46. The following table provides the average rate of exchange received by Ha'avara clients:

Year	Percentage of Reichsmark Holdings
1934–35	80.0–85.0
1936	73.0
1937	62.5
1938 (1st half)	62.0
1938 (2nd half)	48.5
1939 (1st half)	33.3

Compare to exchange figures for those who immigrated to other countries, see n. 133 below.

132. Sperrkonto zur Verwendung im Inlande.

133. Central Bureau, *Report to the Twenty-first Zionist Congress*, 46. The following table provides Sperrmark exchange rates:

Year	Average Rate of Exchange (in percentages)
1935	37.70
1936	26.80
1937	20.38
1938	10.83
1939 (first half)	6.50

134. Arbeitsgemeinschaft *Postbericht*, February 22–28, 1936, CZA S75/188.

135. Beyth to Landauer, January 2, 1936, CZA S75/259; Ilse Caro to Ernst Simon, February 15, 1936, CZA S75/260.

136. Arbeitsgemeinschaft *Postbericht*, February 1–8, 1936, CZA S75/188.

137. Article titled "Tee der Kinder-Alijah," reprinted in Arbeitsgemeinschaft *Postbericht*, February 15–21, 1936, CZA S75/188.

138. Josephthal to Merkaz Hechaluz, November 1936, quoted in *Livnot u-Lehibanot*. 206.

139. *Report on the Second Youth Aliyah Conference (Including Financial Report), Zurich August 23 to 25, 1937* (Berlin, n.d.), 15–18.

140. Bat-Rachel, *Ba-Nativ she-Halachti*, 161.

141. Stern to Landauer, November 2, 1937, CZA S75/506.

142. Protocol of January 6, 1936, meeting of Arbeitsgemeinschaft, CZA S75/191.

143. Report by Arthur Hantke on meeting with Stern, May 18, 1936, CZA S75/129.

144. Letter from group leaders Rachel and Heinz, December 20, 1935, included in "Youth Aliyah in Letters," CZA A440/Box 2.

CHAPTER 4

1. "Interview with Youth Aliyah Representative from Austria—Strictly Confidential," undated (likely November 1938), CZA S75/774.

2. Avraham Barkai, "The Fateful Year 1938: The Continuation and Acceleration of Plunder," in *November 1938: From "Reichskristallnacht" to Genocide,* ed. Walter H. Pehle (Oxford: Berg, 1991), 95–97, noted the significance of this period in terms of economic policy vis-à-vis the Jews. Schleunes, *Twisted Road,* 214, noted that the winter of 1937–38 saw the removal of the last moderate voices in positions of authority within the German government and their replacement by uncompromising National Socialists. He further remarked that during the course of 1938 Hitler centralized control over Jewish policy (216). In his study of the Reichsvertretung, Otto Dov Kulka used March 1938 as a chronological dividing point, *Deutsches Judentum,* 24.

3. Bruce Pauley, *Hitler and the Forgotten Nazis: A History of Austrian National Socialism* (Chapel Hill, 1981), 16–31, 225. On German and Austrian anti-Semitism, see Pulzer, *Political Anti-Semitism;* John Weiss, in *The Ideology of Death: Why the Holocaust Happened in Germany* (Chicago, 1996), repeatedly stressed the importance of Austrian alongside German anti-Semitism in understanding why the Holocaust happened in Germany.

4. George Berkley, *Vienna and Its Jews: The Tragedy of Success, 1880s–1980s* (Cambridge, Mass., 1988), 259.

5. Jonny Moser, "Die Katastrophe," 109–11; Gertrude Schneider, *Exile and Destruction: The Fate of Austrian Jews, 1938–1945* (Westport, Conn., 1995), 16–17.

6. Gerhard Botz, "The Jews of Vienna," 185–89; Berkley, *Vienna and Its Jews,* 259.

7. Schneider, *Exile and Destruction,* 15.

8. Case history recorded December 2, 1938, CZA S75/774.

9. Arthur Ruppin, *Memoirs, Diaries, Letters,* ed. Alex Bein (New York, 1971), 293.

10. According to Kulka, the text for this law along with other enactments had been prepared prior to the Anschluss, *Deutsches Judentum,* 383.

11. Schattner, "Al P'nei Eiropa ha-Mesu'eret," in *Sefer Aliyat ha-No'ar,* 161.

12. Berkley, *Vienna and Its Jews,* 266.

13. Correspondence between Vienna and Szold, March and April 1938, CZA S75/627; April 8, 1938, edition of *Selbstwehr,* Prague, 1.

14. Josephthal to Szold, April 22, 1938, and Ritter, Hechaluz, Vienna, to Georg Landauer, July 9, 1938, CZA S75/627.

15. Josephthal to Szold, April 22, 1938, CZA S75/627.

16. Vienna Hechaluz to Youth Aliyah, Jerusalem, May 19, 1938, CZA S75/627.

17. Testimony by Yehuda Brott [Juda Weissbrod], YVA 03/3912. See also Beyth to Jüdische Jugendhilfe, May 25, 1938, CZA S75/462.

18. Vienna Hechaluz to Youth Aliyah, May 19, 1938, Jerusalem, CZA S75/627.

19. "Interview with a Youth Aliyah Representative in Austria," undated (likely November 1938), CZA S75/816.

20. See articles in *JR* (April 7, 1933; April 5, 1934; March 15, 1935; March 6, 1936; March 2, 1937).

21. "322 Jugend-Alija-Zertifikate," *Gemeindeblatt der Deutsch-Israelitischen Gemeinde zu Hamburg,* March 11, 1938, 6; "Zur Schulentlassung," *JR* (March 4, 1938): 7.

22. See, for example, the case of Privaten Waldschule Kaliski's *Palästina-Gruppe* in Werner Fölling, *Zwischen deutscher und jüdischer Identität: Eine jüdische Reformschule in Berlin zwischen 1932 und 1939* (Opladen, 1995), 181–85.

23. Memo or press release from the Arbeitsgemeinschaft titled, "Die neue Einwanderung-Schedule: Jugend-Alijah-Zertifikate Unbegrenzt," undated, CZA S6/3359; "Jugend nach Palästina: Aus der Arbeit der Jüdischen Jugendhilfe," *JR* (July 26, 1938): 7; "800 Jugend nach Palästina: Die Zertifikatszahl des Sommer-Halbjahres," *JR* (August 16, 1938): 1.

24. Beyth, "1937–1941," in *Sefer Aliyat Ha-No'ar,* 97–98.

25. Undated Eva Michaelis-Stern report, CZA S75/506. "Sie sind so daran gewöhnt, in einer feindlich gesinnten Umgebung zu leben, dass es oft einer wochenlangen Erziehung bedarf, bis sie wieder zum Sprechen und zu einer vertrauensvollen Unterhaltung veranlasst werden können."

26. Case history recorded June 1, 1938, CZA S75/774.

27. Memorandum dated June 1, 1938, CZA S75/439.

28. Gaertner, "Problems of Jewish Schools," 139; Hilde David to Beyth, June 2, 1938, CZA S75/627.

29. Robert Weltsch [then in Prague] to Landauer, June 1, 1938, CZA S75/627.

30. Ruth Kluger, *Still Alive: A Holocaust Girlhood Remembered* (New York, 2001), 57.

31. Viktor Kellner, director of the Chajesrealgymnasium, to Werner Senator, June 30, 1938, CZA S75/627. "Briefe aus Palaestina beweisen mir immer wieder, wie unzureichend die Vorstellung ist, die man unserer Lage hat, wie wenig man begreift, in welchem Ausmass und in welchem Tempo sich der Prozess der Liquidation der oesterreichischen Judentums vollzieht."

32. Edelheit, *Yishuv in the Shadow of the Holocaust,* 180–81.

33. "The Situation of the Jews in Austria, April, 1938," in *Documents on the Holocaust,* 92–93. "A clear policy with regard to the Jewish problem in Austria has neither been announced in public, nor was it conveyed to us in the few interviews we succeeded in having. One cannot, however, avoid the impression that this policy will be essentially different from that adopted in Germany and that it may aim at a complete annihilation of Austrian Jewry" (92–93).

34. YVA 03/3912.

35. Hilde David to Beyth, June 21, 1938, CZA S75/632. The Mandatory government only permitted general Youth Aliyah certificates to the "open" settlements to Jewish youth from Germany or German-controlled lands.

36. Beyth to Chaim Hoffman, September 30, 1938, CZA S75/632.

37. Beyth, "1937–1941," in *Sefer Aliyat Ha-No'ar,* 98; Chaim Hoffman, "Mah Karah be-Czechoslovakia," in *Sefer Aliyat ha-Noar,* 169; Fini Brada, "Emigration to Palestine," in *The Jews of Czechoslovakia: Historical Studies and Surveys* (Philadelphia, 1971), 2:592.

38. This *Irgun* expanded its activity following the establishment of a German *Protektorat* in Bohemia and Moravia and an independent satellite state in Slovakia.

39. "Tasks of a Jewish Youth Leader," in Halpern and Wurm, *The Responsible Attitude*, 63.

40. Beyth to Landauer, April 18, 1938, CZA S75/438.

41. The first transports to arrive at the border were permitted to enter, but Polish guards soon closed the border. Trude Maurer, "The Background for Kristallnacht: The Expulsion of Polish Jews," in Pehle, *November 1938*, 61.

42. Case history recorded 1939, CZA S75/1109.

43. Helga Krohn, "Aus dem Israelitischen Waisenhaus in Frankfurt nach Palästina—eine dramatische Rettungsaktion," *Schriftenreihe des jüdischen Museums Frankfurt am Main* 3 (1995): 23–24. I. Giterman, American Joint Distribution Committee, Warsaw, to American Joint Distribution Committee, Paris, December 7, 1938, in American Jewish Joint Distribution Committee, *American Jewish Joint Distribution Committee, New York*, pt. 1, vol. 10 of *Archives of the Holocaust: An International Collection of Selected Documents*, ed. Sybil Milton and Frederick D. Bogin (New York and London, 1995), 517–21.

44. Unsigned article from *Hanoar Haoleh*, 1940, reprinted in *Sefer Aliyat Ha-No'ar*, 363–64.

45. Irma Landesdorf to Werner Senator, November 29, 1938, CZA S75/719.

46. Children and Youth Aliyah, *Freedom and Work for Jewish Youth: Report for the Third World Youth Aliyah Conference* (London, 1939), 12. See also ICJOHP, interview with Yocheved Bat-Rachel, May 5, 1966; Beyth to Jüdische Jugendhilfe, December 5, 1938; and Devorah Feldman, Ayelet Ha-Shachar, to Youth Aliyah Office, Jerusalem, March 1939, CZA S75/714.

47. Case history recorded December 2, 1938, CZA S75/774.

48. Ibid.

49. Document titled "A War Story with a Happy Ending," by Anita Engle, CZA S75/1071.

50. David to Beyth, October 27, 1938, CZA S75/686.

51. "First Attempt of the Nazi Party to Expel Viennese Jewry, October, 1938," in *Documents on the Holocaust*, 101–2.

52. Testimony of Ze'ev Willy Ritter, YVA 03/3982. Ritter was general secretary of Vienna Hechaluz.

53. For detailed accounts of the November pogrom, see Wolfgang Benz, "The Relapse into Barbarism," in Pehle, *November 1938*, 1–43; Hermann Graml, *Reichskristallnacht: Antisemitismus und Judenverfolgung im Dritten Reich* (Munich, 1988); *Nazism, 1919–1945: A History in Documents and Eyewitness Accounts*, ed. Jeremy Noakes and Geoffrey Pridham (New York, 1990), 1:553–60; *Documents on the Holocaust*, 102–7.

54. Statistics on arrests vary: 20,000, based on a report prepared by the Nazi Party Supreme Court, in *Nazism*, 1:554; 25,000, in Schleunes, *Twisted Road*, 239; 30,000, in Pehle, *November 1938*, vii. The murder statistics vary as well. *Nazism*, 1:554, referring to the supreme court report estimated number of dead at 91, whereas Heydrich referred to 34 Jews killed in the pogrom, in Schleunes, *Twisted Road*, 242.

55. The following account is supported by "Report of the Youth Aliyah Work during the Past Few Months in Berlin," (undated), CZA S75/686.

56. Ibid.

57. Werner Angress, *Between Fear and Hope: Jewish Youth in the Third Reich* (New York, 1988), 25, noted that ninety-four training centers preparing young Jews for emigration operated in Germany in September 1938. By the end of that year only sixty-one sites continued to function; the remainder had fallen victim to the pogrom.

58. Again the evidence reflects the unpredictable nature of Nazi actions, and also demonstrates that vague orders from higher authorities elicited varied responses from local Nazi leaders. Maurer, "Background for Kristallnacht," 56–60, noted this same phenomenon with regard to the deportation of Polish Jews in late October.

59. "Report of the Youth Aliyah Work during the Past Few Months in Berlin," (dated November 10, but obviously written later), CZA S75/686.

60. Case history recorded December 2, 1938, CZA S75/774.

61. "Report of the Youth Aliyah Work during the Past Few Months in Berlin." The Berlin office of Youth Aliyah was sealed off by the Gestapo, thus they were surprised to learn that work continued as before in Vienna, CZA S75/686.

62. Kurt Goldmann, "le-Achar ha-Tish'i be-November," in *Sefer Aliyat ha-Noar,* 159.

63. Report on work of Vienna *Beratungsstelle,* written in London, December 28, 1938, CZA S75/860.

64. Hedwig Eppstein to Stern, November 25, 1938, CZA S75/739, and Children and Youth Aliyah, *Freedom and Work for Jewish Youth,* 18.

65. Noack to Beratungsstelle der Jugendalijah, August 28, 1938, CZA S75/628.

66. Dina Porat, *Blue and Yellow Stars,* 245.

67. Report by Kurt Goldmann, May 1, 1939, CZA S75/687.

68. Szold to Goldmann, January 19, 1939, CZA S75/759.

69. "Schniebinchen," in *Sefer Aliyat ha-No'ar,* 155–56, reprinted from *Alim,* May 3, 1940.

70. Hilde David to Szold, November 21, 1938, CZA S75/686.

71. "Schniebinchen," in *Sefer Aliyat Ha-No'ar,* 156.

72. Ibid.

73. Nicosia, *Third Reich and Palestine,* 144, 266, noted the government's waning enthusiasm for Ha'avara from early 1938 to 1939 and cited the decreasing levels of Jewish capital transferred to Palestine during those years.

74. Hedwig Eppstein to Eva Michaelis, February 27, 1939, CZA S75/641.

75. Szold to Goldmann, June 6, 1939, CZA S75/687.

76. "Informationsrundschreiben an alle Mitarbeiter der Jüdischen Jugendhilfe E.V.," May 10, 1939, 3, CZA S75/687.

77. Perez Leshem, *Strasse zur Rettung: 1933–1939 Aus Deutschland Vertrieben— Bereitet sich jüdische Jugend auf Palästina vor* (Tel Aviv, 1973), 23.

78. Jewish immigration to Palestine was sharply curtailed while the British government prepared the 1939 white paper that would limit total Jewish immigration to seventy-five thousand over the next five years. Even as Great Britain sheltered many young Jews as the need for refuge increased (becoming even more intense as greater numbers of Jews came under Nazi control after the outbreak of the war), the possibilities for legal immigration to Palestine decreased.

79. Karen Gershon, *We Came as Children: A Collective Autobiography* (New York, 1966), 22, 26.

80. Amy Zahn Gottlieb, *Men of Vision: Anglo-Jewry's Aid to Victims of the Nazi Regime, 1933–1945* (London, 1998), 112. This situation contrasts effectively with descriptions of Freier's first groups departing for Ben Shemen in 1932. Kadosh, "Ideology vs. Reality," 22.

81. Cable received by Moshe Shertok from "Joseph" (likely Josephthal), November 17, 1938, A125/102.

82. Szold to Landauer, November 18, 1938, CZA A125/102. "I am appalled by the plan proposed. I remind you . . . that the sum needed for the erection and staffing of an educational institution is far beyond our powers to secure; that the care of several thousand children requires still larger sums; that the adoption of several thousand children is a process so involved, from the point of view of the search for the prospective parents, and from the point of view of the necessary negotiations with the natural parents that it staggers me."

83. "Informationsrundschreiben an alle Mitarbeiter der Jüdischen Jugendhilfe E.V.," May 10, 1939, 4, CZA S75/687.

84. Goldmann to Szold, April 24, 1939, CZA S75/686. The Jugendhilfe in Berlin calculated that about twice as many young Jews were living in the Altreich as in Austria. Though the Jewish populations of the *Protektorat* and Slovakia were about equal, the Jewish youth in Slovakia had stronger numbers. Goldmann suggested the following breakdown for certificates: Germany, 45 percent; Austria, 25 percent; *Protektorat*, 15 percent; and Slovakia, 15 percent.

85. "Materialien zur Irgun-Sitzung," May 24–25, 1939, CZA S75/687.

86. Report by Recha Freier, including protocol of Irgun, May 30 and 31, 1939, CZA S75/687. "The only rescue for the ten thousands, for whom we are responsible, is and remains, *Eretz Israel.* Any attempt to block this final hope of ours must fail. Together with Jewish youth of the world, we will overcome all hindrances to make our way to *Aliyah.*" This passage clearly demonstrates Freier's passion, but also exemplifies her oft-noted impractical single-mindedness.

87. Bela Vago, "Some Aspects of the *Yishuv* Leadership's Activities during the Holocaust," in *Jewish Leadership during the Nazi Era: Patterns of Behavior in the Free World,* ed. Randolph L. Braham (New York, 1985), 46.

88. Beyth to Jüdische Jugendhilfe, August 2, 1939, CZA S75/721.

89. Goldmann to Beyth, August 14, 1939, CZA S75/721.

90. Report by Freier, May 30 and 31, 1939, CZA S75/687. The fact that many Jewish refugees were housed by non-Jews remains a contentious issue in the United Kingdom.

91. Vago, "Some Aspects of the *Yishuv* Leadership's Activities," 47–48. This statement must be recognized as rhetorical, made without knowledge of the ultimate catastrophe that engulfed European Jewry.

92. Michaelis-Stern, "Erinnerungen," 64; Beyth, "1937–1941," in *Sefer Aliyat Ha-No'ar,* 99.

92. Schattner, "Al P'nei Eiropa," in *Sefer Aliyat Ha-No'ar,* 164. Judith Tydor-Baumel, "Ba-Derech la-Aretz ha-Bechirah: Aliyat ha-No'ar ve-ha-Yeladim ha-Plitim bi-Britaniah bi-Milchemet ha-'Olam ha-Shniyah," *Masu'ah* 12 (1984), 71.

94. Baratz to Szold, December 16, 1938, CZA S75/718. Hebrew Original.

95. Children and Youth Aliyah, *Freedom and Work for Jewish Youth*, 18.

96. Schattner, "Al P'nei Eiropa," in *Sefer Aliyat Ha-No'ar*, 162.

97. Goldmann, "le-Achar ha-Tish'i be-November," in *Sefer Aliyat Ha-No'ar*, 160.

98. Untitled report by Kurt Goldmann on work of Jüdische Jugendhilfe, May 1, 1939, CZA S75/687.

99. "Informationsrundschreiben an alle Mitarbeiter der Jüdischen Jugendhilfe E.V.," May 10, 1939, 4, CZA S75/687.

100. Jewish Agency for Palestine, *Political Report of the Executive of the Jewish Agency Submitted to the Twenty-First Zionist Congress and the Sixth Session of the Council of the Jewish Agency at Geneva, August, 1939* (Jerusalem, 1939), 53.

101. Szold to Greenberg, April 2, 1938, YAA 10/46.

102. Szold to Edwin Samuel, June 30, 1939, CZA S75/717.

103. Szold to Samuel, July 17, 1939, CZA S75/717. I could not determine whether Lotte was ever brought to Palestine on a labor certificate or where she went after receiving the order to leave France.

104. A. Reifenberg, Palästina-Amt, to Beyth, July 24, 1939, CZA S75/687. At this point Nazi functionaries focused their attention on emigration of poor Jews, who represented a burden on the economy, and also targeted capitalists in order to facilitate the expropriation of property.

105. Beyth to Reifenberg, August 10, 1939, CZA S75/687.

106. See, for example, letters between Hans Beyth and the Jüdische Jugendhilfe, CZA S75/718.

107. Devorah Feldman, Ayelet Ha-Shachar, to Youth Aliyah Office, Jerusalem, March 1939; Memo from Dora Strauss-Weigert, April 5, 1939, CZA S75/714. Beyth to Jüdische Jugendhilfe, December 2, 1938; Szold to Juda Weisbrod, December 16, 1938, CZA S75/715; undated Beyth to Schattner, CZA S75/712.

108. Beyth to Jüdische Jugendhilfe, June 1, 1939. Telegram from Szold to Jugendhilfe, June 6, 1939, both in CZA S75/716.

109. Beyth to Jüdische Jugendhilfe, August 7, 1939, CZA S75/716.

110. See Idith Zertal, *Zehavam shel ha-Yehudim: ha-Hagirah ha-Yehudit ha-Machtartit le-Eretz Yisrael, 1945–1948* (Tel Aviv, 1996), and Yosef Grodzinski, *Chomer Enoshi Tov: Yehudim mul Tzionim, 1945–1951* (Jerusalem, 1998). Porat, *Blue and Yellow Stars*, 245.

111. Sara Loewenthal, Jüdische Jugendhilfe, to Beyth, January 3, 1939.

112. Szold to Goldmann, August 17, 1939, CZA S75/687.

113. Beyth, "1937–1941," in *Sefer Aliyat Ha-No'ar*, 101; Leni Yahil, *Hatzalat ha-Yehudim be-Deniah—Demokratiah she-Amdah ba-Mivchan* (Jerusalem, 1967), 16.

114. Goldmann, "le-Achar ha-Tish'i be-November," in *Sefer Aliyat Ha-No'ar*, 160; Goldmann to Szold, July 27, 1939, CZA S75/687.

CHAPTER 5

1. Freier, *Let the Children Come*, 18. Hapoel Hamizrachi was the pioneer wing of the Orthodox Zionist movement and emerged as a distinct party from the parent Mizrachi.

2. Document dated August 27, 1933, from *Va'ad le-hachsharat ha-no'ar ha-dati me-germanyah be-eretz yisrael* (unspecified recipient), CZA S75/12.

3. Rodges, founded by *olim* from Germany, seemed the ideal location to host religious Youth Aliyah groups. See Yossi Katz, *Torah ve-Avodah be-Vinyan ha-Aretz: Ha-Kibbutz Ha-Dati be-Tekufat ha-Mandat* (Ramat Gan, 1996).

4. Freier to Ernst Simon, undated (1933), CZA S75/159.

5. Jüdische Jugendhilfe to de Beer, December 6, 1933, refers to a letter dated November 29 and a telegram dated December 4 from de Beer criticizing Jugendhilfe's decision. See also Kommittee für Ausbildung deutscher religiöser Jugend in Erez Jisrael to Landauer, November 23, 1933, CZA S75/12.

6. Thus the Mizrachi party adopted an antilabor position in 1933 and refused to join the governing coalition of the World Zionist Organization. See Shabtai Teveth, *Ben-Gurion: The Burning Ground, 1886–1948* (Boston, 1987), 446.

7. Quite likely the explicit support for Orthodox institutions reflected the dominant position of Orthodoxy within British Judaism. On the history of the Central British Fund, see Gottlieb, *Men of Vision.*

8. Anita Müller Cohen to Szold, November 1933, CZA S75/12. Disregarding capital investments, the average maintenance cost for religious youths was estimated to be 30 percent higher than average costs for nonreligious teens.

9. Szold to Hans Lubinski, December 19, 1933, CZA S75/12; Stern to Alexander Adler, Religious Committee, December 9, 1935, CZA S75/191.

10. Kommittee für Ausbildung deutscher religiöser Jugend in Erez Jisrael to Landauer, November 23, 1933, CZA S75/12.

11. The majority of German Jews identified religiously as Liberal. According to Mordechai Breuer, *Modernity within Tradition: The Social History of Orthodox Jewry in Imperial Germany* (New York, 1992), 397–98, the ratio of Jews identifying as Orthodox before 1933 can be estimated at somewhere between 10 and 20 percent. Michael Shashar, *Ke-Chalom Ya'of: Terumat Yehudei Germanyah le-Chayim ha-Dati'im be-Eretz Yisrael* (Jerusalem, 1997), 31, wrote that the figure never numbered more than 15 percent in the twentieth century.

12. Kitzinger to Beyth, February 25, 1937, CZA S75/417. See Bat-Rachel's description of Sabbath atmosphere in the Schniebinchen training camp in Bat-Rachel, "Tachat ha-Magaf ha-Nazi," in *Sefer Aliyat Ha-No'ar,* 149.

13. Letter from Gerd in Berlin, dated November 28, 1935, included in "Youth Aliyah in Letters," CZA A440/Box 2.

14. Schatzker, *No'ar Yehudi,* 298–99.

15. Adolf Arensfeld to Szold, December 25, 1938, CZA S75/697. Considering the difficulties in placing Orthodox groups in Palestine, Szold, on practical grounds, rejected this demand to find special accommodations for a "religious stream" within an otherwise homogeneous youth group, Szold to Arensfeld, January 17, 1939, CZA S75/697. Pinchas Rosenblüth, "Darcho shel ha-No'ar ha-Dati," in *Sefer Aliyat ha-No'ar,* 218.

16. Beyth to Jüdische Jugendhilfe, December 24, 1935, CZA S75/50.

17. Szold to Martin Rosenblüth, January 17, 1934, CZA S75/12; Jüdische Jugendhilfe to de Beer, December 6, 1933, CZA S75/12; DeBeer to Szold, December 24, 1933, CZA S75/12.

18. Kommittee für Ausbildung deutscher religiöser Jugend in Erez Jisrael to Landauer, November 23, 1933, CZA S75/12; see also Arbeitsausschuss für religiöse Jugend-Alija to Szold, March 14, 1933, CZA S75/12.

19. Szold to Arbeitsgemeinschaft, March 14, 1934, CZA S75/12.

20. Ibid., April 1, 1934, CZA S75/6; Szold to Müller-Cohen, March 4, 1934, CZA S75/12.

21. At the Nineteenth Zionist Congress, Zalman Rubishov recognized the importance of Youth Aliyah in being able to draw support from seemingly opposing factions, *Nineteenth Zionist Congress and the Fourth Sitting of the Council,* 173. An internal Arbeitsgemeinschaft memorandum, signed by Stern and Schattner dated August 27, 1934, reflects this attitude, saying, "Es ist unumgänglich notwendig, dass die Tatsache, dass durch die AG auch *religiöse Gruppen* und Investitionen finanziert werden, in weiten Kreisen des In- und Auslandes bekanntgemacht wird" (emphasis in original), CZA S75/17.

22. Arbeitsausschuß für religiöse Jugendalijah to Szold, March 14, 1934, CZA S75/12. Szold to Arbeitsgemeinschaft, March 22, 1934, CZA S75/16.

23. Landauer to Martin Rosenblüth, February 20, 1934, CZA S75/12, refers to a January 23 protest letter from "gesetztreuen Rabbinerverbandes."

24. Simonson to Szold, April 11, 1934, CZA A125/98.

25. Szold to Landauer, June 15, 1934, CZA A125/98.

26. Siegfried Ucko, Margot Altmann, and Ruth Ucko to Szold, March 10, 1935, CZA S75/45.

27. Szold to Landauer, June 15, 1934, CZA A125/98.

28. Central Bureau, *Report to the Nineteenth Zionist Congress,* 45. Even if one discounts the individuals brought in under the auspices of closed institutions, Orthodox Jews still received only 88 certificates out of 425.

29. S. Eliezer, "Bein Shki'ah le-Zerichah," in *Sefer Aliyat ha-No'ar,* 154.

30. Eva Stern, ed., *Jugend-Alijah* (Berlin, 1935), 17. "Durch körperliche Arbeit und gesunde Lebensweise verändern sich die jüdischen Typen."

31. In Haifa a religious group was apprenticed to an iron foundry; another group was enrolled in the trade school of the Haifa Technical Institute.

32. Schattner to Beyth, July 1935, CZA S75/75.

33. Gross, "1932–1937," in *Sefer Aliyat Ha-No'ar,* 92–95.

34. Szold to Olga Epstein, March 8, 1935, CZA A125/98. Szold to Rose Jacobs, April 21, 1936, CZA S75/160.

35. Simon to Robert Waley Cohen, August 9, 1936, CZA A125/98.

36. Herzog to Hertz, February 25, 1936, CZA S75/159. Even if these statistics were accurate for Frankfurt, which seems unlikely, they do not represent the outlook of the larger German Jewish community unless one differentiates between religious, which could include Liberal Judaism, and Orthodoxy.

37. Chief Rabbinate of Jaffa and Tel Aviv District to Szold, 7 Adar 5699 (February 26, 1939), CZA S75/697. Szold to Hertz, April 8, 1936, CZA S75/116, "I have the impression . . . that things have been grossly misinterpreted to you."

38. Möller to Beyth, October 22, 1935, CZA S75/159.

39. See exchange of letters between Szold and Religious Committee of Jüdische Jugendhilfe, November–December 1935, CZA S75/159.

40. Beyth, "1937–1941," in *Sefer Aliyat Ha-No'ar*, 98. This sum included a special donation of $15,000 from Hadassah, as well as more than $11,000 raised by Orthodox circles in Germany and transferred via Ha'avara.

41. Arbeitsgemeinschaft *Postbericht*, July 1 and July 9, 1935, CZA S75/78.

42. Stern to Alexander Adler, Religious Committee, December 9, 1935, CZA S75/191.

43. Beyth, "1937–1941," in *Sefer Aliyat Ha-No'ar*, 98–99; Children and Youth Aliyah, *Freedom and Work for Jewish Youth*, 14, 23; Central Bureau, *Report to the Twenty-first Zionist Congress*, 50–51.

44. Szold to Rose Jacobs, April 21, 1936, CZA A125/98.

45. Marion Greenberg to Michaelis-Stern, September 26, 1939, CZA S75/712.

46. Szold to Jüdische Jugendhilfe, January 20, 1935, and undated letter (likely January 30, 1935), CZA S75/43.

47. Szold to Jüdische Jugendhilfe, February 28, 1935, CZA S75/45.

48. Reinharz, "Hashomer Hazair in Nazi Germany," 335.

49. Marion Kaplan, *The Jewish Feminist Movement in Germany: The Campaigns of the Jüdischer Frauenbund, 1904–1938* (Westport, Conn., 1979).

50. Elfride Bergel-Gronemann, "Erinnerung einer Zionistin an Bertha Pappenheim," *Blätter des jüdischen Frauenbundes*, October 6–7, 1936; and testimony of Ottilie Schönewald in Monika Richarz, ed., *Jüdisches Leben in Deutschland: Selbstzeugnisse zur Sozialgeschichte, 1918–1945* (Stuttgart, 1982), 3:215.

51. Melinda Given Guttman, *The Enigma of Anna O.: A Biography of Bertha Pappenheim* (Wickford, R.I., 2000), 312.

52. Kaplan, *Jewish Feminist Movement*, 186.

53. Kaplan, *Between Dignity and Despair*, 138–39.

54. See Gillerman, "Crisis of the Jewish Family," 93.

55. On the widely recognized success of Hadassah, see Michael Berkowitz, *Western Jewry and the Zionist Project, 1914–1933* (Cambridge, 1997), 187–88.

56. Bat-Rachel, *Ba-Nativ she-Halachti*, 138.

57. Josephthal to Merkaz Hechalutz, in *Livnot u-Lehibanot*, 206.

58. Tom Segev, *One Palestine, Complete: Jews and Arabs under the Mandate* (New York, 2000), 229.

59. "113 Zertifikate für Deutschland," *JR* (November 11, 1932): 436.

60. "Arbeitsbericht des Zentralausschusses der Deutschen Juden für Hilfe und Aufbau," January 1–June 30, 1934, IfZ Fa 723/1, 6.

61. See "Vermischtes" section of *JR* (March 18, 1932): 108.

62. Kaplan, *Jewish Feminist Movement*, 169–84.

63. Kaplan, *Between Dignity and Despair*, 139–40. On Jewish women as victims, see Gisela Bock, "Ordinary Women in Nazi Germany: Perpetrators, Victims, Followers, and Bystanders," in *Women in the Holocaust*, ed. Dalia Ofer and Lenore J. Weitzman (New Haven, 1998), 85–100.

64. "Proposals of the Jewish Agency for Palestine for the Settlement of German Jews in Palestine, submitted to the Allocations Committee of the CBF," September 3, 1933, CZA S75/1.

65. "Palästina-Wirtschaftsblatt," *JR* (May 12, 1933): 193.

66. Deborah Bernstein, "Daughters of the Nation: Between the Public and Private Spheres in Pre-State Israel," in Judith Baskin, ed. *Jewish Women in Historical Perspective* (Detroit, 1998), 289.

67. "Die Mädchen aus Deutschland," *JR* (January 8, 1935): 3.

68. "Neue Ausbildungsmöglichkeiten," *Blätter des JFB* (April 1936): 15–16.

69. Kaplan, *Jewish Feminist Movement*, 173–181.

70. "Confidential Report," January 1935, CZA L13/57.

71. Untitled, undated (mid-1938) plan for Beth Sefer Lanoar Haoleh in Vienna, CZA S75/686.

72. Kaplan, *Between Dignity and Despair*, 117.

73. Ibid., 138–40.

74. Segev, *One Palestine*, 394.

75. "Although men and women immigrated to Palestine in similar numbers, two-thirds to 90 percent of all women came as dependents, as compared to 10 to 20 percent of all men. Labor permits, on the other hand, were allocated to over 50 percent of all men and only to 10 percent of the immigrant women," Bernstein, "Daughters of the Nation," 290.

76. Szold to Josephthal, August 6, 1934, CZA S75/7.

77. "Jugend-Alijah," *Blätter des jüdischen Frauenbundes*, July 1934, 8.

78. Ottilie Schönewald, "Erste Jugend-Alijah Konferenz in Amsterdam, 9–11. IX. 1935," *Blätter des JFB* (December 1935): 4–5.

79. Arbeitsgemeinschaft *Postbericht*, December 13–20, 1935, CZA S75/188.

80. Paula Fürst, "Die Schule als Vorbereitung für Palästina," *Blätter des JFB*, September 1935, 4–5.

81. Quoted in Guttman, *Enigma of Anna O.*, 316–17.

82. Arbeitsgemeinschaft *Postbericht*, November 24–December 4, 1936, CZA S75/333; Kaplan, *Between Dignity and Despair*, 115.

83. Koonz, "Courage and Choice," 285; Kaplan, *Between Dignity and Despair*, 115.

84. Hedwig Eppstein, "Vorbereitungsmöglichkeiten der weiblichen Jugend für Palästina," *Blätter des JFB* (February 1937): 8. See also 1938 issues from March 1, 8; May 6–7; June 11; July 12; August 10–12.

85. Minutes of Jüdische Jugendhilfe meeting in Berlin, September 16, 1935, CZA S75/152.

86. Nazi authorities even recognized the growing rift between these camps, Bankier, "Jewish Society through Nazi Eyes," 117.

87. See comments by Josephthal and Stern, Minutes of Arbeitsgemeinschaft Board of Directors Meeting, September 23, 1935, CZA S75/185, 1.

88. Arbeitsgemeinschaft *Postbericht*, July 15, 1935, CZA S75/188.

89. Minutes of Arbeitsgemeinschaft Board of Directors Meeting, September 23, 1935, CZA S75/185, 2–3.

90. Beyth, "1937–1941," in *Sefer Aliyat Ha-No'ar*, 99.

91. Socialists blamed Jabotinsky and Revisionism for the murder of Arlosoroff in 1933 and essentially barred their participation in the Zionist Congress that summer. In 1935 Jabotinsky finally broke completely from the official Zionist body and founded the New Zionist Organization.

92. Jüdische Jugendhilfe to Staatszionistische Organisation, June 8, 1936, CZA S75/149.

93. "Offener Brief an Miss Szold," CZA S75/298.

94. Szold to Jüdische Jugendhilfe and Arbeitsgemeinschaft, February 19, 1937, CZA S75/291.

95. Ibid.

96. Szold to Kitzinger, March 8, 1937, CZA S75/292.

97. Beyth to Jüdische Jugendhilfe, April 13, 1937, refers to letter dated March 25, in which this request was made, CZA S75/293.

98. Beyth referred to such work as *Aussenarbeit.* Beyth to Jüdische Jugendhilfe, April 13, 1937, CZA S75/293; and May 2, 1937, CZA S75/294.

99. Szold to Jüdische Jugendhilfe, May 13, 1937, CZA S75/294.

100. Szold to Beyth, August 28, 1939, CZA S75/858.

101. On Revisionist Zionism during the 1930s, see Francis Nicosia, "Revisionist Zionism in Germany (II): Georg Kareski and the Staatszionistische Organisation, 1933–1938," *LBIY* 32 (1987): 231–67.

102. Hechaluz actively worked to establish Youth Aliyah in Vienna and was strongly represented among those who would lead the movement.

103. Vienna Hechaluz to Youth Aliyah, Jerusalem, June 8, 1938, CZA S75/627.

104. Ibid.

105. "Sie haben in die Liste der Jugendalijah Muttersöhnchen zionistischen Advokaten und Aerzte aufgenommen und in den letzten Wochen in den Noar Hazioni eingetragen," Hechaluz Austria (illegible signature) to Hilde David, June 10, 1938, CZA S75/627.

106. Zionistischer Landesverband für Österreich to Landauer, July 7, 1938, CZA S75/627.

107. The difficulties of distribution reflected a widespread problem in the Zionist movement as a whole in that the competition for certificates was a constant source of mistrust and enmity, as Yehuda Brott recalled, "Wir wissen ganz genau, dass die Zertifikaten-Politik, nicht nur bei der Jugendalijah, sondern in der zionistischen Bewegung immer ein Punkt des Misstrauens von beiden Seiten war, und dass die Stellen, die die Zertifikate, ich will nicht sagen, verteilt haben, aber die Verteiligung genommen haben, immer parteiisch orientiert waren," YVA 03/3912.

108. Gat, "Miph'al Aliyat Ha-no'ar," 167.

109. Since the Revisionist youth group Betar had been disbanded by order of the Gestapo, the former members reorganized themselves, without changing their political orientation, under the name Barak.

110. Barak, Vienna, to Szold, August 17, 1938, CZA S75/628. Their request also seems well founded in that the Jewish Agency recognized the strength of Revisionist Zionism in Austria as opposed to Germany. An agreement was reached to give the New Zionist Organization 12 percent of the worker certificates set aside for Vienna, an achievement the Revisionists did not attain for potential German *olim,* CZA S6/3120.

111. Arbeitsgemeinschaft *Postbericht,* October 17–23, 1936, report by Levy-Stein and Preiss, CZA S75/333.

112. Comments by Lola Hahn-Warburg at meeting of small board of Arbeits-gemeinschaft, August 18, 1936, CZA S75/190, 4.

113. Stern to Beyth, October 18, 1935, CZA S75/191.

114. "Aktennotiz," May 22, 1936, CZA S75/189. Comments by Rose Jacobs at small board of Arbeitsgemeinschaft, August 18, 1936, CZA S75/190, 4. On tensions between Keren Hayesod and Hadassah, see Berkowitz, *Western Jewry*, 65–66, 187–89.

115. Report on fund-raising and relationship with Keren Hayesod, signed by Stern and Hahn-Warburg, January 13, 1936, CZA S75/116.

116. Report by Levi in Arbeitsgemeinschaft *Postbericht*, March 28, 1935, CZA S75/78.

117. Ilse Wechsler reported this phenomenon for Essen. See Arbeitsgemein-schaft *Postbericht*, March 30–April 1, 1935, CZA S75/78.

118. Report of meeting between Stern, Hahn-Warburg, and Adler-Rudel, for Youth Aliyah, and Michael Traub and Rachel Holder of Keren Hayesod, January 17, 1936, CZA S75/116.

119. Report by Stern and Hahn-Warburg, January 13, 1936, CZA S75/116.

120. Rau to Jewish Agency, September 25, 1935, CZA S6/3359.

121. Arbeitsgemeinschaft *Postbericht*, February 16, 1937, CZA S75/333. Stern to Marion Greenberg, YAA 1/4.

122. Arbeitsgemeinschaft *Postbericht*, July 13, 1937, CZA S75/333.

123. Ibid., October 20 and November 5, 1937, CZA S75/508.

124. Undated document (probably September 1933) titled "Proposals of the Jewish Agency for Palestine for the Settlement of German Jews in Palestine, Submitted to the Allocations Committee of the Central British Fund for German Jewry," CZA S75/35; S75/1.

125. Adler-Rudel, "Ten Years Youth Aliyah," CZA A140/203.

126. Landauer to Louis Lipsky, July 12, 1934, CZA S75/17 (German original).

EPILOGUE

1. Case history recorded in April 1940, CZA S75/1109.

2. *Aliyat Ha-No'ar: Korot ha-Miph'al*, 25–26; Kadosh, "Ideology vs. Reality," 329–49.

3. Michaelis-Stern, "Erinnerungen," 64–65.

4. Gelber, "Origins of Youth Aliya," 171; Chaim Schatzker, "The Role of Aliyat Hanoar in the Rescue, Absorption, and Rehabilitation of Refugee Children," in *She'erit Hapletah, 1944–1948: Rehabilitation and Political Struggle*, ed. Yisrael Gutman and Avital Saf (Jerusalem, 1990), 370–87.

5. Case history recorded December 2, 1938, CZA S75/774.

6. Schwersenz, *Die versteckte Gruppe*, 50.

7. Jewish Agency for Israel, *Youth Aliyah: Statistical Abstract, 1933–1983* (Jerusalem, 1984), 4.

8. Arnold Paucker and Konrad Kwiet, "Jewish Leadership and Jewish Resistance," in *Probing the Depths of German Antisemitism: German Society and the Persecution of the Jews, 1933–1941*, ed. David Bankier (New York, 2000), 379. Sandra

Kadosh stated in her doctoral dissertation: "Unfortunately, there were many deficiencies in Youth Aliyah's response to the Holocaust. The Youth Aliyah leadership in Palestine failed to realize the extent of the tragedy in Europe, and showed little flexibility in adjusting the Youth Aliyah program," Kadosh, "Ideology vs. Reality," 4.

9. Yechiam Weitz, "Revisionist Criticism of the Yishuv Leadership during the Holocaust," *YVS* 23 (1993): 377–82. For other recent scholarship, see chapter 4, n. 110.

10. Vago, "Some Aspects of the *Yishuv* Leadership's Activities," 49.

11. For a historiographical review of how Zionism confronted the Holocaust, see Dan Michman, "Cheker ha-Tzionut le-Nochach ha-Shoah: Ba'ayot, Pulmusim, u-Munachei Yesod," in *Bein Chazon le-Reviziah: Me'ah Shenot Historiographia Tzionit,* ed. Yechiam Weitz (Jerusalem, 1997). Michman noted the controversial issue of collaboration with Nazi leaders and the important though difficult challenge of distinguishing between cooperation and collaboration, 167–68.

12. "Memorandum of Conversation between E. Samuel and Government Immigration Department," July 26, 1938, YAA 1/46. The memo continues, "The government realizes that there are 3,000,000 Jews in Poland and if we are already beginning to arrange for the immigration of hundreds of children from there, requests for certificates will, in the course of time, amount to many thousands; the Government is not prepared for this at the present time. It is desirable therefore—in his opinion—to restrict the Youth Aliyah in the colonies to Germans and Austrians only because of the unusual humanitarian phase of their situation."

13. "Arbeitsbericht des Zentralausschusses der Deutschen Juden für Hilfe und Aufbau," 1 January 1–June 30, 1934, IfZ Fa 723/1, 6.

14. Gelber, "Origins of Youth Aliya," 164.

15. Though total figures surpass 5,600, that statistic includes 140 from Poland, 30 from Romania, and an additional 40 from other lands, Jewish Agency, *Youth Aliyah: Statistical Abstract.*

16. During that time Youth Aliyah collected $1.9 million, out of a total Central Bureau income of $5.1 million, Jewish Agency, *Report to the Twenty-first Zionist Congress,* 80–81.

17. On the Wagner-Rogers Bill, see David Wyman, *Paper Walls: America and the Refugee Crisis, 1938–1941* (New York, 1985), 75–97.

Glossary

aliyah. Ascent. Jewish immigration to the land of Israel.

Altreich. Germany proper.

chaluz (pl. *chaluzim, chalutzim*). Pioneer(s). Agricultural laborers in Palestine.

dati. Religious.

Deutschtum. German-ness.

Eretz Israel. The land of Israel.

Gemeinde. Official Jewish community. The Jewish communities of Germany were organized as legally recognized corporate entities.

hachsharah. Preparation. Agricultural training in preparing for *aliyah.*

halachah. Jewish law.

Histadrut. Federation of Jewish workers in Palestine. Essentially a large worker's union integrally tied to the *yishuv's* labor Zionist political leadership.

Keren Hayesod. Foundation Fund. Philanthropic body instituted to foster the upbuilding of a Jewish homeland in Palestine.

Keren Kayemet Leyisrael. Jewish National Fund. Philanthropic body organized for the purpose of purchasing land in Palestine for eventual Jewish settlement.

kevutzot. Collective settlements, smaller than kibbutzim.

Kindertransporte. Child transports that rescued more than ten thousand children from Germany.

madrich (fem. *madrichah;* pl. *madrichim*). Leader. Title applied to instructors in the Jewish youth groups.

oleh (pl. *olim*). Jewish immigrant to Palestine/Israel.

shaliach (fem. *shlichah;* pl. *shlichim, schlichot*). Emissary. Representative
   from the *yishuv* assigned to promote *aliyah* from the diaspora.
Va'ad Le'umi. National Council. Elected leadership of the *yishuv.*
yishuv. Settlement; refers to the Jewish community of Palestine.

Bibliography

PRIMARY SOURCES

Unpublished Material

YAA, American Jewish Historical Society/New York

Group No. 1, Archives of Youth Aliyah, 1933–1960

Central Archives for the History of the Jewish People/Jerusalem

M12	Bund deutsch jüdischer Jugend
TD 873	Reichsausschuss jüdischer Jugend
TD1083	Jüdischen Frauenbund
279	Zionistische Vereinigung für Deutschland
5708	Der Ring- Bund Jüdischer Jugend

CZA/Jerusalem

A107	Ruppin, Arthur
A125	Szold, Henrietta
A140	Adler-Rudel, Shalom
A256	Freier, Recha
A344	Josephthal, Giora
A440	Michaelis-Stern, Eva
A474	Rinott, Chanoch
F49	Women's International Zionist Organization
S6	Immigration Department
S7	Central Bureau for the Settlement of German Jewry
S75	Youth Aliyah Department

Ha-Kibbutz Ha-Me'uchad

Diaspora Group

ICJOHP—Hebrew University, Jerusalem

Bat-Rachel, Yocheved
Eisner, Izzi
Freier, Recha
Herz, Rudi
Melitz, Ra'anan (Rudolph)
Michaelis-Stern, Eva
Ross, Avner

IfZ/Munich

F71	Reichsicherheitshauptamt
Fa119	Bayerische Politische Polizei
Fa303	Gestapo—Berlin
Fa373	Reichsvertretung
1182	Eichmann, A.

LBIJ

157	Pappenheim, B.
159	Adler-Rudel, S.
161	von Mildenstein, L.
409	Auswanderung und Rückwanderung
536	Religious Zionist Youth Movements
555	Reichsvertretung der Juden in Deutschland
557	Erziehungs- und Schulwesen

YIVO Archives

249	German Jewish Children's Aid

YVA/Jerusalem

JM/11388	Central British Fund
M38	Eichmann
01	Testimonies
051.0SO/82	Hachscharah

Newspapers and Periodicals

Blätter des JFB.
CV-Zeitung.
Der Angriff.
Der Israelit.
Gemeindeblatt der Deutsch-Israelitischen Gemeinde zu Hamburg.
Gemeinde-Zeitung für die israelitischen Gemeinden Württembergs.
Hamburger Israelitisches Familienblatt.
Informationsblätter im Auftrage des Zentralausschusses der deutschen Juden für Hilfe und Aufbau.

Israelitisches Gemeindeblatt (Berlin).
JR (Jüdische Rundschau).
Jüdische Wohlfahrtspflege und Sozialpolitik.
Selbstwehr.
Völkischer Beobachter.

Published Material

American Jewish Joint Distribution Committee. *American Jewish Joint Distribution Committee, New York.* Pt. 1. Vol. 10 of *Archives of the Holocaust: An International Collection of Selected Documents.* Ed. Sybil Milton and Frederick D. Bogin. New York and London: Garland Publishing, 1995.

Arlosoroff, Chaim. *Mivchar Ketavim u-Firkei Chaim.* Jerusalem: Ha-Sifriyah ha-Tsiyonit, 1958.

Bat-Rachel, Yocheved. *Ba-Nativ she-Halachti.* Tel Aviv: Ha-Kibbutz Ha-Me'uchad, 1981.

Beard, Charles. "Education under the Nazis." *Foreign Affairs* 14, no. 3 (April 1936): 437–52.

Ben-Menachem, Michael. "Zionism in Germany." *New Judea* 12, no. 4: 33–35.

Bentwich, Norman. *Jewish Youth Come Home.* London: Gollancz, 1944.

Bericht über die Erste Jugend-Alijah-Weltkonferenz, Amsterdam 9–12 September 1935. Berlin: Arbeitsgemeinschaft für Kinder- und Jugend-Alijah, n.d.

Bonin, Adelyn. *Allegiances.* Santa Barbara, Calif.: Fithian, 1993.

Central Bureau for the Settlement of German Jews in Palestine. *Report to the Nineteenth Zionist Congress and to the Fourth Council of the Jewish Agency in Lucerne.* London, 1935.

——. *Report to the Twentieth Zionist Congress and to the Council of the Jewish Agency in Zurich.* Jerusalem, 1937.

——. *Report to the Twenty-first Zionist Congress and to the Council of the Jewish Agency for Palestine in Geneva.* Jerusalem, 1939.

Central Zionist Archives, Jerusalem, 1933–39. Ed. Francis Nicosia. Vol. 3 of *Archives of the Holocaust: An International Collection of Selected Documents.* Henry Friedlander and Sybil Milton, gen. eds. New York and London: Garland Publishing, 1990.

Children and Youth Aliyah. *Freedom and Work for Jewish Youth: Report for the Third World Youth Aliyah Conference.* London: Children and Youth Aliyah, 1939.

Dawidowicz, Lucy, ed. *A Holocaust Reader.* New York: Behrman House, 1976.

Die jüdische Emigration aus Deutschland 1933–1941: Die Geschichte einer Austreibung. Frankfurt am Main: Buchhändler Vereinigung, 1985.

Documents on the Holocaust: Selected Sources on the Destruction of the Jews of Germany and Austria, Poland, and the Soviet Union. Ed. Yitzhak Arad, Yisrael Gutman, and Abraham Margaliot. Jerusalem: Yad Vashem, 1981.

Freier, Recha. *Le-Korot Aliyat Ha-No'ar. Reshumot.* Vol. 4. Tel Aviv, 1947.

——. *Let the Children Come.* London: Weidenfeld and Nicolson, 1961.

——. *Yashresh: Al Yesod Aliyat Ha-No'ar u-Shnoteyhah ha-Rishonot.* Tel Aviv: Am Oved, 1953.

Friedländer, Günter. *Jüdische Jugend zwischen Gestern und Morgen.* Berlin: Jüdischer Buchverlag, 1938.

Gemeinschaftsarbeit der jüdischen Jugend. Berlin: Zentralwohlfahrtsstelle der Juden in Deutschland, 1937.

Gershon, Karen. *A Lesser Child: An Autobiography.* London: P. Owen, 1994.

———. *We Came as Children: A Collective Autobiography.* New York: Harcourt, Brace and World, 1966.

Haffner, Sebastian. *Defying Hitler: A Memoir.* New York: Picador, 2003.

Halpern, Ben, and Shalum Wurm, eds. *The Responsible Attitude: Life and Opinions of Giora Josephthal.* New York: Schocken, 1966.

"The Hehaluz Movement in Germany." *Hamigdal* 2, no. 6: 7, 9.

Herzberg, Arno. "The Jewish Press under the Nazi Regime—Its Mission, Suppression, and Defiance—A Memoir." *LBIY* 36 (1991): 367–88.

Jewish Agency for Palestine. *Political Report of the Executive of the Jewish Agency Submitted to the Twenty-First Zionist Congress and the Sixth Session of the Council of the Jewish Agency at Geneva, August, 1939.* Jerusalem: Executive of the Jewish Agency, 1939.

———. *Report of the Executive of the Jewish Agency for Palestine Submitted to the Fourth Meeting of the Council at Lucerne, September 4th–5th, 1935.* London, 1935.

"The Jewish Social Question in Germany." *Jewish Review* no. 6: 70–76.

Kellermann, Henry J. "From Imperial to National-Socialist Germany: Recollections of a German-Jewish Youth Leader." *LBIY* 39 (1994): 305–30.

Kulka, Otto Dov, ed. *Deutsches Judentum unter dem Nationalsozialismus, I: Dokumente zur Geschichte der Reichsvertretung der deutschen Juden, 1933–1939.* Tübingen: Mohr Siebeck, 1997.

Landauer, Georg. *Der Zionismus im Wandel: Dreier Jahrzehnte.* Tel Aviv: Bitaon-Verlag, 1957.

Lubinski, Georg, and Irene Eger, eds. *Richtlinien für die Berufsausbildung von Juden in Deutschland.* Berlin: Reichsvertretung der Juden in Deutschland, n.d.

Melitz, Rudolph. *Das ist unser Weg: Junge Juden Schildern Umschichtung und Hachscharah.* Berlin: Joachim Goldstein Verlag, 1937.

Michaelis-Stern, Eva. "Errinerungen an die Anfänge der Jugendalijah in Deutschland." *Bulletin des Leo Baeck Instituts,* 70 (1985): 55–66.

Nazism, 1919–1945: A History in Documents and Eyewitness Accounts. Ed. Jeremy Noakes and Geoffrey Pridham. 2 vols. New York: Schocken, 1990.

The Nineteenth Zionist Congress and the Fourth Sitting of the Council of the Jewish Agency, Lucerne, August 20–September 6, 1935, Stenographic Report. Tel Aviv: Dvir, 1937.

Report of the Executive of the Jewish Agency for Palestine Submitted to the Third Meeting of the Council at Prague, August 31–September 1, 1933. London: Central Office of the Jewish Agency for Palestine, 1933.

Report of the Executive of the Zionist Organisation and of the Jewish Agency for Palestine Submitted to the Twenty-first Zionist Congress and the Sixth Session of the Council of the Jewish Agency at Geneva, August, 1939. Jerusalem: Executive of the Zionist Organisation and of the Jewish Agency for Palestine, 1939.

Report of the Executive of the Zionist Organisation Submitted to the Nineteenth Zionist Congress at Lucerne, August 20–30, 1935. London: Central Office of the Zionist Organisation, 1935.

Report on the Second Youth Aliyah Conference (Including Financial Report), Zurich, August 23 to 25, 1937. Berlin: Arbeitsgemeinschaft für Kinder und Jugendalijah, n.d.

Resolutions of the Eighteenth Zionist Congress, Prague, August 21 to September 3, 1933, with a Summary Report of the Proceedings. London: Central Office of the Zionist Organisation, 1934.

Resolutions of the Nineteenth Zionist Congress at Lucerne, August 20–September 3, 1935. London: Central Office of the Zionist Organisation, 1937.

Richarz, Monika, ed. *Jüdisches Leben in Deutschland.* 3 vols. Vol. 1, *Selbstzeugnisse zur Sozialgeschichte, 1780–1871.* Vol. 2, *Selbstzeugnisse zur Sozialgeschicht eim Kaiserreich.* Vol. 3, *Selbstzeugnisse zur Sozialgeschichte, 1918–1945.* Stuttgart: Deutsch Verlags-Anstalt, 1976–82.

Rosenbluth, Martin. *Go Forth and Serve: Early Years and Public Life.* New York: Schocken, 1976.

Ruppin, Arthur. *Memoirs, Diaries, Letters.* Ed. with an intro. Alex Bein. New York: Herzl Press, 1971.

Schwersenz, Jizchak. *Die versteckte Gruppe: Ein jüdische Lehrer erinnert sich an Deutschland.* Berlin: Wichern, 1988.

Sefer Aliyat Ha-No'ar. Ed. Bracha Habas. Jerusalem: Ha-Misrad ha-Merkazi le-Yishuv Yehudei Germanyah be-Eretz Yisrael, ha-Lishkah le-Aliyat ha-No'ar le-yad ha-Sochnut ha-Yehudit le-Eretz Yisrael, 1941.

Sholem, Gershom. *On Jews and Judaism in Crisis: Selected Essays.* New York: Schocken, 1976.

Stahl, Rudolph. "Vocational Training of Jews in Nazi Germany 1933–38." *Jewish Social Studies* 1, no. 2 (1939): 169–99.

Stenographisches Protokoll der Verhandlungen des XVIII. Zionistenkongresses und der dritten Tagung des Council der Jewish Agency für Palästina., Prag, 21. August bis 4 September 1933. Vienna: Fiba Verlag, 1934.

Stern, Eva. "Beginn der Jugend-Alija." In *Zur Eröffnung der Ludwig Tietz Lehrwerkstätte in Jagur,* ed. Friedrich Brodnitz, 31–33. Berlin: Reichsvertretung der Juden in Deutschland, 1937.

———. *Jugend-Alijah* Berlin: Arbeitsgemeinschaft für Kinder und Jugendalijah, 1934.

———, ed. *Jugend-Alijah.* Berlin: Arbeitsgemeinschaft für Kinder und Jugendalijah, 1935.

———. *Youth Aliyah: A Review of Three Years' Achievement: Realizing an Idea.* Berlin: Arbeitsgemeinschaft für Kinder und Jugendalijah, n.d.

———. See also Michaelis-Stern, Eva.

Szold, Henrietta. *Five Years of Youth Immigration into Palestine, 1934–1939.* Jerusalem: Jewish Agency for Palestine, Central Bureau for the Settlement of German Jews in Palestine, 1939.

———. *Youth Immigration from Germany to Palestine.* Jerusalem: Jewish Agency for Palestine, Central Bureau for the Settlement of German Jews in Palestine, May 1934.

Tofahrn, Klaus W., ed. *Vergessen kann man es nie—: Erinnerungen an Nazi-Deutschland.* Frankfurt and New York: Lang, 2002.

The Twenty-first Zionist Congress, Geneva, August 16–25, 1939, Stenographic Report. Jerusalem: Weiss, 1939–40.

Warburg, G. *Six Years of Hitler: The Jews under the Nazi Regime.* London: George Allen and Unwin, 1939.

Was ist der Hechaluz? Einige Worte an jeden jungen Juden. Berlin: Hechaluz, May 1933.

Weigert, Oscar. *Administration of Placement and Unemployment Insurance in Germany.* New York: Industrial Relations Counselors, 1934.

Werk und Werden: Ein chaluzische Sammelschrift. Berlin: Hechaluz, September 1934.

SECONDARY SOURCES

Books and Articles

Adiel, S. *Al Sifrut Aliyat Ha-No'ar: Bibliographia Muvcheret, Memuyenet, u–Mu'eret (1934–1984).* Jerusalem: Youth Aliyah Department, 1984.

Adler-Rudel, S. *Jüdische Selbsthilfe unter dem Naziregime, 1933–1939: Im Spiegel der Berichte der Reichsvertretung der Juden in Deutschland.* Tübingen: J. C. B. Mohr, 1974.

Aliyat Ha-No'ar: Korot Ha-Miph'al. Jerusalem: Ha-Histadrut ha-Tsiyonit; ha-Machlakah le-Inyanei ha-No'ar ve-Hechalutz; ha-Machlakah le-Aliyat Yeladim ve-No'ar, 1968.

Aly, Götz, and Susan Heim. "Forced Emigration, War, Deportation, and Holocaust." In *The Fate of the European Jews, 1939–1945: Continuity or Contingency?* ed. Jonathan Frankel. New York: Oxford University Press, 1997.

Angress, Werner T. *Between Fear and Hope: Jewish Youth in the Third Reich.* New York: Columbia University Press, 1988.

——. "Erfahrungen jüdischer Jugendlicher und Kinder mit der nichtjüdischen Umwelt 1933–1945." In *Die Deutschen und die Judenverfolgung im Dritten Reich,* ed. Ursula Büttner, 89–104. Hamburg: Christians, 1992.

——. "Jüdische Jugend zwischen nationalsozialistischer Verfolgung und jüdischer Wiedergeburt." In *Die Juden im Nationalsozialistischen Deutschland: The Jews in Nazi Germany 1933–1943,* ed. Arnold Paucker, 211–21. Tübingen: J. C. B. Mohr, 1986.

Ankum, Katharina von, ed. *Women in the Metropolis: Gender and Modernity in Weimar Culture.* Berkeley: University of California Press, 1997.

Baldwin, Peter. "Zionist and Non-Zionist Jews in the Last Years before the Nazi Regime." *LBIY* 27 (1982): 87–108.

Ball-Kaduri, K. Y. "The National Representation of Jews in Germany—Obstacles and Accomplishments at Its Establishment." *YVS* 2(1958): 159–78.

Bankier, David. *The Germans and the Final Solution: Public Opinion under Nazism.* Oxford: Blackwell, 1992.

——. "Jewish Society through Nazi Eyes, 1933–1936." *Holocaust and Genocide Studies* 6, no. 2 (1991): 111–27.

Bar-Gil, Shlomo. *Mechapsim Bayit Motz'im Moledet Aliyat Ha-No'ar be-Chinuch uve-Shikum Sh'erit Ha-Pleitah 1945–1955.* Jerusalem: Yad Yitzchak Ben-Zvi, 1999.

Barkai, Avraham. "The Fateful Year 1938: The Continuation and Acceleration of Plunder." In *November 1938: From "Reichskristallnacht" to Genocide,* ed. Walter H. Pehle, 95–122. Oxford: Berg, 1991.

———. "Jewish Cultural Life under National Socialism." In *German-Jewish History in Modern Times,* ed. Michael Meyer, 4:45–71. New York: Columbia University Press, 1998.

———. "Population Decline and Economic Stagnation." In *German-Jewish History in Modern Times* 4: 30–44. New York: Columbia University Press, 1998.

———. *Vom Boykott zur "Entjudung": Der wirtschaftliche Existenzkampf der Juden im Dritten Reich 1933–1943.* Frankfurt am Main: Fischer, 1988.

Bauer, Yehuda. *A History of the Holocaust.* New York: Franklin Watts, 1982.

———. *Jews for Sale? Nazi-Jewish Negotiations, 1933–1945.* New Haven: Yale University Press, 1994.

Beit-Zvi, Shabtai. *Ha-Tzionut ha-post-Ugandit be-Mashber ha-Shoah.* Tel Aviv, 1977.

Bennathan, Esra. "Die demographische und wirtschaftliche Struktur der Juden." In *Entscheidungsjahr, 1932,* ed. Werner Mosse, 87–131. Tübingen: J. C. B. Mohr, 1966.

Bentwich, Norman. *Ben-Shemen: A Children's Village in Israel.* Jerusalem: Fedération Internationale des Communautés d'Enfants, 1958.

———. "The Destruction of the Jewish Community in Austria, 1938–1942." In *The Jews of Austria: Essays on their Life, History, and Destruction,* ed. Josef Fraenkel, 267–78. London: Vallentine, Mitchell, 1967.

Benz, Wolfgang. *The Holocaust: A German Historian Examines the Genocide.* New York: Columbia University Press, 1999.

———. "The Relapse into Barbarism." In *November 1938: From "Reichskristallnacht" to Genocide,* ed. Walter H. Pehle, 1–43. Oxford: Berg, 1991.

———, ed. *Die Juden in Deutschland, 1933–1945: Leben unter nationalsozialistischer Herrschaft.* Munich: Beck, 1988.

Berkley, George. *Vienna and Its Jews: The Tragedy of Success, 1880s–1980s.* Cambridge, Mass.: Harvard University Press, 1988.

Berkowitz, Michael. *Western Jewry and the Zionist Project, 1914–1933.* Cambridge: Cambridge University Press, 1997.

Bernstein, Deborah. "Daughters of the Nation: Between the Public and Private Spheres in Pre-State Israel." In *Jewish Women in Historical Perspective,* ed. Judith Baskin, 287–311. Detroit: Wayne State University Press, 1998.

Biletzky, Eliyahu. *Chaim Arlosoroff: Iyunim be-Mishnato ha-Yehudit.* Tel Aviv: Tarbut ve-Chinuch, 1966.

Black, Edwin. *The Transfer Agreement. The Untold Story of the Secret Agreement between the Third Reich and Jewish Palestine.* New York: Macmillan, 1984.

Blasius, Dirk. "Zwischen Rechtsvertrauen und Rechtszerstörung: Deutsche Juden 1933–1935." In *Zerbrochene Geschichte: Leben und Selbstverständnis der Juden in Deutschland,* ed. Dirk Blasius and Dan Diner, 121–37. Frankfurt am Main: Fischer, 1991.

Blumenfeld, Kurt. "Ursprünge und Art einer zionistischen Bewegung." *Bulletin des Leo Baeck Instituts* 1 (1957): 129–40.

Boas, Jacob. "German-Jewish Internal Politics under Hitler, 1933–1938." *LBIY* 29 (1984): 3–25.

———. "Germany or Diaspora? German Jewry's Shifting Perceptions in the Nazi Era (1933–1938)." *LBIY* 27 (1982): 109–26.

———. "The Jews of Germany: Self-Perceptions in the Nazi Era as Reflected in the German Jewish Press, 1933–1938." Ph.D. diss., University of California, Riverside, 1977.

———. "A Nazi Travels to Palestine." *History Today* 30 (January 1980): 33–38.

Bock, Gisela. "Ordinary Women in Nazi Germany: Perpetrators, Victims, Followers, and Bystanders." In *Women in the Holocaust,* ed. Dalia Ofer and Lenore J. Weitzman, 85–100. New Haven: Yale University Press, 1998.

Bolkosky, Sidney M. *The Distorted Image: German Jewish Perceptions of Germans and Germany, 1918–1935.* New York: Elsevier, 1975.

Bondy, Ruth. *The Emissary: A Life of Enzo Sereni.* Boston: Little, Brown, 1977.

Botz, Gerhard. "The Jews of Vienna from the *Anschluss* to the Holocaust." In *Jews, Antisemitism, and Culture in Vienna,* ed. Ivar Oxaal, Michael Pollak, and Gerhard Botz, 185–204. New York: Routledge and Kegan Paul, 1987.

Bracher, Karl Dietrich. "The Stages of Totalitarian Integration (*gleichschaltung*)." In *Republic to Reich, the Making of the Nazi Revolution,* ed. Hajo Holborn, 109–28. New York: Vintage, 1973.

Brada, Fini. "Emigration to Palestine." In *The Jews of Czechoslovakia: Historical Studies and Surveys,* 2:589–98. Philadelphia: Jewish Publication Society, 1971.

Brenner, Lenni. *Zionism in the Age of the Dictators.* Westport, Conn.: Lawrence Hill, 1983.

Brenner, Michael. *The Renaissance of Jewish Culture in Weimar Germany.* New Haven: Yale University Press, 1996.

———. "Turning Inward: Jewish Youth in Weimar Germany." In *In Search of Jewish Community: Jewish Identities in Germany and Austria, 1918–1933,* ed. Michael Brenner and Derek J. Penslar, 56–73. Bloomington: Indiana University Press.

Breuer, Mordechai. *Modernity within Tradition: The Social History of Orthodox Jewry in Imperial Germany.* New York: Columbia University Press, 1992.

Brook-Shepherd, Gordon. *Anschluss: The Rape of Austria.* London: Macmillan, 1963.

Browning, Christopher. *The Origins of the Final Solution: The Evolution of Nazi Jewish Policy, September 1939–March 1942.* Lincoln: Yad Vashem and University of Nebraska Press, 2004.

Burgess, Greg. "France and the German Refugee Crisis of 1933." *French History* 16, no. 2 (June 2002): 203–29.

Carr, William. "Nazi Policy against the Jews." In *Life in the Third Reich,* ed. Richard Bessel, 69–82. Oxford: Oxford University Press, 1987.

Cesarani, David. *Eichmann: His Life and Crimes.* London: W. Heinemann, 2004.

Cochavi, Yehoyakim. "Liberals and Zionists on the Eve of the National Socialist Seizure of Power." *LBIY* 39 (1994): 113–29.

Cohen, Asher, and Yehoyakim Cochavi, eds. *Zionist Youth Movements during the Shoah.* New York: Peter Lang, 1995.

Cohen, Naomi W. *American Jews and the Zionist Idea.* New York: Ktav, 1975.

Colodner, Solomon. *Jewish Education in Germany under the Nazis.* New York: Jewish Education Committee Press, 1964.

———. "Jewish Education under National Socialism." *YVS* 3 (1959): 161–86.

Crane, Cynthia. *Divided Lives: The Untold Stories of Jewish-Christian Women in Nazi Germany.* New York: St. Martin's Press, 2000.

Dash, Joan. *Summoned to Jerusalem: The Life of Henrietta Szold.* New York: Harper and Row, 1979.

Dawidowicz, Lucy. *The War against the Jews, 1933–1945.* New York: Bantam, 1986.

Doron, Yehoyakim. *Ne'urim ba-Tenu'ah: Mekorot le-Toldot Tenu'ot ha-No'ar ha-Yehudiyot be-Germanyah, 1909–1933.* Jerusalem: Yad Ya'ari and the Leo Baeck Institute, 1996.

Dwork, Debórah. *Children with a Star: Jewish Youth in Nazi Europe.* New Haven: Yale University Press, 1991.

Eckstein, George Gunther. "The Frei Deutsch-Jüdische Jugend (FDJJ), 1932–1933." *LBIY* 26 (1981): 231–39.

Edelheit, Abraham. *The Yishuv in the Shadow of the Holocaust: Zionist Politics and Rescue Aliya, 1933–1939.* Boulder, Colo.: Westview Press, 1996.

Elon, Amos. *The Pity of It All: A History of Jews in Germany, 1743–1933.* New York: Metropolitan Books/Henry Holt, 2002.

Eloni, Yehuda. "German Zionism and the Rise to Power of National Socialism." *Studies in Zionism* 6, no. 2 (1985): 247–62.

Esh, Shaul. "The Establishment of the Reichsvereinigung der Juden in Deutschland and Its Main Activities." *YVS* 7 (1963): 19–38.

———. "Ha-Ha'avara." In *Iyunim be-Cheker ha-Shoah ve-Yehadut Zemanenu,* 33–106. Jerusalem: Institute for Contemporary Jewry, Yad Vashem, and the Leo Baeck Institute, 1973.

Eshkoli, Hava (Wegman). *Elem: Mapai le—nochach ha-Shoah, 1939–1942.* Jerusalem: Yad Yitzchak Ben-Zvi, 1994.

———. "Three Attitudes toward the Holocaust within Mapai, 1933–1945." *Studies in Zionism* 14, no. 1 (1993): 73–94.

Evans, Richard. *The Coming of the Third Reich: A History.* London: Allen Lane, 2003.

Feilchenfeld, Werner, Dolf Michaelis, and Ludwig Pinner. *Haavara-Transfer nach Palästina und Einwanderung Deutscher Juden, 1933–1939.* Tübingen, J. C. B. Mohr, 1972.

Feinberg, Nathan. "The Activities of Central Jewish Organizations Following Hitler's Rise to Power." *YVS* 1 (1957): 67–84.

Feldman, Gerald. "Industrialists, Bankers, and the Problem of Unemployment in the Weimar Republic." *Central European History* 25 (1992): 76–96.

Fineman, Irving. *Woman of Valor: The Life of Henrietta Szold, 1860–1945.* New York: Simon and Schuster, 1961.

Fölling, Werner. *Zwischen deutscher und jüdischer Identität: Eine jüdische Reformschule in Berlin zwischen 1932 und 1939.* Opladen: Leske u. B., 1995.

Fraenkel, Daniel. *Al Pi Tehom: ha-Mediniyut ha-Tsiyonit u-She'elat Yehudei Germanyah 1933–1938.* Jerusalem: Magnes Press and Leo Baeck Institute, 1994.

———. "Bein Hagshama le-Hatzalah ve-'Irgun, Hechalutz le-Nochach Metzukat ha-Yehudim be-Germaniah ha-Natzit (1933–1935)." *Yahadut Zemanenu* 6 (1990): 215–44.

Fraenkel, Josef, ed. *The Jews of Austria: Essays on Their Life, History, and Destruction.* London: Vallentine, Mitchell, 1967.

Freeden, Herbert. *The Jewish Press in the Third Reich.* Providence, R.I.: Berg, 1993.

Friedland, Fritz. "Trials and Tribulations of Education in Nazi Germany." *LBIY* 3 (1958): 187–201.

Friedländer, Saul. *Nazi Germany and the Jews.* Vol. 1, *The Years of Persecution, 1933–1939.* New York: HarperCollins, 1997.

Friedman, Jonathan. *The Lion and the Star: Gentile-Jewish Relations in Three Hessian Communities, 1919–1945.* Lexington: University Press of Kentucky, 1998.

Gaertner, Hans. "Bildungsprobleme der jüdischen Schule während der Nazizeit." *Bulletin des Leo Baeck Instituts* 2–3 (1958): 83–86.

———. "Problems of Jewish Schools in Germany during the Hitler Regime." *LBIY* 1 (1956): 123–41.

Gat, Raphael. "Miph'al Aliyat Ha-No'ar 1933–1939." *Kathedra* 37 (1985): 149–76.

Gay, Peter. *Weimar Culture: The Outsider as Insider.* New York: Harper Torchbooks, 1968.

Gelber, Yoav. "The Historical Role of the Central European Immigration to Israel." *LBIY* 38 (1993): 323–41.

———. *Moledet Chadasha.* Jerusalem: Yad Yitzhak Ben-Zvi, 1990.

———. "The Origins of Youth Aliyah." *Studies in Zionism* 9, no. 2 (1988): 147–71.

———. "The Reactions of the Zionist Movement and the Yishuv to the Nazis' Rise to Power." *YVS* 18 (1987): 41–101.

Gellately, Robert. *Backing Hitler: Consent and Coercion in Nazi Germany.* New York: Oxford University Press, 2001.

———. *The Gestapo and German Society: Enforcing Racial Policy, 1933–1945.* Oxford: Clarendon Press, 1990.

Genschel, Helmut. *Die Verdrängung der Juden aus der Wirtschaft im Dritten Reich.* Göttingen: Musterschmidt, 1966.

Gessner, Dieter. *Die Weimarer Republik.* Darmstadt: Wissenschaftliche Buchgesellschaft, 2002.

Getter, Miriam. *Chaim Arlosoroff: Biographia Politit.* Tel Aviv: Universitat Tel-Aviv, 1977.

Gidal, Nachum T. *Henrietta Szold: A Documentation in Photos and Text.* New York: Gefen Publishing, 1996.

Gillerman, Sharon Ilise. "Between Public and Private: Family, Community, and Jewish Identity in Weimar Berlin." Ph.D. diss., UCLA, 1996.

———. "The Crisis of the Jewish Family in Weimar Germany: Social Conditions and Cultural Representations." In *In Search of Jewish Community: Jewish Identities in Germany and Austria, 1918–1939,* ed. Michael Brenner and Derek J. Penslar, 176–99. Bloomington: Indiana University Press, 1998.

Glasenapp, Gabriele von, and Michael Nagel. *Das jüdische Jugendbuch: Von der Aufklärung bis zum Dritten Reich.* Stuttgart: J. B. Metzler, 1996.

Göpfert, Rebekka. *Der jüdische Kindertransport: Von Deutschland nach England, 1938/39.* Frankfurt am Main: Campus, 1999.

Gordon, Sarah. *Hitler, Germans, and "the Jewish Question."* Princeton: Princeton University Press, 1984.

Gottlieb, Amy Zahn. *Men of Vision: Anglo-Jewry's Aid to Victims of the Nazi Regime, 1933–1945.* London: Weidenfeld and Nicolson, 1998.

Graml, Hermann. *Reichskristallnacht: Antisemitismus und Judenverfolgung im Dritten Reich.* Munich: Deutscher Taschenbuch Verlag, 1988.

Grevelhörster, Ludger. *Kleine Geschichte der Weimarer Republik, 1918–1933: Ein Problemgeschichtlicher Überblick.* Münster: Aschendorff, 2000.

Grodzinski, Yosef. *Chomer Enoshi Tov: Yehudim mul Tzionim, 1945–1951.* Jerusalem: Hed Artzi, 1998.

Gross, Walther. "The Zionist Students' Movement." *LBIY* 4 (1959): 143–164.

Grossman, Kurt R. "Zionists and Non-Zionists under Nazi Rule in the 1930s." *Herzl Year Book* 4 (1962): 329–44.

Gruenewald, Max. "The Beginning of the Reichsvertretung." *LBIY* 1 (1956): 57–67.

Gruner, Wolf. "Die Reichshauptstadt und die Verfolgung der Berliner Juden 1933–1945." In *Jüdische Geschichte in Berlin*, ed. Reinhard Rürup, 229–66. Berlin: Hentrich, 1995.

Gutman, Yisrael, ed. *Major Changes within the Jewish People in the Wake of the Holocaust: Proceedings of the Ninth Yad Vashem International Historical Conference, Jerusalem, June 1993.* Jerusalem: Yad Vashem, 1996.

Gutman, Yisrael, and Gideon Greif, eds. *The Historiography of the Holocaust Period: Proceedings of the Fifth Yad Vashem International Historical Conference.* Jerusalem: Yad Vashem, 1988.

Gutman, Yisrael, and Cynthia Haft, eds. *Patterns of Jewish Leadership in Nazi Europe 1933–1945: Proceedings of the Third Yad Vashem International Historical Conference.* Jerusalem: Yad Vashem, 1979.

Guttman, Melinda Given. *The Enigma of Anna O.: A Biography of Bertha Pappenheim.* Wickford, R.I.: Moyer Bell, 2000.

Hadomi, Leah. "Jüdische Identität und der zionistische Utopieroman." *Bulletin des Leo Baeck Instituts* 86 (1990): 23–66.

Hæstrup, Jorgen. *Passage to Palestine: Young Jews in Denmark, 1932–45.* [Odense,] Denmark: Odense University Press, 1983.

Harvey, Elizabeth. "Youth Unemployment and the State: Public Policies towards Unemployed Youth in Hamburg during the World Economic Crisis." In *The German Unemployed: Experiences and Consequences of Mass Unemployment from the Weimar Republic to the Third Reich*, ed. Richard J. Evans and Dick Geary, 142–71. New York: St. Martin's Press, 1987.

Heer, Friedrich. *Challenge of Youth.* University: University of Alabama Press, 1974.

Heilbronner, Oded. "Georg Lubinski: Ein Leben für die Sozialarbeit." In *Zedaka: Jüdische Sozialarbeit im Wandel der Zeit*, 129–34. Frankfurt am Main: Jüdisches Museum, 1992.

Helmreich, Ernst. "Jewish Education in the Third Reich." *Journal of Central European Affairs* 15, no. 2 (1955): 134–47.

Hetkamp, Jutta. *Die jüdische Jugendbewegung in Deutschland von 1913–1933.* Münster: Lit, 1994.

Hilberg, Raul. *The Destruction of the European Jews.* Rev. and definitive ed. 3 vols. New York: Holmes and Meier, 1985.

Hildesheimer, Esriel. "Ha-Irgun ha-Merkazi shel Yehudei Germanyah ba-Shanim, 1933 and 1945: Ma'amado ba-Medinah u-va-Chevrah ha-Yehudit." Ph.D. diss., Hebrew University, Jerusalem, 1982.

———. *Jüdische Selbstverwaltung unter dem NS-Regime: Der Existenzkampf der Reichsvertretung und Reichsvereinigung der Juden in Deutschland.* Tübingen: J. C. B. Mohr, 1994.

Holzer, Willi. *Jüdische Schulen in Berlin: Am Beispiel der privaten Volksschle der jüdischen Gemeinde Rykestraße.* Berlin: Hentrich, 1992.

Horowitz, Dan, and Moshe Lissak. *Origins of the Israeli Polity: Palestine under the Mandate.* Chicago: University of Chicago Press, 1978.

Inbar, Ester Ziv. *Le-'olam Tiheyeh 'atsmecha: Sipurah shel Henrietta Szold.* Jerusalem: Yad Yitzchak Ben Zvi; Tel Aviv: Am Oved, 1996.

Jewish Agency for Israel. *Youth Aliyah: Statistical Abstract, 1933–1983.* Jerusalem: Youth Aliyah, 1984.

Johnson, Eric A. *Nazi Terror: The Gestapo, Jews, and Ordinary Germans.* New York: Basic Books, 1999.

Kadosh, Sandra. "Ideology vs. Reality: Youth Aliyah and the Rescue of Jewish Children during the Holocaust Era, 1933–1945." Ph.D. diss., Columbia University, 1995.

Kaelter, David F. "Das jüdische Schulwerk in Deutschland nach 1933." *Bulletin des Leo Baecks Instituts* 2/3 (1958): 86–88.

Kamron, Ephraim. "Ha-Chazit ha-Me'uchedet shel ha-No'ar ha-Yehudi neged ha-Natzim ba-Shanim 1934–38." *Masu'ah* 2 (1974): 112–16.

Kaplan, Marion A. *Between Dignity and Despair: Jewish Life in Nazi Germany.* New York: Oxford University Press, 1998.

———. *The Jewish Feminist Movement in Germany: The Campaigns of the Jüdischer Frauenbund, 1904–1938.* Westport, Conn.: Greenwood Press, 1979.

Katz, Yossi. *Torah ve-Avodah be-Vinyan ha-Aretz: Ha-Kibbutz Ha-Dati be-Tekufat ha-Mandat.* Ramat Gan: Bar-Ilan University, 1996.

Kershaw, Ian. *The Nazi Dictatorship: Problems and Perspectives of Interpretation.* London: Edward Arnold, 1985.

Klönne, Arno. *Jugend im Dritten Reich: Die Hitler-Jugend und ihrer Gegner.* Cologne: PapyRossa, 2003.

Kluger, Ruth. *Still Alive: A Holocaust Girlhood Remembered.* New York: Feminist Press at CUNY, 2001.

Kol, Moshe. "Ma-amatzei Hatzalah ve-'Ezrah." *Masu'ah* 2 (1974): 30–43.

———. *Masechet Aliyat Ha-No'ar.* Tel Aviv: M. Neumann, 1961.

Koonz, Claudia. "Courage and Choice among German-Jewish Women and Men." In *Die Juden im Nationalsozialistischen Deutschland: The Jews in Nazi Germany, 1933–1943,* ed. Arnold Paucker, 283–93. Tübingen: J. C. B. Mohr, 1986.

Kramer, David. "Jewish Welfare Work." In *Die Juden im Nationalsozialistischen Deutschland: The Jews in Nazi Germany, 1933–1943,* ed. Arnold Paucker, 173–88. Tübingen: J. C. B. Mohr, 1986.

Kraus, Hertha. *Work Relief in Germany.* New York: Russel Sage Foundation, 1934.

Krohn, Helga. "Aus dem Israelitischen Waisenhaus in Frankfurt nach Palästina—eine dramatische Rettungsaktion." *Schriftenreihe des jüdischen Museums Frankfurt am Main* 3 (1995): 11–55.

Kwiet, Konrad. "Gehen oder Bleiben? Die deutschen Juden am Wendepunkt." In *Der Judenpogrom 1938: Von der "Reichskristallnacht" zum Völkermord*, ed. Walter H. Pehle, 132–45. Frankfurt am Main: Fischer, 1988.

Lacina, Evelyn. *Emigration, 1933–1945: Sozialhistorische Darstellung der deutschsprachigen Emigration und einiger ihrer Asylländer aufgrund ausgewählter zeitgenössischer Selbstzeugnisse.* Stuttgart: Klett-Cota, 1982.

Laqueur, Walter. *Generation Exodus: The Fate of Young Jewish Refugees from Nazi Germany.* Hanover, N.H.: Brandeis University Press, 2001.

———. "The German Youth Movement and the Jewish Question: A Preliminary Survey." *LBIY* 6 (1961): 193–205.

———. *A History of Zionism.* New York: Schocken, 1989.

Lavsky, Hagit. *Before Catastrophe: The Distinctive Path of German Zionism.* Jerusalem: Magnes Press, 1996.

Leshem, Perez. *Strasse zur Rettung: 1933–1939 Aus Deutschland Vertrieben—Bereitet sich jüdische Jugend auf Palästina vor.* Tel-Aviv: Verbande der Freunde der Histadrut, 1973.

Levin, Nora. *The Holocaust: The Destruction of European Jewry, 1933–1945.* New York: Thomas Y. Crowell, 1968.

Leyens, Erich, and Lotte Andor. *Years of Estrangement.* Evanston, Ill.: Northwestern University Press, 1996.

Livnot u-Lehibanot: Tenu'at "Habonim" be-Germanyah, 1920–1942. Tel Aviv: Ghetto Fighters' House, 1990.

Loewenstein, Kurt. "Die innerjüdische Reaktion auf die Krise der deutschen Demokratie." In *Entscheidungsjahr, 1932,* ed. Werner Mosse, 349–403. Tübingen: J. C. B. Mohr, 1966.

Longerich, Peter. *Politik der Vernichtung: Eine Gesamtdarstellung der nationalsozialistischen Judenverfolgung.* Munich: Piper, 1998.

Lotan, Giora [Georg Lubinski]. "The Zentralwohlfahrtsstelle." *LBIY* 4 (1959): 185–207.

Lowenthal, Marvin. *Henrietta Szold, Life and Letters.* New York: Viking Press, 1942.

Maor, Aharon. "The Influence of Political, Social, Economic, and Religious Procedures on the 'Religious Youth Aliyah' in Its Initial Stage." Master's thesis, Bar-Ilan University, 1987.

Maoz (Mosbacher), Eliyahu. "The Werkleute." *LBIY* 4 (1959): 165–82.

Marcus, Ernst. "The German Foreign Office and the Palestine Question in the Period 1933–1939." *YVS* 2 (1958): 179–204.

Margaliot, Avraham. *Ben Hatzalah le-Ovdan: Iyunim be-Toldot Yehudei Germanyah, 1932–1938.* Jerusalem: Yad Vashem, the Institute of Contemporary Jewry, and the Leo Baeck Institute, 1990.

———. "The Dispute over the Leadership of German Jewry." *YVS* 10 (1974): 129–48.

———. "Hagirat Yehudei Germanyah—Tichnun u-Metzi'ut." *Yahadut Zemanenu* 5 (1989): 287–300.

———. "The Problem of the Rescue of German Jewry during the Years 1933–1939:

The Reasons for the Delay in Their Emigration from the Third Reich." In *Rescue Attempts during the Holocaust: Proceedings of the Second Yad Vashem International Historical Conference, April 1974.* Jerusalem: Yad Vashem, 1974.

———. "Teguvat Mosdoteyhah shel Yahadut Germanyah ve-Irguneyha el ha-Mishtar ha-Natzional-Sotzialisti ba-Shanim 1933–1938," ed. and completed by Yehoyakim Cochavi. In *Toldot ha-Shoah: Germanyah,* ed. Avraham Margaliot and Yehoyakim Cochavi, 1:69–233. Jerusalem: Yad Vashem, 1998.

Markel, Richard. "Brith Haolim. Der Weg der Alija des Jung-Jüdischer Wander-bundes (JJWB)." *Bulletin des Leo Baeck Instituts,* 9 (1966): 119–89.

Marrus, Michael. *The Holocaust in History.* New York: Meridian, 1989.

———. "Varieties of Jewish Resistance: Some Categories and Comparisons in His-toriographical Perspective." In *Major Changes within the Jewish People in the Wake of the Holocaust: Proceedings of the Ninth Yad Vashem International Historical Con-ference, Jerusalem, June 1993,* ed. Yisrael Gutman, 269–99. Jerusalem: Yad Vashem, 1996.

Maurer, Trude. "The Background for Kristallnacht: The Expulsion of Polish Jews." In *November 1938: From "Reichskristallnacht" to Genocide,* ed. Walter H. Pehle, 44–72. Oxford: Berg, 1991.

McKale, Donald M. "From Weimar to Nazism: Abteilung III of the German Foreign Office and the Support of Antisemitism, 1931–1935." *LBIY* 32 (1987): 297–307.

Melka, R. L. "Nazi Germany and the Palestine Question." *Middle Eastern Studies* 5, no. 3 (1969): 221–33.

Mendelsohn, Ezra. *The Jews of East Central Europe between the World Wars.* Bloom-ington: Indiana University Press, 1983.

Meyhöfer, Rita. *Gäste in Berlin? Jüdisches Schülerleben in der Weimarer Republik und im Nationalsozialismus.* Hamburg: Verlag Dr. Kovac, 1996.

Michman, Dan. "Cheker ha-Tzionut le-Nochach ha-Shoah: Ba'ayot, Pulmusim, u-Munachei Yesod." In *Bein Chazon le-Reviziah: Me'ah Shenot Historiographia Tzionit.* Ed. Yechiam Weitz. Jerusalem: Zalman Shazar Center, 1997.

———. "Le-Verur ha-Musag 'Hatzalah' bi-Tekufat ha-Shoah." *Yalkut Moreshet* 28 (1979): 55–76.

Milton, Sybil. "The Expulsion of Polish Jews from Germany, October 1938 to July 1939: A Documentation." *LBIY* 29 (1984): 169–99.

Mommsen, Hans. "The Failure of the Weimar Republic and the Rise of Hitler." In *The Burden of German History: Essays for the Goethe Institute,* ed. Michael Laffan, 116–30. London: Methuen, 1988.

Morgenthaler, Sibylle. "Countering the Pre-1933 Nazi Boycott against the Jews." *LBIY* 36 (1991): 127–49.

Morris, Benny. "Response of the Jewish Daily Press in Palestine to the Accession of Hitler, 1933." *YVS* 27 (1999): 363–407

Moser, Jonny. "Depriving Jews of Their Legal Rights in the Third Reich." In *No-vember 1938: From "Reichskristallnacht" to Genocide,* ed. Walter H. Pehle, 123–38. Oxford: Berg, 1991.

———. "Die Katastrophe der Juden in Österreich 1938–1945—Ihre Voraussetzung und ihre Überwindung." In *Der Gelbe Stern in Österreich: Katalog und Einführung zu einer Dokumentation.* Vol. 5 of *Studia Judaica Austriaca,* 67–133. Eisenstadt: Roetzer, 1977.

Mosse, George L. *German Jews beyond Judaism.* Bloomington and Cincinnati: Indiana University Press and Hebrew Union College Press, 1985.

Mosse, Werner E., ed. *Entscheidungsjahr, 1932: Zur Judenfrage in der Endphase der Weimarer Republik.* Tübingen: J. C. B. Mohr, 1966.

Nicosia, Francis. "The End of Emancipation and the Illusion of Preferential Treatment: German Zionism, 1933–1938." *LBIY* 36 (1991): 243–65.

———. "Revisionist Zionism in Germany (II): Georg Kareski and the Staatszionistische Organisation, 1933–1938." *LBIY* 32 (1987): 231–67.

———. *The Third Reich and the Palestine Question.* Austin: University of Texas Press, 1985.

Niederland, Doron. *Yehudei Germanyah—Mehagrim 'o Plitim? Iyun bi-D'fusei ha-Hagirah bein shtei Milchemot ha-Olam.* Jerusalem: Magnes Press, 1996.

Niewyk, Donald L. "The Impact of Inflation and Depression on the German Jews." *LBIY* 28 (1983): 19–36.

———. *The Jews in Weimar Germany.* Baton Rouge: Louisiana State University Press, 1980.

Ofer, Dalia. "Fifty Years After: The Yishuv, Zionism, and the Holocaust, 1933–1948." In *Major Changes within the Jewish People in the Wake of the Holocaust: Proceedings of the Ninth Yad Vashem International Historical Conference, Jerusalem, June 1993,* ed. Yisrael Gutman, 463–95. Jerusalem: yad Vashem, 1996.

Oppenheim, Israel. *The Struggle of Jewish Youth for Productivization: The Zionist Youth Movement in Poland.* Boulder, Colo.: East European Monographs, 1989.

Out of the Fire. Ed. Alan Sillitoe. Collated by Meir Gottesman. London: Children and Youth Aliyah, Committee of Great Britain and Eire, 1979.

Paucker, Arnold. "Das Berliner liberale jüdische Bürgertum im Centralverein deutscher Staatsbürger jüdischen Glaubens." In *Jüdische Geschichte in Berlin: Essays und Studien,* ed. Reinhard Rürup, 215–28. Berlin: Hentrich, 1995.

———, ed. *Die Juden in Nationalsozialistischen Deutschland: The Jews in Nazi Germany, 1933–1943.* Tübingen: J. C. B. Mohr, 1986.

Pauker, Arnold, and Konrad Kwiet. "Jewish Leadership and Jewish Resistance." In *Probing the Depths of German Antisemitism: German Society and the Persecution of the Jews, 1933–1941,* ed. David Bankier. New York: Berghahn Books, 2000.

Pauley, Bruce F. *Hitler and the Forgotten Nazis: A History of Austrian National Socialism.* Chapel Hill: University of North Carolina Press, 1981.

Pehle, Walter H., ed. *November 1938: From "Reichskristallnacht" to Genocide.* Oxford: Oxford University Press, 1991.

Peukert, Detlev J. K. *Inside Nazi Germany: Conformity, Opposition, and Racism in Everyday Life.* New Haven: Yale University Press, 1987.

———. "The Lost Generation: Youth Unemployment at the End of the Weimar Republic." In *The German Unemployed: Experiences and Consequences of Mass Unemployment from the Weimar Republic to the Third Reich,* ed. Richard J. Evans and Dick Geary, 172–91. New York: St. Martin's Press, 1987.

Pincus, Chasya. *Come from the Four Winds.* New York: Herzl Press, 1970.

Poppel, Stephen M. *Zionism in Germany, 1897–1933: The Shaping of a Jewish Identity.* Philadelphia: Jewish Publication Society, 1977.

Porat, Dina. *The Blue and Yellow Stars of David: The Zionist Leadership and the Holocaust, 1939–1945.* Cambridge, Mass.: Harvard University Press, 1990.

Prestel, Claudia. "'Youth in Need': Correctional Education and Family Breakdown in German Jewish Families." In *In Search of Jewish Community: Jewish Identities in Austria and Germany, 1918–1933,* ed. Michael Brenner and Derek J. Penslar, 200–222. Bloomington: Indiana University Press, 1998.

Prinz, Arthur. "The Role of the Gestapo in Obstructing and Promoting Jewish Emigration." *YVS* 2 (1958): 205–18.

Pulzer, Peter. *The Rise of Political Anti-Semitism in Germany and Austria.* Cambridge, Mass.: Harvard University Press, 1988.

Reinharz, Jehuda. *Fatherland or Promised Land: The Dilemma of the German Jew, 1893–1914.* Ann Arbor: University of Michigan Press, 1975.

———. "Hashomer Hazair in Germany (II): Under the Shadow of the Swastika, 1933–1938." *LBIY* 32 (1987): 183–229.

———. "Hashomer Hazair in Nazi Germany." In *Die Juden in Nationalsozialistischen Deutschland: The Jews in Nazi Germany, 1933–1943,* ed. Arnold Paucker, 317–50. Tübingen: J. C. B. Mohr, 1986.

———. "Zionisten und Liberaler in der Deutschsprachigen Ländern." *Bulletin des Leo Baeck Instituts* 82 (1989): 49–63.

Reinhold, Chanoch. *No'ar Boneh Baito: Aliyat ha-No'ar ke-Tenu'ah Chinuchit.* Tel Aviv: Am Oved, 1953.

Reissner, H. G. "The Histories of 'Kaufhaus N. Israel' and of Wilfrid Israel." *LBIY* 3 (1958): 227–56.

Rheins, Carl J. "The Schwarzes Fähnlein, Jungenschaft, 1932–1934." *LBIY* 23 (1978): 173–97.

Rinott, Chanoch. "Jüdische Jugendbewegung in Deutschland: Entstehung, Entwicklung und Ende (1912–1942)." *Neue Sammlung* 17 (1977): 75–94.

———. "Major Trends in Jewish Youth Movements in Germany." *LBIY* 19 (1974): 77–96.

Ritter, Gerhard. "The Historical Foundations of the Rise of National Socialism." In *The Third Reich,* published for the International Council for Philosophy and Humanistic Studies, 381–417. London: Weidenfeld and Nicolson, 1955.

Röcher, Ruth. *Die jüdische Schule im nationalsozialistischen Deutschland, 1933–1942.* Frankfurt am Main: Dipa-Verlag, 1992.

Rosenbaum, Ron. *Explaining Hitler: The Search for the Origins of His Evil.* New York: Random House, 1998.

Rosenkranz, Herbert. "The Anschluss and the Tragedy of Austrian Jewry, 1938–1945." In *The Jews of Austria: Essays on their Life, History, and Destruction,* ed. Josef Fraenkel, 479–545. London: Vallentine, Mitchell, 1967.

———. "Austrian Jewry: Between Forced Emigration and Deportation." In *Patterns of Jewish Leadership in Nazi Europe 1933–1945: Proceedings of the Third Yad Vashem*

International Historical Conference, ed. Yisrael Gutman and Cynthia Haft, 65–74. Jerusalem: Yad Vashem, 1979.

———. *Verfolgung und Selbstbehauptung: Die Juden in Österreich 1938–1945.* Vienna: Herold, 1978.

Rosenstock, Werner. "Exodus, 1933–39—A Survey of Jewish Emigration from Germany." *LBIY* 1 (1956): 373–92.

———. "The Jewish Youth Movements." *LBIY* 19 (1974): 97–106.

Rubinstein, William D. *The Myth of Rescue: Why the Democracies Could Not Have Saved More Jews from the Nazis.* London and New York: Routledge, 1997.

Sandler, Ahron. "The Struggle for Unification." *LBIY* 2 (1957): 76–84.

Schachne, Lucie. *Erziehung zum geistigen Widerstand: Das jüdische Landschulheim Herrlingen, 1933–1939.* Frankfurt am Main: Dipa-Verlag, 1986.

Schatzker, Chaim. "The Jewish Youth Movements in Germany in the Holocaust Period: Youth in Confrontation with a New Reality." *LBIY* 32 (1987): 157–81.

———. "The Jewish Youth Movements in Germany in the Holocaust Period (II): The Relations between the Youth Movement and Hechaluz." *LBIY* 33 (1988): 301–25.

———. "Makkabi Hazair—Tenu'at ha-No'ar ha-Yehudit ha-Achronah be-Germanyah." In *Tenu'ot ha-No'ar ha-Tziyoni'ot ba-Shoah,* ed. Yehoyakim Cochavi, 81–83. Haifa: Ha-Machon le-Cheker Tekufat ha-Shoah, 1989.

———. *No'ar Yehudi be-Germanyah bein Yahadut le-Germaniut, 1870–1945.* Jerusalem: Zalman Shazar Center for Jewish History, 1998.

———. "The Role of Aliyat Hanoar in the Rescue, Absorption, and Rehabilitation of Refugee Children." In *She'erit Hapletah, 1944–1948: Rehabilitation and Political Struggle,* ed. Yisrael Gutman and Avital Saf, 365–87. Jerusalem: Yad Vashem, 1990.

Schechtman, Joseph B. *The Life and Times of Vladimir Jabotinsky.* 2 vols. Vol 1, *Rebel and Statesman, the Early Years.* Vol. 2, *Fighter and Prophet, the Last Years.* Silver Spring, Md.: Eshel Books, 1986.

Schiratzki, Selma. "The Rykestrasse School in Berlin: A Jewish Elementary School during the Hitler Period." *LBIY* 5 (1960): 299–307.

Schleunes, Karl A. *The Twisted Road to Auschwitz: Nazi Policy toward German Jews, 1933–1939.* Urbana and Chicago: University of Illinois Press, 1970.

Schlör, Joachim. *Tel Aviv: From Dream to City.* London: Reaktion Books, 1999.

Schneider, Gertrude. *Exile and Destruction: The Fate of Austrian Jews, 1938–1945.* Westport, Conn.: Praeger, 1995.

Schorsch, Ismar. *Jewish Reactions to German Anti-Semitism, 1870–1914.* New York: Columbia University Press, 1972.

Segev, Tom. *One Palestine, Complete: Jews and Arabs under the Mandate.* New York: Henry Holt, 2000.

———. *The Seventh Million: The Israelis and the Holocaust.* New York: Hill and Wang, 1993.

Shapiro, Yosef. *Chaim Arlosoroff.* Tel Aviv: Am Oved, 1975.

Sharfman, Glenn Richard. "The Jewish Youth Movement in Germany, 1900–1936:

A Study in Ideology and Organization." Ph.D. diss., University of North Carolina, 1989.

Shashar, Michael. *Ke-Chalom Ya'of: Terumat Yehudei Germanyah le-Chayim ha-Dati'im be-Eretz Yisrael.* Jerusalem: Shashar Publishing, 1997.

Shepherd, Naomi. *Wilfrid Israel: German Jewry's Secret Ambassador.* London: Weidenfeld and Nicolson, 1984.

Shirer, William. *The Rise and Fall of the Third Reich: A History of Nazi Germany.* New York: Simon and Schuster, 1960.

Silberklang, David. "Jewish Politics and Rescue: The Founding of the Council for German Jewry." *Holocaust and Genocide Studies* 7, no. 3 (winter 1993): 333–71.

Silver, Daniel B. *Refuge in Hell: How Berlin's Jewish Hospital Outlasted the Nazis.* Boston: Houghton Mifflin, 2003.

Sorkin, David. *The Transformation of German Jewry.* New York: Oxford University Press, 1987.

Stachura, Peter. "Introduction: The Development of Unemployment in Modern German History." In *Unemployment and the Great Depression in Weimar Germany,* ed. Peter Stachura, 1–28. New York: St. Martin's Press, 1986.

——. "The Social and Welfare Implications of Youth Unemployment in Weimar Germany, 1929–1933." In *Unemployment and the Great Depression in Weimar Germany,* ed. Peter Stachura, 121–47. New York: St. Martin's Press, 1986.

Strauss, Herbert. "Jewish Emigration from Germany: Nazi Policies and Jewish Responses." *LBIY* 25 (1980): 313–61.

——. "The Jugendverband: A Social and Intellectual History." *LBIY* 6 (1961): 206–35.

Sykes, Christopher. *Crossroads to Israel.* Bloomington: Indiana University Press, 1965.

Szanto, A. "Economic Aid in the Nazi Era: The Work of the Berlin Wirtschaftshilfe." *LBIY* 4 (1959): 208–19.

Teveth, Shabtai. *Ben-Gurion and the Holocaust.* New York: Harcourt Brace, 1996.

——. *Ben-Gurion: The Burning Ground, 1886–1948.* Boston: Houghton Mifflin, 1987.

Toury, Jacob. "Organizational Problems of German Jewry—Steps towards the Establishment of a Central Organization (1893–1920)." *LBIY* 13 (1968): 57–90.

Trefz, Bernhard. *Jugendbewegung und Juden in Deutschland: Eine historische Untersuchung mit besonderer Berücksichtigung des Deutsch-Jüdischen Wanderbundes "Kameraden."* Frankfurt am Main: Peter Lang, 1999.

Tydor-Baumel, Judith. "Ba-Derech la-Aretz ha-Bechirah: Aliyat ha-No'ar ve-ha-Yeladim ha-Plitim bi-Britaniah bi-Milchemet ha-'Olam ha-Shniyah." *Masu'ah* 12 (1984): 71–80.

——. *Unfulfilled Promise: Rescue and Resettlement of Refugee Children in the United States, 1934–1945.* Juneau, Alaska: Denali Press, 1990.

Tzur, Ya'akov. "Bein Tzionut le-Ortodoksyah be-Germanyah." In *Ha-Tzionut u-Mitnagdeyha ba-Am ha-Yehudi,* ed. Haim Avni and Gideon Shimoni, 75–85. Jerusalem: Bialik Institute, 1990.

——. "Tenu'ot ha-No'ar ha-Dati'ot be-Germanyah ba-Shanim 1933–1939." In

Tenu'ot ha-No'ar ha-Tziyoni'ot ba-Shoah, ed. Yehoyakim Cochavi, 73–79. Haifa: Ghetto Fighters House, 1989.

Vago, Bela. "Some Aspects of the *Yishuv* Leadership's Activities during the Holocaust." In *Jewish Leadership during the Nazi Era: Patterns of Behavior in the Free World,* ed. Randolph L. Braham, 45–65. New York: Columbia University Press, 1985.

Volkmann, Michael. *Neuorientierung in Palästina: Erwachsenenbildung deutschsprachiger jüdischer Einwanderer, 1933 bis 1948.* Cologne: Böhlau Verlag, 1994.

Volkov, Shulamit. "German Jews between Fulfillment and Delusion: The Individual and the Community." In *In Search of Community: Jewish Identities in Austria and Germany, 1918–1933,* ed. Michael Brenner and Derek J. Penslar, 1–14. Bloomington: Indiana University Press, 1998

Walk, Joseph. *Jüdische Schule und Erziehung in dritten Reich.* Frankfurt am Main: Hain, 1991.

Weiner, Hannah. *No'ar Toses be-Eidah She'anenah: Tenu'ot ha-No'ar ha-Tzioniot ve-"Hechalutz" be-Germanyah.* Ramat Eph'al and Tel Aviv: Yad Tabenkin and the Institute for Zionist Research at Tel Aviv University, 1996.

Weiss, John. *The Ideology of Death: Why the Holocaust Happened in Germany.* Chicago: I. R. Dee, 1996.

Weiss, Yfaat. *Schicksalsgemeinschaft im Wandel.* Hamburg: Christians Verlag, 1991.

——. "The Transfer Agreement and the Boycott Movement: A Jewish Dilemma on the Eve of the Holocaust." *YVS* 26 (1998): 129–71.

Weitz, Yechiam. "Revisionist Criticism of the Yishuv Leadership during the Holocaust." *YVS* 23 (1993): 377–82.

——. "Yishuv, Golah, Shoah—Mitus u-Metzi'ut." *Yahadut Zemanenu* 6 (1990): 133–50.

——, ed. *Bein Chazon le-Reviziah: Meah Shenot Historiographia Tzionit.* Jerusalem, Zalman Shazar Center, 1997.

Weizmann, Vera. "The Great Choice." In *Palestine's Economic Future,* ed. J. B. Hobman, 277–80. London: Percy, Lund, Humphries, 1946.

Wetzel, Juliane. "Auswanderung aus Deutschland." In *Die Juden in Deutschland, 1933–1945: Leben unter nationalsozialistischer Herrschaft,* ed. Wolfgang Benz, 413–98. Munich: Beck, 1988.

Wollenberg, Jörg. "The Expropriation of the Rapacious Capital by Productive Capital." In *The German Public and the Persecution of the Jews, 1933–1945,* ed. Jörg Wollenberg, 118–40. Atlantic Highlands, N.J.: Humanities Press, 1996.

Wyman, David. *Paper Walls: America and the Refugee Crisis, 1938–1941.* New York: Pantheon Books, 1985.

Yahil, Leni. *Hatzalat ha-Yehudim be-Deniah—Demokratiah she-Amdah ba-Mivchan.* Jerusalem: Magnes Press, 1967.

——. *The Holocaust: The Fate of European Jewry, 1932–1945.* New York: Oxford University Press, 1990.

Yisraeli, David. "The Third Reich and Palestine." *Middle Eastern Studies* 7, no. 3 (1971): 343–53.

Zariz, Ruth. *Breichah be-Terem Shoah.* Tel Aviv: Ghetto Fighter's House, 1990.

Zertal, Idith. *Zehavam shel ha-Yehudim: ha-Hagirah ha-Yehudit ha-Machtartit le-Eretz Yisrael, 1945–1948.* Tel Aviv: Am Oved, 1996.

Zukas, Alex. "Lazy, Apathetic, and Dangerous: The Social Construction of Unemployed Workers during the Late Weimar Republic." *Contemporary European History* 10, no. 1 (March 2001): 25–49.

Index